Urban Images of Kyoto:
Kyoto Culture and
its Cultural Resources

シリーズ｜日本文化デジタル・ヒューマニティーズ

05

京都イメージ バイリンガル版
文化資源と京都文化

文部科学省グローバルCOEプログラム
「日本文化デジタル・ヒューマニティーズ拠点」(立命館大学) 監修
冨田美香・木立雅朗・松本郁代・杉橋隆夫 編

ナカニシヤ出版

はじめに

　「日本文化デジタル・ヒューマニティーズ」シリーズの第5冊にあたる本書は、人文学のなかでも歴史、芸術領域の研究者による、京都文化のデジタル・アーカイブの取り組みと、そこに蓄積された文化資源や情報をとおして可視化された京都文化や都市イメージに関する論考で構成している。
　この「デジタル・ヒューマニティーズ」という複合領域の名称は、デジタル技術の急激な革新を背景に欧米の大学を中心に拡がり、日本においてもこの数年でかなり耳にする機会が多くなったといってよいだろう。本シリーズを監修している立命館大学グローバルCOEプログラム「日本文化デジタル・ヒューマニティーズ拠点」も、その一つのムーブメントをなしている教育・研究拠点である。ここでは、人文学と情報技術のさまざまな分野の研究者が参加・連携しながら、京都や日本の有形・無形文化財を対象としたデジタル・アーカイブを推進し、マルチメディア技術やGISなどの情報技術を用いた新しい人文学の教育・研究活動をプロジェクトごとに展開している。なかでも、複数のプロジェクトで構成している日本文化研究班と京都文化研究班は、人文学の研究者が中心になって、自らの研究領域に必要な文化資源や情報のデジタル・アーカイブの構築に励みながら、デジタル・アーカイブの技術や、伝統的な知に根ざした史料批判や研究方法など、多様なアプローチによる教育・研究活動をおこなっている。
　本書の目的は、その京都文化班の教育・研究活動をとおして深め得た、デジタル・アーカイブの手法と各時代と分野におけるあらたな知見を、広く共有するとともに、海外の日本文化研究者や拠点、デジタル・ヒューマニティーズを志向する若手研究者らも含めた研究ネットワークを広げることにある。ただし、京都文化班の大きな特徴の一つでもあるイメージデータベースの構築やそれらを用いた研究手法は、本シリーズ第2冊の『イメージデータベースと日本文化研究』（赤間亮・冨田美香編、2010年3月）において既に発表しているため、本書では対象外とした。本書で向き合ったのは、蓄積した膨大な史料や文化財および文化資源の一点一点と、その背後にある京都という都市の空間と歴史の時

間軸、そこから浮かびあがってくる日本文化である。

　全8章からなる本書の構成は、前半の1章から4章を中世から19世紀まで、後半の5章から8章を大正から戦時期までとし、それぞれ二つの研究プロジェクトが執筆している。
　1章の「古筆と極め―その歴史的意義―」と、3章の「仏教的世界観における都と天皇―中世日本の世界認識―」、4章の「19世紀英国における円山四条派理解について―英国人蒐集家が京都の画師に寄せた思い―」は、『洛中洛外図屏風の総合的アーカイブと都市風俗の変遷』プロジェクトの研究者が、歴史や宗教、絵画など、さまざまなテクストの分析をとおして展開した都市イメージ論である。1章では、当プロジェクトの研究対象でもある立命館大学アート・リサーチセンター所蔵の藤井永観文庫を例にとりあげながら、古筆への憧憬が生成される背景への考察をとおして、その流通と社会的ネットワークの存在をあらたに指摘している。3章では、中世の天皇を中心とした京都の都市空間と仏教的世界観との関係を読み解きながら、天皇を絶対視する世界認識を論攷し、4章では、近代以降に日本から海外へ大量に流出した日本美術の中から円山四条派の絵画に着目して、それらをめぐる英国人蒐集家の批評の視軸となっている価値観を描出した。
　2章の「中世平安京の都市構造―GISを用いた貴族の移動経路分析―」は、『平安貴族の行動と見聞―古典史料アーカイブ利用の試み―』プロジェクトによる論文である。当プロジェクトでは、平安京・京都の都市構造と、貴族社会における空間移動の問題とその諸要件を明らかにすることを目的とし、伝統的な歴史研究の手法とGIS技術を用いてアプローチしている。本論でも、摂関期から鎌倉期までの儀式と人の移動記録をデータベース化すると同時にGISで可視化し、時代ごとの都市空間の変容を明らかにした。同時代を扱った3章の都市論や、本シリーズの第3冊『京都の歴史GIS』（矢野桂司・中谷友樹・河角龍典・田中覚編、2011年3月）と併せて読むことで、京都という都市空間がより立体感をもって立ち上がってくることを補足したい。
　5章の「「韓国併合」を祝賀した友禅染」と6章の「立命館大学アート・リサーチセンター所蔵友禅図案資料群の整理作業」は、『京都における工芸の民俗考古

学的研究』プロジェクトの論文である。このプロジェクトでは、窯業や西陣織・友禅染といった京都の伝統工芸に関する基礎資料のデジタル・アーカイブ化を推進しており、本書ではその中から友禅染を対象にとりあげた。5章では、貴重な文化資源である型友禅の絵摺りへの詳細な分析をとおして「韓国併合」を祝賀した社会とその意識を浮き彫りにし、6章では、立命館大学アート・リサーチセンターのデジタル・アーカイブの手法を、実際に活動している学生たちの教育プログラムも含めて報告し、デジタル・ヒューマニティーズの教育実践の成果をも明らかにした。

　7章の「俄興行がもたらした映画受容の場への影響―京都新京極の事例―」と、8章の「戦間期日本における小型映画文化の様相―映画都市京都のもう一つの顔―」は、『近代京都における映画文化とそのアーカイブス』プロジェクトの論文である。このプロジェクトでは、近代京都の映画文化のアーカイブ活動を行っており、その中から本書では、大正期の新京極の映画興行情報と、蒐集した戦前の小型映画を考察対象にとりあげた。7章では、京都日出新聞から興行情報を収集して作成した京都興行情報データベースを用いて、新京極の映画常設館の変遷をトレースしながら、館や地域固有の興行特徴を指摘している。8章では、先行研究の少ない日本における小型映画文化の概要を論じながら、稀有な映画都市京都の一面を明らかにした。

　各執筆者とプロジェクトの研究活動は、多くの国内外の研究者や専門機関の協力、連携体制を得てこそ、すすめることができたものである。記して感謝の意を表したい。

編者代表　冨田美香

Foreword

This is the fifth book of the "Digital Humanities for Japanese Arts and Cultures" series. It is an achievement of the Digital Archives for Kyoto Culture project by researchers of history and the arts. The book consists of articles about Kyoto culture and its urban images made manifest through use of archived cultural resources and information.

The genre-spanning term, "digital humanities," originated in Western universities as digital technologies have rapidly advanced, and, even in Japan, we encounter this term more and more often recently. Ritsumeikan University's Global COE Program, "The Digital Humanities Center for Japanese Arts and Cultures," is one of the research and educational centers involved in this trend. At this center, researchers from different genres in the humanities and information technologies cooperate together to promote the creation of digital archives of tangible and intangible cultural assets. The center's activities also extend to many projects that engage in new educational and research activities in the humanities using information technologies such as multi-media technologies and GIS (Graphic Information Systems). Among these, the Research Group of Japanese Culture and the Research Group of Kyoto Culture, both centered around humanities researchers, are made up of multiple projects; Each researcher establishes a digital archive of the cultural resources and information necessary for his or her own specialty. They engage in educational and research activities utilizing different methods, such as digital archiving technologies, as well as the traditional critical approach to the historical resources and research.

This book aims to achieve two goals: to share widely our discoveries about digital archiving methods, each specialized genre, and period through the research and educational activities of the Research Group of Kyoto Culture, and to broaden the research network of digital humanities to include the researchers and research centers of Japanese culture abroad, as well as young scholars. The construction of an image database and the related methods that characterize the Research Group of Kyoto Culture are already published in *Image-Database and Studies for Japanese Arts and Cultures* (Ryō Akama and Mika Tomita, eds. March 2010). The Research Group of Kyoto Culture has encountered an enormous amount of historical resources, cultural assets, and cultural resources through the project. This book introduces these resources, on the individual level; their background formed by the urban space and history of the city of Kyoto; and the overall Japanese culture that takes shape from them.

This book has eight chapters. The first four chapters cover materials from the medieval period to the nineteenth century, and the latter four chapters cover materials from the Taishō period to the post-war period. Each half is written by researchers from two research projects, with a total of four projects.

Chapters One, Three, and Four ("Kohitsu and Kiwame—Their Historical Meanings," "Emperor and Capital in the Buddhist Worldview: The Perception of the World in Medieval Japan," and "The Art of the Maruyama-Shijō School in 19th century Britain: British Collectors on Kyoto Painters") are discussions of urban images that were developed from analyses of texts on history, religion, and paintings by the researchers of the "Comprehensive Archive of *Rakuchū rakugai zu* Folding Screens and Transformations of Urban Customs" project. The first chapter takes as an example the Fujii Eikan Bunko Library, one of the research objects of this project owned by Ritsumeikan University Art Research Center. Through examining the background of the early development of the appreciation of *kohitsu* calligraphy, this chapter breaks new ground by examining the emergent social network that encouraged the circulation of the art pieces. The third chapter discusses the world-view of placing absolute importance on the emperors by examining the relationship between the urban space of Kyoto that centered around medieval emperors and the Buddhist world-view. The fourth chapter explains the British collectors' sense of artistic value, paying particular attention to the art of the Maruyama-Shijō School among the Japanese art that flowed abroad after the modern era.

Chapter Two, "Urban Construction in Medieval Heian-Kyō: Analysis of Nobility Transit Routes Using GIS," is a product of the "Activities and Observation of the Heian Aristocracy: Attempts to Archive Classical Historical Documents" project. This project aims to clarify the urban construction in Heian-kyō and the entirety of Kyoto, the issue of transit of the aristocratic society, and other related issues, using both traditional methods of historical studies and GIS technologies. This article concerns a database of the records of the ceremonies from the Sekkan period (982-1081) to the Kamakura period (1185 - 1332) and people's movements, and makes them manifest using GIS technology, in order to display the changes of urban space over time. I would like to add that the urban space of Kyoto appears more multi-dimensionally by reading this article in conjunction with Chapter Three, which discusses urban images, and with the third book of this series, *Historical GIS of Kyoto* (Keiji Yano, Tomoki Nakaya, Tatsunori Kawasumi, and Satoshi Tanaka, eds. March, 2011).

Chapters Five and Six, "Yuzen Dyeing Works that Celebrated Japan's Annexation of Korea" and "Sorting of the Collection of Yuzen Designs and Related Materials at Ritsumeikan University's Art Research Center" are achievements of "Ethnoarchaeological

Research on Crafts in Kyoto" project. This project promotes the digital archiving of basic resources of traditional craft works such as ceramics, Nishijin textiles, and Yuzen dyeing; and the chapters in this book focus on Yuzen dyeing. The fifth chapter analyzes in detail the test prints of stenciled Yuzen and the *e-zuri*(the test printing), which are important cultural resources, and discusses contemporary society and the mindset of people who celebrated the "annexation of Korea." The sixth chapter reports on the digital archiving methods of the Ritsumeikan University Art Research Center, including the active educational programs for students, and the achievements of such educational activities of the digital humanities.

Chapters Seven and Eight, "The Influence of *Niwaka* Improvisational Entertainment on Movie Theatres: a Case Study on Kyoto's Shinkyōgoku District" and "Aspects of Small-Gauge Film in Interwar Japan: Another Face of the 'Cinema City' Kyoto," are products of the "Research and Archiving of the Film Culture in Modern Kyoto" project. This project makes archives of cinematic cultural assets of modern Kyoto, and this book introduces the examinations of the Shinkyōgoku district during the Taishō period (1912-1926) and collections of the interwar small-gauge films. Utilizing the informational database of the performances in Kyoto that the project compiled from the information on performances appearing in the *Kyoto Hinode Shinbun* newspaper, the authors of the seventh chapter track the evolution of permanent movie theaters in the Shinkyōgoku district, and point out the characteristics of performances unique to each theater and local area. The eighth chapter discusses the overview of the little-studied culture of small-gauge films, and discovers a new face of the unique "cinema city" Kyoto.

The research of each author and project could only be achieved thanks to the cooperation and understanding of domestic and international researchers and institutions. We would like to acknowledge and show our gratitude to everyone who helped make this book possible.

Mika Tomita, Primary Editor
(Translated by Shiho Takai)

目　次

はじめに　i／Foreword　iv

Chap.1 古筆と極め
　　　　―その歴史的意義―·· 1
　　　川嶋將生

Chap.2 中世平安京の都市構造
　　　　―GISを用いた貴族の移動経路分析―·························· 14
　　　田中　誠

Chap.3 仏教的世界観における都と天皇
　　　　―中世日本の世界認識―·· 28
　　　松本郁代

Chap.4 19世紀英国における円山四条派理解について
　　　　―英国人蒐集家が京都の画師に寄せた思い―·················· 44
　　　彬子女王

Chap.5 「韓国併合」を祝賀した友禅染·· 58
　　　木立雅朗

Chap.6 立命館大学アート・リサーチセンター所蔵友禅図案
　　　資料群の整理作業··· 74
　　　山本真紗子

Chap.7 俄興行がもたらした映画受容の場への影響
　　　　―京都新京極の事例―··· 88
　　　大矢敦子

Chap.8 戦間期日本における小型映画文化の様相
　　　　―映画都市京都のもう一つの顔―································ 103
　　　冨田美香

Chap.9 *Kohitsu* and *Kiwame*-Their Historical Meanings ············ 119
　　　Masao Kawashima (Translated by Shiho Takai)

Chap.10 Urban Construction in Medieval *Heian-Kyō*:
　　　Analysis of Nobility Transit Routes Using GIS ················ 132
　　　Makoto Tanaka (Translated by Michael Chan)

Chap.11 Emperor and Capital in the Buddhist Worldview:
The Perception of the World in Medieval Japan ·············· 146
Ikuyo Matsumoto (Translated by Elizabeth Tinsley)

Chap.12 The Art of the Maruyama-Shijō School in 19th century
Britain: British Collectors on Kyoto Painters ············· 164
Princess Akiko of Mikasa (Translated by Elizabeth Tinsley)

Chap.13 Yuzen Dyeing Works that Celebrated Japan's
Annexation of Korea ··· 176
Masa'aki Kidachi (Translated by Eddy Y. L. Chang)

Chap.14 Sorting of the Collection of Yuzen Designs and Related
Materials at Ritsumeikan University's Art Research
Center ··· 195
Masako Yamamoto (Translated by Eddy Y. L. Chang)

Chap.15 The Influence of *Niwaka* Improvisational
Entertainment on Movie Theatres: a Case Study
on Kyoto's Shinkyōgoku District ························· 209
Atsuko Oya (Translated by Eddy Y. L. Chang)

Chap.16 Aspects of Small-Gauge Film in Interwar Japan: Another
Face of the "Cinema City" Kyoto ························· 223
Mika Tomita (Translated by Takuya Tsunoda)

おわりに　241／Afterword　243
索　引　245

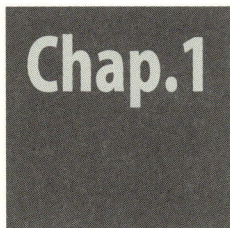

Chap.1 古筆と極め
―その歴史的意義―

川嶋將生　Masao Kawashima

はじめに

　本稿は、古筆に対する憧憬が生み出されてきた歴史的背景について、また古筆の筆者を鑑定する意味と、それを必要とした背景には、どのような事情があったのかなどを、近世初期の公家や古筆了佐等の活動を通して考察することを目的とする。

　古筆や古筆切、あるいは古筆を鑑定した極めなどに関連する研究の蓄積は、近年きわめて顕著であり、それに関する展覧会の開催も多い[1]。あるいは鶴見大学附属図書館などは、古筆切の収集を積極的に行っているという。

　そうしたなかで、古筆切に限定してみても、国文学研究資料館の「古筆切所収情報データベース」[2]や「早稲田大学蔵古筆切データベース」[3]、さらには名古屋大学後藤文庫の「古筆切データベースについて」などをはじめとして、幾つかのデータベースも公開されて、この分野の研究環境も徐々に整えられつつある。あるいは古筆・古筆切とは称していなくとも、各機関所蔵の貴重資料をweb上で公開するのは、もはや常識といっていい状況である。つまりは立命館大学GCOE「日本文化デジタル・ヒューマニティーズ拠点」が、日本のなかで先駆けて推し進めてきたデジタル・ヒューマニティーズの環境が、この研究分野のなかでも急速に広がりつつあるといってよい。

　ただし本稿は、古筆切や極めそのものの分析を目的としているわけではなく、冒頭に記した内容にアプローチすることを目指している。

こうした問題については、私もかつて「古筆需要の社会的背景」という小論を書いて[4]、歴史学の立場から古筆がどのような歴史状況のなかで需要されてきたのか、その分析を試みたことがある。結果、安土・桃山時代以降こそがその需要がもっとも大きな広がりをみせるようになった時期であり、それ故に、古筆家などの専門の鑑定家などを生み出すにいたったことを述べた。したがってこの問題を考察するうえにおいては、安土・桃山時代以降の近世初頭時期が、いわばターニングポイントともいうべき時であることが、改めて実感された。
　本稿が近世初期を中心として、この問題を分析しようとするのも、以上のような理由による。

(1)　古筆観賞の歴史的背景
　古人の能筆を観賞することは、すでに平安時代後期にははじまっていたことは小松茂美氏をはじめとして諸氏の指摘するところだし[5]、またそれらの能筆を切断して古筆切として愛でる行為が室町時代後期になって盛んとなっていったこともまた、指摘されているところである。小松氏によると、古人の筆跡という意味での「古筆」語が、文献上にはじめて登場するのは、14世紀になってからのことであるという。
　なぜこの時期、そうしたことへの関心が高まったのか。この問題についてはこれまで、侘び茶の湯の隆盛と、茶人武野紹鷗が、それまで茶掛けに主として用いられていた墨跡や唐絵から、代わって和歌や歌書を用いるようになったことが、古筆を愛でる行為の隆盛に結びついていったと指摘されている。私もそうした新たな動向が重要な要因であったと考えるが、それとともに考慮しなければならないことは、南北朝から室町時代には、武士をはじめとする諸階層に連歌が広く浸透し、その連歌の隆盛とともに『源氏物語』や『古今和歌集』をはじめとする、いわゆる古典への憧憬が一段と高まっていたことも大きな要因としてあっただろう、点である。
　連歌を詠むためには古典の素養が不可欠であり、それがために都鄙を問わず、古典に対する知識の欲求が高まったのが、この時代のことであった。それをもっとも象徴的に示しているのが、歌僧正徹が応永25年（1415）頃に著したという、『なくさめ草』のなかの、尾張に滞在した際の次のエピソードである。

さても光源氏の物がたりといふこと。よく人に尋しりたるとなむきゝをよびたまひぬる。年久しくあわれ連歌の道にすきはべりしを。あるときは世の中にさはり。ある時はすきごとならずして。詞の花色すくなく。心のいづみみなもととぼしきのみにて。ちかくはこれをとゞまりにき。さはあれどもこの物がたりゆへ聞きはべりたき。ひまあらば片端にてもいかゞなどあり。

　連歌をするには自分は詞の花色がすくないため、『源氏物語』を教えてほしいと、織田氏が正徹に依頼しているのである。
　以上のことをきわめて単純化していえば、古典への憧憬が、歌人への憧憬を生み、そしてその歌人が認（したた）めた筆跡への憧憬へと発展していくのであり、さらにそうした風潮が名蹟への憧れとその収集へと結びついていくことになったのである。
　さらにいまひとつ指摘しておかなければならないのは、入木道（じゅぼくどう）における名筆再確認の現れであろう。
　嵯峨天皇・空海・橘逸勢をもってする三筆は、いうまでもなく後世の仮託である。その原型は『江談抄』巻2に、大内裏の門額が、この三人に小野美材を加えた4名でもって書いたとされるものだが、三筆の名は17世紀後半に成った『和漢名数』にはじめて登場する。しかし三筆が17世紀になって現れるのは、この時期の王朝文化再認識の動向と密接に関わってのことと考えるが、それについては、指摘するに止めて、その前に入木道における名筆再確認の問題に簡単にふれておこう。
　日本の書の流れについて語ることは本稿の主旨ではないが、三筆とともに書の歴史上では確固とした地位を保っているのが、いうまでもなく三蹟である。そしてこの三蹟の名も後世になって名付けられたものだが、平安時代末、『夜鶴庭訓抄（やかくていきんしょう）』や『才葉抄（さいようしょう）』などの書論書が著されたにもかかわらず[6]、その後、藤原定家などの出現はあるものの、入木道そのものは停滞する。
　そうした状況のなかで出現したのが、伏見天皇皇子の尊円親王（1298〜1356）によって著された『入木抄』である。本書は日本の入木道（書道史）を体系的に論じた最初の書物で、宋風の書風を批判するとともに、親王自身も学んだ和様

1　古筆と極め　　3

の世尊寺流書風の正統性を主張したものである。これによって和様名筆の再確認がこの時期以降、進んでいったといえよう。ちなみに伏見天皇自身の筆跡も、歴代天皇のなかでは屈指の名筆として知られ、『増鏡』巻12に「御手もいとめでたく、昔の行成大納言にもまさり給へるなど、時の人申けり」と語られるほどであった。

(2) 古筆の鑑定行為

能筆を観賞するには、その筆跡が間違いなく誰のものであるかの判断が古くから行われていたものと考えられるが、残念ながら、そのことを明らかにできる史料には恵まれていない。

江戸時代初期になって、古筆家によって小さな短冊形の極札が用いられ、それがある種、ステータスとなって古筆家の名を高めたが、極札こそ用いられなくとも、それに類似した行為は古筆家以前からもちろん行われていたことである。

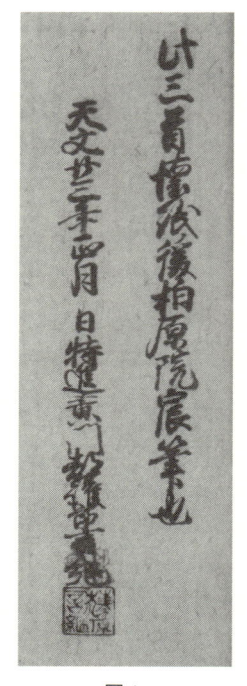

図1

例えば立命館大学アート・リサーチセンター所蔵の藤井永観文庫に、後柏原天皇宸翰和歌懐紙一幅が所蔵されている。そして本幅の裏には山科言継(ときつぐ)の「此三首懐紙後柏原院宸筆也、天文廿三年正月日特進黄門都護節言継(朱印)(黒印)」との極めがあり(7)(図1参照)、それに関連して言継の『言継卿記』同月25日条にも、「早瀬民部丞に申付、先皇三首御懐紙并正親町被誂年代記等、今日表法会出来到」との記事を確認することができる。つまり古筆家による短冊形の極札ではなくとも、かつてはこうした形式での鑑定が行われていたのである。ただしその行為が「極め」とは呼ばれてはいなかっただけである(8)。

『実隆公記』大永8年(1528)5月25日条には、先に述べるところがあった、青蓮院流の書風を開いたといわれる尊円親王(青蓮院門跡・天台座主)の手蹟を能登三宅なるものが入手し、尊円親王のものであることを証明するため、実隆の一筆を所望する、との記事がある。そして6月7

日に出来上がった証明を受け取りにきたが、実隆はそれを単に「奥書を加えた」と語っているにすぎない。つまり別紙にその証明を行ったのではなく、尊円親王の手蹟の奥にそのまま、証明を記したのである。言継が後柏原天皇の和歌懐紙の紙背に極めを行ったのと同様の行為であったと言っていいだろう。
　『実隆公記』によると、こうした鑑定の行為は、単に「書き遣わす」とか「奥書を加え」といった言葉で表現されており、のちにみられるような真贋の鑑定としての意味での「極」語は、用いられてはいない。あるいは奥書という言葉にこだわるならば、伝醍醐天皇宸翰「白氏句巻」の巻末余白に、伏見天皇による「延喜聖主宸筆也」の極めがあることが、報告されている(9)。
　ちなみに能登三宅なる人物は不詳で、『実隆公記』によると、この能登三宅と実隆との仲介をしたのが、「下京の者」であった。おそらく町衆と考えてよかろう。古筆への関心はこの時期、こうした階層の者にまで拡大していたのである。
　ところで、和歌の家でもない山科家が、なぜこうした鑑定を行ったのだろうか。言継が実隆の子三条西実条の和歌の門人であったとしても、また天文2年(1533)、尾張の織田信秀やその家来に和歌や蹴鞠の教授を行っていたとしても、実隆のように、『源氏物語』や『古今和歌集』などの研究で名声を博していたわけでもない。しかし言継は、『源氏物語』を所蔵して、享禄2年(1529)6月には叡覧に供しているし、また後奈良天皇からは享禄2年7月4日と天文22年2月22日の二度、『源氏物語』の書写を命じられている。それだけではなく、天文14年7月には、やはり天皇から法華経紙背の書写も命じられているのである(10)。
　以上のことは、つまるところ言継が、その名筆ぶりを天皇によって認められていたからでろう（彼の書風については図1を参照のこと）。そしてこうした環境が、言継をして、筆跡鑑定能力の涵養となって働いていたのではないか。その彼が、誰の依頼をうけて、なんのために後柏原天皇和歌懐紙の極めを行ったのか、その状況は不明である。
　なお言継の子言経もしばしば古筆の鑑定を行っていたことが、その日記『言経卿記』によって知られるから(11)、歌道の家、あるいは能筆家を輩出した家に拘わることなく、鑑定の力が認められた者がそうした行為を行っていたことが、以上の山科家の事例によって知ることができる。

(3) 藤谷為賢と古筆了佐

　江戸時代初期、冷泉家がしばしば藤原俊成や定家の鑑定を行っていたことは、『言経卿記』にみえるところだが、これは冷泉家にとっては、いわば先祖の筆跡の鑑定を依頼されたものであって、例えその依頼によってなにがしかの収入を得ていたとしても、それで家の経済を成り立たせていたわけではない。ところがこの冷泉家から分家した初代藤谷為賢（1583～1653）は、古筆の売買などの活動を行い、かなりの収入を得ていた。藤谷家は冷泉家からの分家だから、もちろん歌道の家である。その具体的な活動についてはかつて論じたことがあるので、詳細はその拙論に譲るが[12]、古筆の売買を行うにあたっては、彼自身に古筆の真贋を見極める力が備わっていることと、その力が他の人からも認められ評価されていることが前提となることは言うまでもなかろう。

　そうした為賢の能力を示す史料はさほど多くないが、それでも幾つかの事例を示すことはできる。例えば『大覚寺文書』下巻、638号にある[13]

　　（前略）御門跡様御取被下哥書筆者ノ事、御門跡様迄可被進候旨、かね〳〵被仰聞候、藤谷殿御状無之候てハ、何者筆跡も不知事候、無御失念、必々急度藤谷殿御状御門跡様御指上様ニ御取成奉頼候（後略）

との、年未詳3月21日付、大覚寺門跡側近宛の加藤正方（風庵）書状などは、その一例である。この書状では、藤谷為賢の文書がなければ、誰の筆跡であるかもわからない、と述べられていて、為賢のそうした面での評価が、公家社会の枠を超えて存在していたことが知られる。ちなみに加藤正方（風庵と号す。1580～1648）は、もと肥後加藤氏の重臣で内牧城代などを勤めたが、その後、加藤家改易とともに京都や大坂で茶の湯や連歌などを嗜んだ人物であり、この書状はおそらく肥後を離れてからのものであろう。

　一方、鹿苑寺住持鳳林承章の日記『隔蓂記』には、「自伊藤九左衛門、頼古今集并龍峯山之悦渓禾上之墨跡、頼相渡、以神辺宗利、令見古筆了佐也」（正保3年10月25日条）のように、あるいはまた「自田源太、被頼、古筆古今集遣了佐」（正保4年3月4日条）のように、鳳林承章が依頼をうけて古筆了佐に対し古今和歌集の古筆の鑑定を仲介することがあったが、しかし鳳林承章自身は、はたして

古筆了佐の鑑定力をどのように評価していたのか。というのも、『隔蓂記』万治4年（1661）3月16日条に、次のような記事が見えるからである。

　　到秉燭之時分、愚渓厚西堂被来、此比弟子取之由、少年同道也、扇子二本入箱与鹿苑院太上天皇之遺像一幅小師之持参也、御影者古絵也、影之上三首和歌書付、而有之也、了佐札者飛鳥井栄雅之筆云、所見非栄雅也、

　つまり足利義満像の上に和歌が三首書き付けられており、その筆者を古筆了佐は足利義政の信任を得ていた飛鳥井栄雅（雅親）と判断していたのに対し[14]、鳳林承章はそれに異を唱えているのである。ただし鳳林の鑑定は誰であったのかは、記されていない。これは単なる意見の相違なのか、それとも了佐に対し全面的な信頼は寄せていないことの現れなのか、この一例だけでの判断は慎むべきだろうが、確実に言えることは、古筆了佐の鑑定に無批判には従わない鳳林の姿勢がここにみてとれることである。
　さらにこの文面で注目すべきことは、「了佐札」とある点である。この「札」はいうまでもなく古筆家によって用いられた小さな短冊形の「極札」であろうが、鳳林はここでは単に「札」とのみ称している。
　先の為賢自身も、了佐に対しては必ずしも良い印象をもっていなかったようだ。やはり大覚寺門跡側近宛の為賢書状中には、「然者内々御物語申上候哥書五色、進上申候、阿仏事、了佐ニミせ申事、能々存候ヘハ、取沙汰迷惑ニ存候間」（236号）とあることや「然者大和物語うた書之物廿五つまりにて御座候、（中略）了佐ニミせ可申由、尤存候得共、正筆かとの内談にてハ御座有間敷候」（266号）といった文言がみられることに、そのことを窺うことができる。
　藤谷為賢はもちろん、鳳林承章も公家の勧修寺家出身である。了佐はこうした公家とは微妙な関係を保ちながらも活動していたようだが、しかし彼は、以上のような公家社会だけではなく、もっと広い活躍の場を得ていたようだ。『伊達家文書』の中には、源頼政の色紙を鑑定した了佐の証状が残されているし[15]、あるいはまた茶人宗旦関連資料のなかに、彼の名がしばしば登場するからである。表千家不審菴文庫から2007年に刊行された『新編元伯宗旦文書』には246点の宗旦書状等が収載されているが、そのうちの22点に了佐が登場する。

その全てを本稿で紹介することはさほど意味はないが、了佐は宗旦とは親しい間柄であったらしく、彼の消息についてその書状のなかに記すことが多い。なかでも両者の関係を端的に示すものを一例だけあげれば、寛永6年（1629）と推定されている銀子2貫630目の宗旦の借用状には、「其上別紙ニモ了佐請状アリ」（『宗』239号。以下、『新編元伯宗旦文書』については、左のように記す）とあり、了佐が宗旦の保証人となっているのである。両者はそうした間柄だったのだろう。

　そして慶安3年（1650）11月18日付、千宗左・玄室宛て宗旦書状には（『宗』182号）、「了佐子勘兵衛きられ果候」との衝撃的な事件が記されているが、この文章に続けて宗旦は、「心中のあしきゆへと見へ申候、両人弥たしなミ尤候、親ノ子ゆへ候、勘兵へ親をませさる天命と見へ申候」と、この事件に関する感想を認めている。文章は難解で、正確な文意は汲みとりにくいが、「心中のあしきゆへと見へ申候」などには、勘兵衛に対する必ずしも好意的ではない感情が読み取れる。しかしこの勘兵衛は、宗旦にとっては34人の弟子の内の一人だったのである[16]。

　いずれにせよ了佐はこうした茶人との交流をもっていたが、『宗旦文書』のなかには、「此廿七日近衛大所様御成事ニ候、了佐御伴ニ被仰候」（『宗』68号）とか、「了佐、長助、近様御父子懇ニ候」（『宗』95号）といった、近衛信尋と結びついている了佐の動向も記されているのである。この記述は一見些細なようだが、慶応3年（1867）再刻の『補正古筆了伴先生和漢書画古筆鑑定家印譜』に記された、「従近衛関白前久公古筆目利伝授遂為古筆鑑定家」とあるような、伝承のなかで語られている了佐と近衛家との関係を、具体的な史料によって実証することができるものなのである。

(4)　裏辻季福(すえとみ)のこと

　さて藤谷為賢の古筆売買という行為は、公家社会においては為賢だけにみられる特別な活動ではなかったようだ。上述で用いてきた『大覚寺文書』からは、実は為賢と同様の行動をとっていた人物として、いま一人に裏辻季福（1604～44）という公家が浮かび上がってくる。

　季福は歴史上、さほどその名前を知られているわけではない。むしろほとん

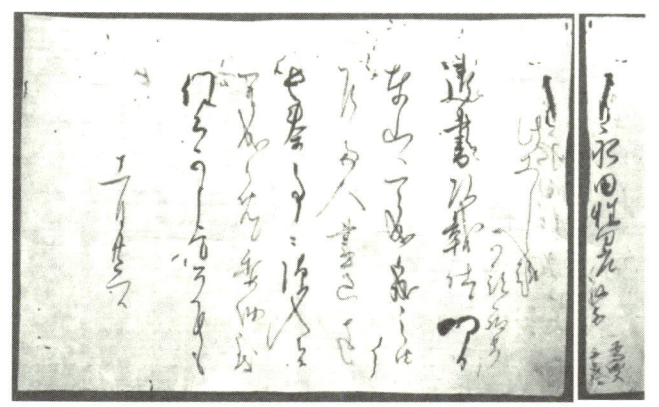

図2　藤谷為賢・裏辻季福連署書状（右下に「為賢・季福」とみえる）

ど知られていないといった方が良いだろう。したがって彼についてはこれまで、管見の限りほとんど語られることはなかったが、季福は正親町季康の息で、家格は羽林家の裏辻家の祖となった人物である。寛永19年（1642）にようやく参議となったが、その2年後には40歳で没しているから、政治的にもなにがしかの働きを行ったわけではなかった。ところが詳細は紙幅の関係で省くが、彼も為賢と同様、大覚寺に対し古筆をはじめとする諸道具の斡旋などを行っているのである[17]。

　『大覚寺文書』には、季福書状が53通残されていて、その内容を通覧すると、彼は為賢ときわめて昵懇であったようで、その書状中に為賢の名がしばしば登場するだけではなく、この期のものとしてはきわめて珍しい為賢・季福二人の連名による書状も残っているほどである（417号。図2）。

　季福は『源氏物語』や短冊その他の斡旋を大覚寺に対し行い、その値段の交渉にも携わっていたことが、書状の内容から知ることができる。しかし彼自身は、為賢のように筆跡の鑑定には当たっていなかったようで、季福の書状中はもちろん、他の人物の史料のなかにも、そうしたことを窺わせる内容のものをみることができない。

　そうした季福書状のなかから一点だけ、彼の活動を示す事例を紹介しておこう。やはり大覚寺門跡側近宛の年未詳2月14日付の書状である（384号）。「（前

略）唯今如申候藤谷殿未一覧無之候へとも、先宗仲ニ御請合被成、其内其許へ藤谷殿伺公候て、是又御談合被遊、如何様とも奉頼候」というもので、某の短冊について斡旋する書状のなかで語られる文面である。

　ここには短冊の斡旋に関わって季福・為賢・宗仲の三人が登場する。前二人はこれまで述べた通りだが、では残る宗仲とは誰か。実はこの宗仲も為賢の書状中にはしばしば登場する人物で、それだけではなく、「宗仲ハ事外口あしき仁ニ候故、迷惑ニ存候」（277号）と為賢によって語られている人物でもある。

　現段階ではこの宗仲とは誰であるかを断定することはできないが、可能性としてここでは、野路宗仲なる人物をあげておこう。野路宗仲とは、江戸時代初期の茶人で茶道宗和流の祖として知られる金森宗和の家来で、彼自身が発給した史料には、「金森宗和内」との肩書きが記されていて、宗和の茶碗などを斡旋していたことを確認することができる(18)。したがって『随流斎延紙ノ書』(19)に「宗旦より金森宗和家来野志七郎衛門へ売り」とみえる「野志七郎衛門」と同一人物とみて間違いなかろう。

　その野路宗仲は京都五山禅院などとの関係ももっていたし、また宗和が近衛家などの公家とも親しい関係にあったことなどを考慮すれば、『大覚寺文書』のなかにみられる「口あしき」宗仲とは、この金森宗和家来野路宗仲であった可能性がある。あるいは、395号の季福書状中に、茶碗のことにつき「乍慮外宗仲へ一覧被仰付候て、五両不苦候由候」とあることも、このように推定する根拠となっている。

　それはともかく、ここで主張しておきたことは、江戸時代初期段階においては、古筆などの売買や斡旋には公家なども深く関与し、またそのネットワークも築かれていたことである。

むすびにかえて

　以上、本稿では近世初期を中心に、公家や古筆了佐などの活動を分析することを通して、古筆や古典の写本などが売買される実態や、鑑定・普及といった問題を分析した。そしてそうした活動を行ううえでのネットワークの存在の可能性も指摘した。とりわけ古筆了佐については、伝承のなかで語られることが

多かった彼の活動の一端を、一次的な史料によって跡づけることができたのではないかと思う。

　もちろん本稿では触れることができなかった問題も多い。本稿は残された史料の関係もあって、公家とその周辺に議論を集中させたが、しかし『実隆公記』に登場した「下京の者」のように、古筆などを愛でる階層はもっと大きな広がりをみせていたはずである。史料的な困難もあろうが、今後はさらなる史料の博捜のうえ、こうした課題に迫っていくことが肝要であろう。あるいは藤谷為賢や裏辻季福だけではなく、公家のなかで同様の活動を行っていた者の追跡と分析も必要であろう。いずれも今後の課題としておきたい。

■注
(1) 大学や資料館・博物館などの研究機関がこうした活動を行っている近年の例としては、2004年（平成16）2月から篆刻美術館において開催された「古筆切と極印」展に、大東文化大学書道研究所が後援として参加しているし、茶道資料館においても2005年4月から特別展「古筆と極め」を開催している。立命館大学アート・リサーチセンターにおいても2008年12月「極め札」展を開催した。なお國學院大學若木書法會では機関誌『若木書法』を刊行するなどの活動を展開している。
(2) 国文学研究資料館のデータベースは、所蔵の古筆切に関するものではなく、説明には「このデータベースは、伊井春樹氏・高田信敬氏編『古筆切提要』（1984年淡交社）以後に影印刊行された古筆切類の所収情報の検索システムです」とある。
(3) 関連する論考として兼築信行「早稲田大学図書館所蔵の古筆切資料」（『早稲田大学図書館紀要』48号、2001）があり、また塩村耕「後藤文庫の古筆切データベースについて」（『名古屋大学附属図書館報』173号、2009）がある。なお兼築信行氏はデータベースの構築意義について、web「早稲田大学蔵古筆切データベース」で、「データベース構築の意図」として「日本古典文学研究の立場から言えば、これら古筆切は貴重な古写本の一部分であり、文献学的に高い資料価値をもっている。バラバラに分断され、分散所蔵されている古筆切を研究するためには、まずツレとなる切を蒐集しなければならない。そのために、古筆切の画像とデータがインターネット上に提供されていれば至便であろう。早稲田大学には、中央図書館特別資料室に古筆手鑑1帖と、幅物や未装の古筆切が若干所蔵されている。また、文学部の兼築信行研究室には、教材用および研究資料として蒐集された古筆切がある。これらを材料に構築しつつあるのが本データベースである。データは今後も逐次追加していく。」と述べられている。

(4) 川嶋將生『室町文化論考―文化史のなかの公武』（法政大学出版局、2008年、初出は2006年）所収。
(5) 小松茂美『古筆』（講談社、1972年）。下坂守「古筆と手鑑」（図録『古筆と手鑑』京都国立博物館、1989年）。
(6) これらの書論書の分析については宮﨑肇「中世書流の成立―世尊寺家と世尊寺流―」（鎌倉遺文研究会編『鎌倉期社会と史料論』東京堂出版、2002年所収）がある。本論文は歴史学的分析から、入木道の家としての世尊寺家の成立を論じている。
(7) 朱印の印文は不明だが、黒印の印文は「藤原言継」とある。
(8) 古筆家による短冊形の極札以前においては、竪紙や切紙等さまざまな形態の紙が鑑定に用いられている。ちなみに『日葡辞書』には「Qiuame. キワメ（極め）」「Qiuame, uru,eta. キワメ、ムル、メタ（極め、むる、めた）」は立項されているが、前者は「極致、終末、あるいは、究極」であり、後者は「ある事を究極のところまでする」などであって、そこには古筆を判定する意味の使用例は示されていない。
(9) 小松氏前掲注(5)。
(10) 以上『言継卿記』。
(11) 例えば『言経卿記』永禄4年（1595）5月13日条には、藤原定家の筆跡であるか否かの鑑定を行っていることや、文禄5年（1596）9月2日条では、『新勅撰集』が正親町三条実雅の大納言の時の筆であることを、連歌師祐恵の依頼によって鑑定していることなどである。
(12) 「藤谷為賢小論―寛永文化期における一公家の活動」（前掲注4拙著所収、1992年初出）。
(13) 『大覚寺文書』下巻（大覚寺発行、1980）。以下、本文書については、文書番号のみを記す。
(14) 飛鳥井栄雅は、足利義満から厚い信頼をうけ、その昇進は前代未聞といわれた飛鳥井雅縁（宋雅）の孫に当たり、栄雅自身も足利義政の信任を得ていた。雅縁は義満の死を悼んで『鹿苑院殿をいためる辞』を著したことで知られている。この肖像画は現在、相国寺承天閣に所蔵されるが、同館においてもこの和歌の筆者を「栄雅」とすることを、時代が合わないとして留保されている。
(15) 『大日本古文書』の『伊達家文書』3307号。承応2年（1653）9月付。ただし、この了佐の証状が伊達家の依頼によって作成されたものか、作成された後になんらかの手段によって伊達家が入手したものか、宛名がないため不明である。なおこの証状は、記された文字の多さからみて、極札に書かれたものではないだろう。
(16) 千宗左監修、千宗員編『江岑宗左茶書』所収「弟子衆控」（主婦の友社、1998年）。
(17) こうした裏辻季福の活動は「昨日者茶碗之義、早々禀奉存候、今朝高直之由申遣候へハ、先取而帰候、（中略）今一軸ハ中将姫と申候、是又細工見事ニ御座候、金一

枚五両と申候、御慰ニ掛御目候、御意ニ不合返し可被下候」(396号) からも、その一端を窺うことができるだろう。

(18)　「東南家文書」(京都市歴史資料館架蔵写真) には、野路宗仲書状一通と同金子請取状一通が収められている。書状の端裏書には「野治宗仲」とあり、『随流斎延紙ノ書』には「野志」とあるが、金子請取状には「野路」との自署があるので、ここではそれに従った。

(19)　『茶道古典全集』第10巻所収。

Chap.2 中世平安京の都市構造
―GISを用いた貴族の移動経路分析―

田中　誠　*Makoto Tanaka*
（研究プロジェクト「平安貴族の行動と見聞」）

はじめに

　平安京の都市構造については、これまでさまざまな角度から分析されてきた。特に本稿で取り上げる天皇・院・貴族の移動経路との関係は、すでに小寺武久（1969）大村拓生（1990）の専論があり[1]、中世平安京における主要道路を割り出すことで、平安京の都市構造が分析されてきた。

　天皇・院・貴族の移動自体、見物の対象になるなど儀式の一環であった（野田、1999）。単なる移動でないが故に、古記録に膨大な数の移動経路が記されてきたのであり、本稿もこうした認識に立つものである。

　移動経路と都市構造との関係で重要なのは、主要道路の抽出だけでなく、異動に伴う道路整備の問題である。平安京の道路は耕地・宅地が発生するなど常に変化していたが（仲村、1968）、移動に際しては京職・検非違使によって掃除や道路整備が行われていたことから（中原、1984）、移動件数の多い道路の整備状況は良好であったと想定される。つまり道路整備の問題は平安京の都市形態を規定する面を有しているといえよう。小寺・大村の研究は移動経路と道路整備の問題にまで踏み込んでおり、高く評価されるものである。

　両氏は、神社行幸・御幸など特定の儀式に用いる移動経路に注目して、その変遷を具体的に追究された。こうした方法は儀式自体と都市構造の変遷を追う上で有効な手段である。しかし、結果的に移動経路の分析に偏りが生じており、貴族社会における移動経路の全体像を掴むことは難しいと思われる。

従来の方法ではこうした移動経路の全容を整理・把握することは困難であった。しかし、GIS（Geographic Information System）を用い、各記録にみえるデータを集積・分析することで、あらゆる儀式にみえる移動経路の網羅的な研究が可能となった。
　したがって本稿では、特定の儀式路に偏ることなく、平安から鎌倉時代の古記録にみえる天皇・院・貴族の移動経路を集積・分析し、平安京の都市構造の変遷を明らかにすることを目的とする。

・GIS を用いた研究方法

　本論に入る前に、研究方法について付言しておく。まず GIS（ソフトウェアは Arc Map10.0、ESRI 社、2010）を用いて基となる地図を作成する。次いで古記録から収集した移動経路データの通過した部分を、その地図に入力する。データの一例を示すと、『中右記』永久2年（1114）11月14日条、鳥羽天皇石清水行幸の「出二東門一騎馬。〈皇居六条殿東門、烏丸面也。〉路経二烏丸・六条・大宮・七条・朱雀一、至二鳥羽北門一」（〈　〉内は割書。以下同じ）といった記事である。本プロジェクトでは、天皇・院・貴族等の京内外への移動に際し、発着地が明記あるいは推定でき、京内の移動経路が明記されている記事を対象にデータベース化した。その上で移動経路を便宜的に摂関期（天元5年（982）～永保元年（1081））、院政期（寛治元年（1087）～元暦元年（1184））、鎌倉期（文治元年（1185）～元弘2年（1332））に区分しそれぞれ地図を作成した[2]。全データ数は590件[3]に登っており、これらのデータを整理・分析できる点が、GIS を利用する大きなメリットである。なお未だ調査の途中であるが、相応の傾向が把握できると考え議論を進めていきたい。

1　摂関期の移動経路

　摂関期における石清水・春日などの神社行幸は大内裏東側諸門から京中に出て、大宮・二条・朱雀という経路をたどることが多かった。院政期に入ると、朱雀大路の利用が減少し、大宮・西洞院・東洞院各大路のいずれかを七条大路まで南下し、七条朱雀から京外に出る経路が多用されるようになった。また春

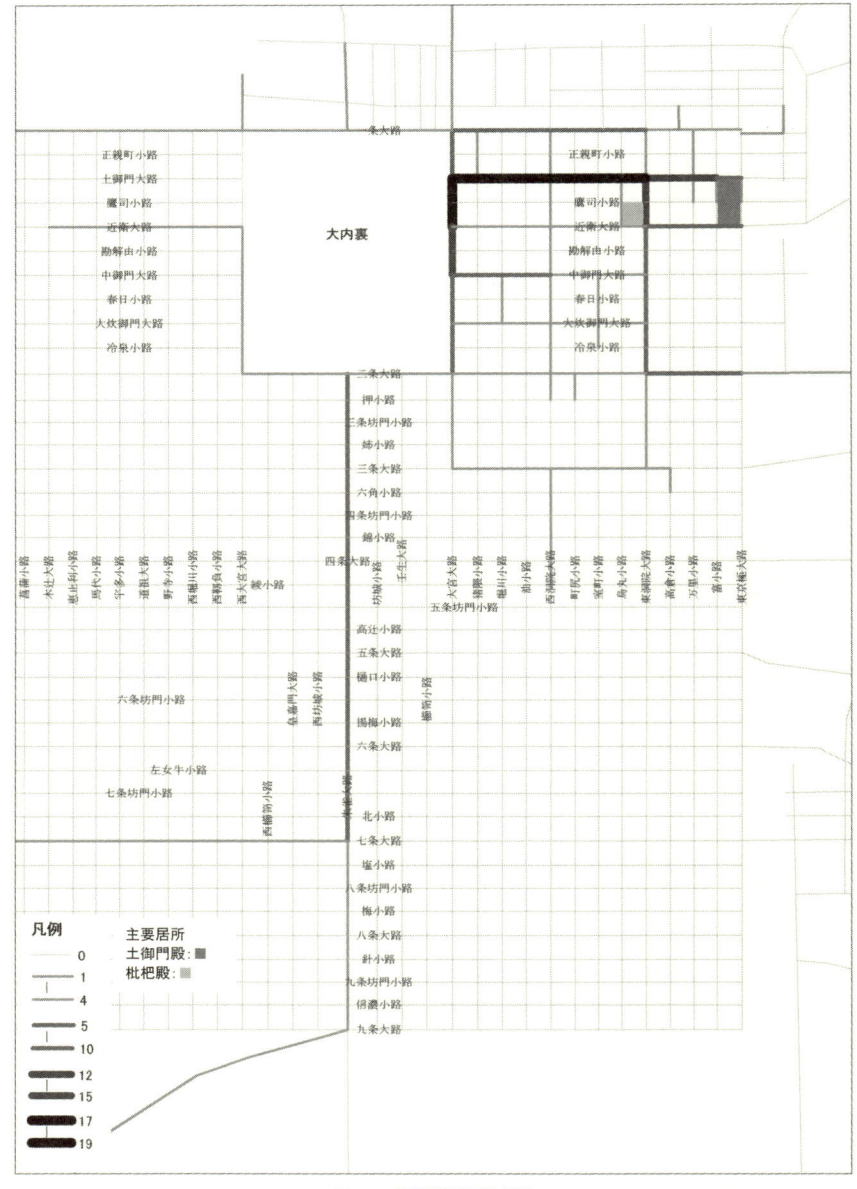

図1　摂関期移動経路
Fig. 1　Transit routes during the Sekkan (regency) period

日社・宇治方面へ行くには九条東京極付近の九条口が利用されるようになる（小寺、1969。大村、1990）。このなかで大村氏は、大宮大路と七条大路が中世京都の境界と重なると指摘された。氏の指摘は平安京の構造を考える上で注目すべき見解である。つまり、先行研究の成果は、中世京都の輪郭を明らかにしたものと読み替えることができる。

そこで本稿では、先行研究の手薄な左京内部の移動経路を網羅的かつ詳細に分析することを課題とする。それによって新たな平安京の構造を提示できると考えられる。そのためにGISを用いて作成した地図が図1～3である。道路一町・京外の経路ごとの天皇・貴族の通行データ件数が多い順に線を太くして表示した。

(1) 摂関期における南北道路と移動経路

当該期にもっとも移動件数の多い道は、大内裏に東面する部分の大宮大路と、土御門大路である（図1）。大宮大路は幅員12丈（約36m）で、南北道路では朱雀大路に次ぐ広さを持ち、二条以北が宮城門と接していた。当該期には大内裏で儀式を行うことも多い上、天皇が内裏に居住していることも多く、大内裏内外への移動のために大宮大路を通行せねばならず、移動件数が多くなるのである。

(2) 摂関期における東西道路と移動経路

土御門大路は道幅10丈（約30m）の道路である。土御門大路の左京部分ほぼ全長に亘って利用が多い。この要因は、藤原道長の邸宅である土御門殿（土御門南東京極西南北二町）と、同じく枇杷殿（鷹司南東洞院西）の存在である。土御門殿は道長がもっともよく利用した邸宅である。枇杷殿も道長の邸宅であるが、三条天皇の御所として使われた（太田、1987）。

大内裏―土御門殿・枇杷殿間を往来する儀式は朝覲行幸・入内・遷幸・葬送など多岐にわたるが、ほとんどが土御門大路を用い、南側の近衛大路はあまり使われない。儀式の性格や通行主体によって通行する道路が選択されていたと考えられる。

このように、道長邸・里内裏が土御門大路の付近に置かれており、これらの邸宅と大内裏を結び、多様な儀式に使われる道路として、土御門大路がもっと

も頻繁に利用されてきたのである。

　以上、当該期においては、南北道路として朱雀・大宮大路が使われ、東西道路としては、藤原道長の邸宅と大内裏を結ぶ土御門大路がもっとも利用されていたことが明らかになった。大村（1990）は天皇の居所と経路が相関関係にあると指摘されたが、天皇だけでなく、摂関家を含む権力者の邸宅の位置と移動経路には相関関係が認められることを指摘しておきたい。

　行幸における道路整備は当該期からすでにみられ、土御門もその対象であった（『小右記』諸事供養部類記　治安2年（1022）7月10日条など）。こうした成果もあり、土御門大路は単に貴人の通行に適するだけでなく、行幸行列を見物する雑踏に耐えうるだけの広さや道路状況を有していたと思われる。この点を踏まえれば、土御門を当該期東西道路における平安京のメインストリートと位置づけることができよう。

2　院政期の移動経路

(1)　院政期の左京

　院政期に入ると、図2を一見してわかるように、貴族の移動件数が増加し、行動半径が拡大する。左京南部、白河・鳥羽への経路が拡大していることが一目瞭然である。神社行幸・御幸の他、方違行幸・御幸、朝覲行幸、拝賀等の増加が移動件数の増加に結び付いている。行動半径の拡大は、五条・六条大路付近における内裏の造営や、左京南部・白河・鳥羽・法住寺殿等の院御所の造営によってそこへ行くための移動が要因であるといえる。また、摂関家による九条大路付近や平氏政権による八条大路付近の開発も見逃すことができない。

(2)　院政期における東西道路と移動経路

　院政期における道路の利用状況の特徴としてまず挙げられるのが、摂関期に多用されていた朱雀大路と土御門大路の利用減少である。東西道路においては、中御門大路（10丈、約30m）・大炊御門大路（同）・二条大路（17丈、約41m）、特に二条大路が用いられるようになる。院政期には二条付近に、堀河殿・閑院・東三条殿・高陽院・二条東洞院内裏など主な里内裏・摂関家邸宅が営まれ、こう

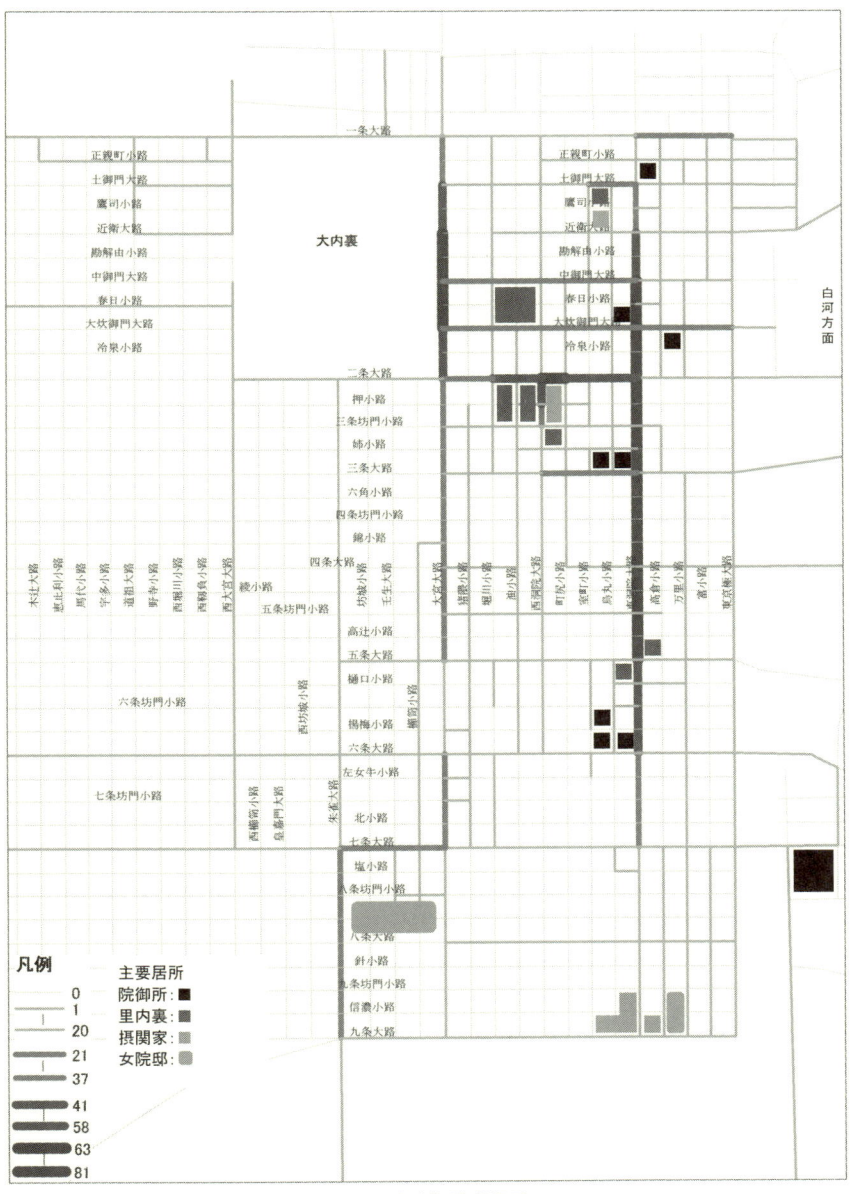

図 2　院政期移動経路
Fig. 2　Transit routes during the Insei (retired emperor) period

した邸宅に接していたことが二条の利用増加に繋がったと考えられる。当該期では二条大路が主要な東西道路であり、それに中御門・大炊御門が続くという状況であった。

(3) 院政期における南北道路と移動経路

それでは南北道路はどうであろうか。朱雀大路が衰退する代りに、顕著な利用状況を示すのが東洞院大路（8丈、約24m）である。特に、中御門―五条間の移動件数が他の南北・東西道路を含めても圧倒的に多い。

東洞院大路を利用する儀式は石清水・春日行幸等の他に、賀茂行幸・御幸・摂関賀茂詣、方違行幸、朝覲行幸、中宮行啓、拝賀など多岐に亘る。東洞院の性格を考える上で参考になるのが次の事例である。『山槐記』治承3年（1179）5月28日高倉天皇方違行幸では「東門、北行、二条東行、東洞院□南行、七条東行、河原〈先々自=五条=至=于京極或四条=、而去比洪水京極東岸壊入、仍用=此路-〉」とあり、閑院から法住寺殿へ至る経路が記録されている。先例とは異なり、洪水で東京極大路の東岸が壊れたため、東洞院を七条まで南下しており、東京極の代替として東洞院が選択されていることがわかる。『中右記』元永元年（1118）7月15日条白河法皇御幸においても同様の事例がみられる。大村（1994）は大規模な神社行幸と方違行幸とは同一視しえないと指摘されたが、移動経路の選択条件を考えた場合、東洞院大路が臨時の代替路として用いられており、普段から行幸・御幸が多い東洞院の道路整備の状況は左京内でとりわけ良好であったと推察される。

経路全体の移動主体は、最多が天皇で、次いで院、中宮、女院、摂関家関係者が多い。この傾向は他の経路でも、後の鎌倉期でも一致しており、記主が天皇・院の儀式を後世に伝えようとする意志の現れとみることができる。

東洞院を用いる際の発着地は、左京三条以北の各邸宅から五条六条の内裏・院御所、法住寺殿、春日・石清水社などである。大宮が主に石清水・春日・鳥羽殿など京都南部への移動に際し利用されるのに対し、東洞院は左京北部から賀茂・左京南部・石清水・春日・鳥羽殿への移動に使われており、その用途は多様であった。したがって、東洞院大路は貴人の移動そのものおよびその見物に耐えうるだけの幅員と良好な路面を持っていたと推定されるのである。

周知のように院政期には右京が衰退し、平安京の左右対称性が喪失される。朱雀大路が衰退し、邸宅が左京に集中したことで、儀式に用いられる道路として東洞院の存在が浮上する。多種多様な主体が多種多様な儀式に用いていたところに東洞院の特徴があり、東洞院はかつての朱雀大路に匹敵するメインストリートとしての地位を与えられたと考えられるのである。

3　鎌倉期の移動経路

(1)　鎌倉期の左京と大宮大路

　次いで、鎌倉期左京の特徴をみていきたい（図3）。鎌倉期に入ると、天皇・院・摂関家の邸宅の位置も変化する。鎌倉前期では閑院内裏、鎌倉後期では左京とその北辺以北に御所が集中するようになる。

　それよりも大きな変化は、大内裏の機能低下である。周知のように鎌倉期以降大内裏は荒廃が進むとされていたが、近年、大内裏の一部の建物は修理・再建・維持されたことが明らかにされている（高橋、2006）。とはいえ、院政期（図2）に比べると大宮の利用が明らかに減少しており、儀式に用いられる道路としての役割が低下している様子が看取されよう。

(2)　鎌倉期における東西道路と移動経路

　次に、東西道路の利用状況を見ていこう。一見して院政期において顕著であった中御門・七条大路の利用が減少していることがわかる。中御門は大内裏の機能低下、七条は石清水・鳥羽・法住寺殿への移動が減少することと（図3）、平安京南部への移動に際し朱雀大路に出る経路が七条に限定されなくなること（大村、1990）が利用低下の要因である。

　大炊御門大路と二条大路は引き続き顕著な利用がみられる。院政期に比べるとより局地的な利用に留まっているものの、二条大路には内裏・院御所が隣接しており、やはり内裏・院御所と経路との関係が想定される。

(3)　鎌倉期における南北道路の利用形態

　朱雀・大宮大路の利用減少とは対照的に、東洞院大路は引き続き顕著な利用

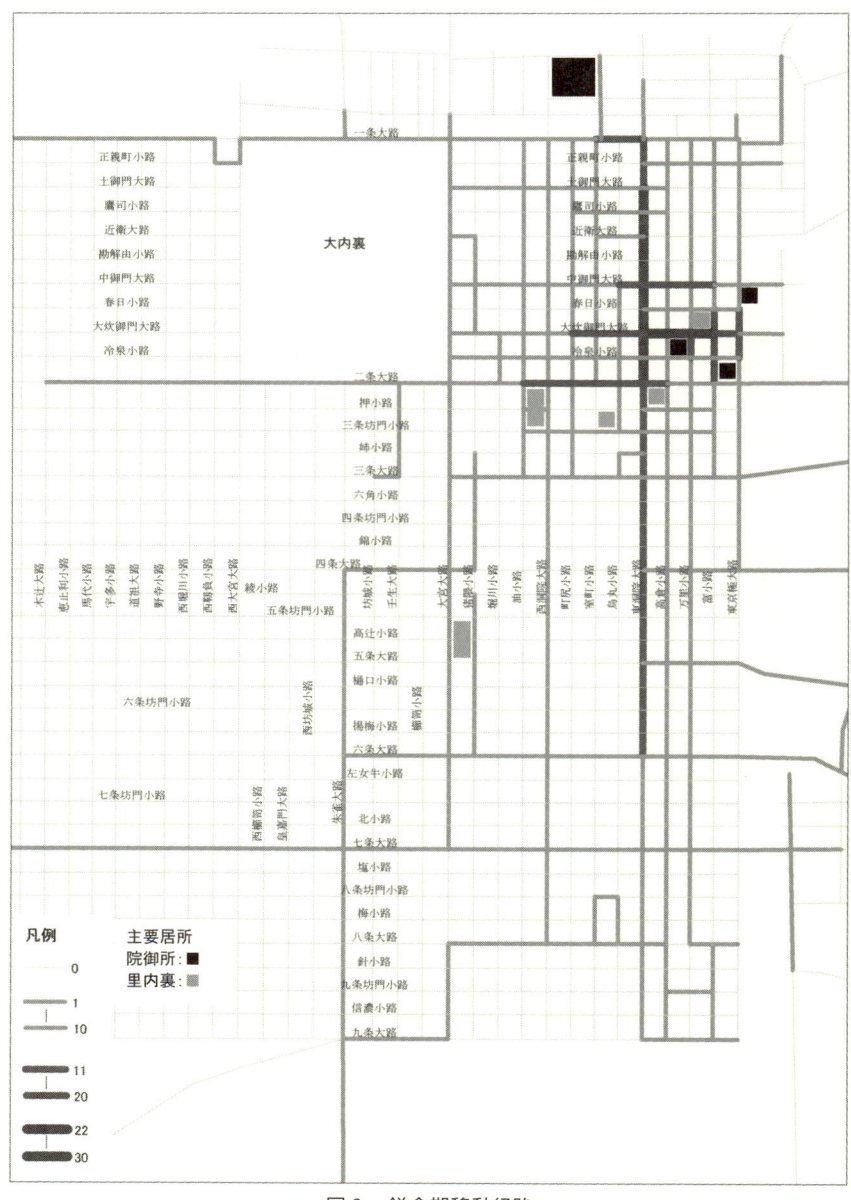

図 3 鎌倉期移動経路
Fig. 3 Transit routes during the Kamakura period

状態を示す。ここを利用した儀式は方違行幸が多いが、石清水・賀茂・松尾など神社行幸もなお確認される。鎌倉期の内裏・院御所は東洞院に隣接していないものが多く、東洞院南部には邸宅等に充てられる建物がない。それでもなお東洞院の利用が顕著であるのは、院政期の例が鎌倉期にも引き継がれたからと考えられる。大村（1990）は当該期において天皇の居所を都市空間の基準とすることはできない、すなわち内裏と経路の相関関係が希薄になると述べておられるが、大炊御門・二条・東洞院の利用が顕著である理由に内裏・院御所が集中する地域であることを想定すべきであろう。右京の荒廃がますます進み、かつ朱雀・大宮大路が利用されなくなるにつれて、東洞院大路の平安京左京におけるメインストリートとしての地位はより確固たるものになっていったのである。院政期から鎌倉期にかけて平安京の再編が進む中で、東洞院大路を軸に左京内部が再編されていったのではなかろうか。

(4) 移動経路と六波羅探題との関係

　最後に六波羅探題との関係に触れておきたい。六波羅探題は承久の乱後に置かれた鎌倉幕府の西国統治機関である。探題が設置される前は平氏の邸宅があり武家ゆかりの地であったが、六波羅への移動例は院政末から鎌倉期を通じて管見に入らなかった。行列の警固に六波羅武士が参加し、さらには天皇の輿を担ぐ事例がみられるが[4]、これは例外的措置であろう。現在までところ、六波羅探題による経路の変更などの直接的な影響は見受けられなかった。

　ここまで、移動経路の時期的な変遷を追い、東洞院が中世前期における平安京左京のメインストリートとして位置づけられる過程を追ってきた。一つ注意しておくべき点として東洞院と同じ道幅を持つ西洞院大路の存在がある。図1〜3でみたように全時代を通じて西洞院はあまり使われていないことがわかる。これは何故であろうか。次にこの問題を検討する。

4　東洞院大路と西洞院大路

(1) 西洞院川について

　東洞院大路と西洞院大路は、同じ8丈（約24m）の道幅を持つ大路である。西

洞院付近には閑院・東三条殿・高松殿・高陽院など主だった邸宅が存在していた。左京を南北に移動する際、西洞院大路を利用できたはずであるが、そうした傾向が見出せないのである。

西洞院が使われないことについては、すでに小寺（1969）が西洞院に沿う川が原因ではないかと指摘されている。氏の指摘を踏まえ、洛中を流れる河川との関係に着目してみよう。

洛中の河川については九条家本『延喜式』所収「左京図」（『平安京提要』所収）を参考にすると、大宮・堀川小路の全長、西洞院・町小路・室町小路・烏丸小路・東洞院の一部に沿って河川があったことがわかる。問題の西洞院川の存在は、室町初期成立の仁和寺本古写本『系図』所収の閑院内裏の陣中図（野口、2005）にもみられ、「左京図」にみえる河川の記載と合致する。

西洞院川は、『中右記』長承3年（1134）5月17日条に「京中堀川・西洞院河大出有₌流死之者₋云々」とあり、また『勘仲記』弘安7年（1284）閏4月17日条「洪水溢₌洛中₋、烏丸川西洞院川等不ﾚ及ﾚ通₋人馬₋云々」とみえ、院政期から鎌倉期にかけて頻繁に洪水が起こる川であったと考えられる。

東洞院川と西洞院川との違いは、川の長さである。西洞院は中御門大路以南に川が沿うのに対し、東洞院は一条から大炊御門までであり、少なくとも大炊御門以南は川の影響を受けなかったと考えられる。

道路全長と並行する川として、大宮川と堀川がある。堀川小路の道幅は、西洞院と同じ8丈である。大宮大路の川幅は不詳だが、道幅は12丈（約36m）であり東・西洞院よりも4丈分広い。図1～3をみると堀川小路の移動件数が少ないに対し、大宮大路の利用件数は多いことがわかる。大内裏における儀式の際にはここを通る必要があることは前述の通りであり、さらに陽明門から郁芳門までの大宮大路と大宮川が並行していなかったという史料もある[5]。道幅の関係からも大宮川が大きな障害にならなかったのではあるまいか。

ところが、西洞院大路の場合は、幅員が狭く川の洪水も頻繁に起こっていた。そのため、道路整備が行き届かなかったと考えられる。貴人の移動の際には車を用いることが多く（天皇は輿）、幅員が狭い上に道路整備が行き届かない西洞院大路は通行しにくく、経路の選択肢から除外されていたのであろう。

(2) 東洞院大路の利用と貴族社会における先例意識

　こうした道路状況とは別に、貴族社会における先例の積み重ねも影響していると考えられる。東洞院大路が代替路として用いられた例があることは前述した。さらに注目されるのは『兵範記』保元元年（1156）3月1日条後白河天皇石清水行幸である。行幸列は高松殿（三条坊門北西洞院東）より出立し「自三条東行、自東洞院南行、自七条西行、其以南如例」と進んだ。続けて「須任先例経大宮大路。而顕輔卿於六条大宮、去年四月薨了。閏年中依有其憚被忌歟」とある。注目されるのは、代替として高松殿に接する西洞院ではなく、東洞院が選択されている点である。

　以上のように、西洞院大路は通行に適していないため早い段階から経路選択の内から除外されており、さらに「西洞院を通らない」という先例が積み重なって西洞院大路が通行されなくなったと考えられる。それと反比例するように目的地との関係上不合理であっても東洞院大路が選択され、通行されるようになっていったのではなかろうか。

おわりに

　以上、本稿では天皇・院・貴族の移動経路から、中世前期における平安京道路利用状況を検討してきた。その結果、院政期を境に朱雀大路が廃れ、東洞院大路が頻繁に利用されるようになり、それが鎌倉期まで引き継がれることを明らかにした。そして、東洞院大路を中世前期における平安京のメインストリートと位置づけた。この東洞院はいわば儀式のための道路であり、中世前期から徐々に発達する町小路に展開した商業地とは異なる性格を持つ[6]。図1～3を見ると二条町小路以南の移動件数は確かに少ない。これは商業圏と儀式空間とが平安京内で分離していたことを示していると考えられ、中世前期平安京の空間構造の特徴の一つと言えるだろう。

　最後に今後の課題を述べておきたい。GISの利用には技術的な問題が多い上、調査中ということもあり事例採録の脱漏が多い。また紙幅の都合から政治史や経済史の動向、武家政権との関係を踏まえた議論を十分に展開することができなかった。しかし、GISを使うメリットは大きいことは確認できたと考える。

今回は果たせなかったが、GIS の特性上現在の街路と重ねることもできるため、京都であるからこそ時期的な変遷を追った研究が可能である。今後もこうした特性を生かして、研究を進めていきたい。

　　［付記］　本稿は、立命館大学グローバル COE デジタルヒューマニティーズ京都文化研究班における研究成果を基に田中が代表して執筆したものである。成稿にあたり 13th EAJS Conference（2011年 8 月、於エストニア国）における口頭報告を行った。プロジェクト代表杉橋隆夫先生、佐古愛已先生には終始ご指導を賜わった。古記録データベースの調査・作成および GIS 地図化作業には本学上島理恵子、花田卓司、谷昇、滑川敦子、吉美悠、池松直樹諸氏に分担・協力していただいた。また GIS 地図の作成・操作について、本学文学部地理学専攻河角龍典先生、今村聡氏のご協力を賜わった。関係者のご厚意に対し、記して深謝申し上げる次第である。

■注
(1)　都市論の他に、葬列と移動経路との関係ついては前嶋（1998）がある。
(2)　地図の作成に際して、摂関期（図 1）…『小右記』『御堂関白記』『左経記』『権記』『春記』、院政期（図 2）…『中右記』『後二条師通記』『兵範記』『山槐記』『玉葉』（元暦元年以前）、鎌倉期（図 3）…『玉葉』（文治元年以後）『明月記』（建久 3 年─元久元年）『民経記』『勘仲記』『冬平公記』『公衡公記』『花園院宸記』を利用した。時期区分は古記録の残存状況と移動経路の変遷を踏まえて、摂関期を堀河天皇即位以前、院政期を堀河天皇即位から平氏都落ちまで、鎌倉期を平氏都落ち以降とした。また各邸宅の位置は、川上（1967）、近藤（1992）、山田（1994）を参照した。また道路名称は寺升（1994）の表記に統一した。
(3)　この内、ある一つの移動経路が複数の記録に採録されている場合、それぞれ別個に採録したものがある。紙幅の都合から説明を省略するが、全体に占める割合はごく少数であるため、論旨に大過ないと考えて議論を進める。
(4)　『民経記』寛喜 3 年（1231）7 月 1 日条。同 8 月 6 日条方違行幸では北条重時に「御供武士」の事を仰せつけているので、7 月 1 日条方違行幸に供奉した武士は明らかに六波羅武士であるといえる。
(5)　「伊勢物語知顕抄」中（『史料京都の歴史』4　市街・生業）。
(6)　『京都の歴史』第 2 巻中世の明暗（京都市、1971年。第 3 章第 3 節、川嶋將生・横井清執筆分）

■参考文献

太田静六（1987）『寝殿造の研究』吉川弘文館［Ota, 1987］
大村拓生（2006、初出1990）「儀式路の変遷と都市空間」『中世京都首都論』吉川弘文館［Omura, 1990］
　　同　　（2006、初出1994）「行幸・御幸の展開」同書［Omura, 1994］
川上貢（2002、初出1967）「鎌倉時代後半期における内裏と院御所の研究」『日本中世住宅の研究〔新訂〕』中央公論美術出版［Kawakami, 1967］
小寺武久（1969）「平安京の空間的変遷に関する考察(1)(2)」『日本建築学会論文報告集』第165号・第166号［Kotera, 1969］
近藤成一（1992）「内裏と院御所」五味文彦編『都市の中世』吉川弘文館［Kondo 1992］
高橋昌明（2006）「大内裏の変貌―平安末から鎌倉中期まで―」高橋昌明編『院政期の内裏・大内裏と院御所』図書出版文理閣［Takahashi, 2006］
寺升初代（1994）「平安京内街路　古今対照表」『平安京提要』角川書店［Teramasu, 1994］
中原俊章（1984）「検非違使と「河」と「路」」『ヒストリア』第105号［Nakahara, 1984］
仲村研（1975、初出1968）「東寺領巷所の存在形態」秋山國三・仲村研『京都「町」の研究』法政大学出版局［Nakamura, 1968］
野口孝子（2005）「仁和寺本『系図』に描かれた閑院内裏の陣中」『仁和寺研究』第5輯［Noguchi, 2005］
野田有紀子（1999）「平安貴族社会の行列―慶賀行列を中心に―」『日本史研究』第447号［Noda, 1999］
前嶋敏（1998）「中世前期の葬列における順路と見物」『大学院研究年報』中央大学、第28号［Maeshima, 1998］
山田邦和（1994）「左京と右京」『平安京提要』角川書店［Yamada, 1994］

Chap.3 仏教的世界観における都と天皇
―中世日本の世界認識―

松本郁代 Ikuyo Matsumoto

はじめに

　中世日本では、記紀神話が仏教的世界観を獲得することで、神祇世界の序列や神格が形成された。それと同様に、平安京という都市空間も天皇を中心とする密教的世界観のなかに観想された。これらは、神と仏による神話的な叙述によって、中世以前に遡る「世界」が保証されているといえる。そして、中世仏教は、現実的な「世界」に理念的意味を与える言説としても登場した。なかでも密教は、仏教を実践的な空間へと導く世界観として理解できる。中世日本の密教が構築する「世界」の範囲は、仏教的理念のみならず、現実的な地理空間にまで及ぶものであった。

　このように、中世仏教に基づく理念が、実際の地理空間と結合して考えられた歴史的な背景は、10世紀以降、中国皇帝を中心とする東アジアの仏教政策と日本仏教が連動しながら形成されていた点と軌を一にする[1]。しかし、実際の地理空間を見立てる宗教的な宇宙観や世界観は、宗教世界の修飾的なアレゴリーや観念的なものとして評価される傾向にある。

　前近代日本における世界観や世界認識の登場は、まず、掌握する必要のある地域や範囲が秩序だてられた「世界」として生み出されたことに始まる。そして、これらの地域は、神話や宗教によってその存在意義が作り出された。このようにして作られた世界観や宇宙観は、時代毎の社会や文化的変遷の影響を受けた大地の「ありよう[2]」を提示している。つまり、宗教的観念の対象となる地

理空間には、ある一定の思想や秩序が込められているのであり、それを「世界認識」として捉えることができるのである。

前近代をとおして、東アジア文化は中国を軸とする華夷秩序に基づきながら展開した。大きな転換点として、中国が明王朝から清王朝へ交替したことで、江戸の思想家たちを中心に「華夷変態」が認識された点が挙げられる。しかし、幕末の開国に至るまで、日本と対比される文明世界は中国であった。そのようななか、グローバリゼーションの初期段階とされる16世紀大航海時代以降の日本は、東南アジアや中国経由でヨーロッパ文化も体験した。そのインパクトが次第に日本の開港を促すことにつながる。しかし日本が正確な「世界図」を獲得するまでの世界認識は、中世以来の「異界」認識と同様、古代中国の地誌である『山海経』などに基づいた空想的な叙述の中にあった[3]。

小稿では、中世日本において仏教的世界観によって表された都と天皇の世界認識について論じる。そして、近代に至り排除された世界観の一端を論じることで、近代にはなかった「世界」の捉え方を提示したい。

1　仏教的世界観における日本

(1) 仏教的世界観と近代の相克

前近代日本における世界観の代表として、須弥山を中心とする仏教的世界観が存在した。虚空に世界が構築されているのが、須弥山を中心とする世界観である。この虚空にある世界を支えるための土台である円盤状の空間が「風輪」であり、風の力で世界を支えているという。そして風輪の上には、この風によって生み出された円盤状の「水輪」の空間があり、さらに、この上に「金輪」という空間があり、そこには、山や海や島が浮かべられているという。これが世界の土台となる部分の説明である。

そしてその土台となる世界の中心が、須弥山である。この須弥山を取り囲むようにして、周囲には、七つの金の山と鉄囲山があった。その山々の間には八つの海が輪のようにあり、この九山八海の外には、海水に浮かぶ四大州があった。この四大洲が浮かぶ海水をたたえているのが金輪であった。そして、その海水を「四海」といった。

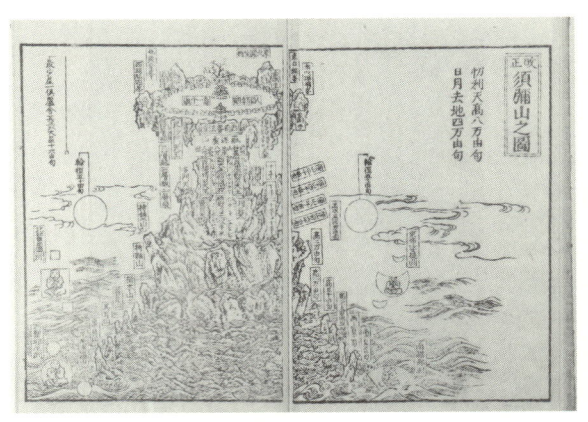

図1　須弥山図解
Fig. 1

　金輪は、大地である須弥山や四大洲の底と接する器でもあった。この四大洲のうち、人間が住む世界を南瞻部洲といい、インド亜大陸の地をモデルにした雪山の頂上にある阿耨達池から四方に川が流れていた。そのイメージ図は、「五天竺図」（法隆寺蔵）などに代表される[4]。

　さて、図1は、文化6年（1809）に刊行された高井蘭山（1762-1839）が著した『須弥山図解』所収の、須弥山を中心とする世界観が図解されたものである[5]。この図に記されているように、須弥山の中腹には、四天王が鎮座し四大洲を守り、日天と月天が回っていた。そして、須弥山頂上である忉利天の善見城には帝釈天が住していた。仏教には、須弥山を中心とする世界が、仏典世界の常識として存在していたのである。

　須弥山が仏教的世界の問題ではなくて、現実的な世界観として取り沙汰されたのは、江戸時代後半に起きた梵暦運動に端を発する。梵暦とは、仏教的な世界観に基づく「仏教天文学」のことを指す。これは、僧の普門円通（1754〜1834）が地動説を含む天文学理論をもとに仏典の天文学理論を体系化したものであった。

　地道説がオランダ書の翻訳をとおして日本に伝えられたのは、1770年代から90年代にかけてであった。その後、物理学や理学のもととなる「窮理学」と関連付けられて論じられた。司馬江漢（1747〜1818）によって寛政8年（1796）に刊

行された『和蘭天説』は、洋学から学んだ天文学や地理学の成果を踏まえ、天文・地理・気象などの原理を分かりやすく図解した書であった。蘭学の影響を受けた知識人たちによって、「世界を象徴的なイメージとして描くのではなく、あるがままの現実を直接に表象することができる[6]」西洋の学問の優越性が説かれた。

これに対し円通は、須弥山を中心とする仏教的世界観を、西洋天文学における世界観と対峙させるイメージで作り出した。円通は、須弥山を中心とする梵暦は「天眼」によるものであり、不変の基準をもった根源的で包括的な理論として考えた。一方で、西暦は「肉眼」に基づくもので、技術に左右される人の観察を重視したものであり理論に統一性がない点を主張し、西暦は梵暦に劣るという論理を展開した[7]。

円通に始まる梵暦は、江戸時代後半から明治5年（1872）に太陽暦が採用されるまで活発に論じられ、昭和初期には世間から全く姿を消した仏教的な世界認識の一つである。梵暦登場の論点とは、仏教的世界観と西洋天文学との関係とは何か、という点にあった。それは、仏の絶対的な第三の眼か人の相対的な眼を信じるか否かにも関わっていた。このような考え方は、それまで「日本人」の思考や行動を独占してきた仏教の存在形態が、外来の新たな知識によって再構築されることを意味した。

梵暦研究者である岡田正彦氏は、「丸い地球の概念と地動説の受容を近代的思考の指標とすれば、平らな世界の実在を主張する世界記述は、反近代的な伝統主義とも見なし得るであろう。しかし、近代的世界記述が人々の意識にもたらしたものは、概念化された世界の見かけ上の変化だけではない。重要なのはむしろ、新しい世界記述の様式によってもたらされた、眼差しの転換と記述された世界の性質上の変化なのである[8]」として、新たな世界観を受容する過程の歴史叙述の転換を近代世界の時代性として評価している。

(2) 和漢梵の世界観

梵暦運動が仏教の近代化の一過程として評価されるのは、それまで常識と考えられていた仏教世界の様式が、幕府や朝廷、諸地域を巻き込みながら価値転換された点に見出される[9]。それは逆に、前近代までの日本では仏教的世界観

が「世界」の論理として展開していたことを意味する。

そこで本節では、前近代的な仏教的世界観をとおした世界認識がどのような「世界」を形成していたのか論じる。具体的には、「世界」がインド・中国・日本から構成されるとする認識である。この認識は、仏教が天竺（インド）から震旦（中国）に伝えられ、日本に伝来したとする仏法の三国東漸に基づく。

日本におけるかかる三国観の認識は、永承7年（1052）以降、日本が末法の時代に入ったとする思想にも影響された。市川浩史氏によると、古代から中世の過渡期における日本の特徴として、震旦や天竺という「世界」との触発によって、自国観や国家意識を生みだした点や、朝鮮半島諸国を軽視する思想表現が顕著になる点、そして、釈迦信仰に基づく天竺に対する憧憬や思慕の念を喚起する点が挙げられるという[10]。また、伊藤聡氏は、平安時代末期から鎌倉時代初頭の天台僧慈円（1155～1225）によって論じられた、仏典翻訳のコトバを通じた特異な三国観の展開について指摘する[11]。

それによると、仏典には、コトバや文学は仏説より誕生すると記されており（『大般涅槃経』巻8文字品第13）、さらに梵字や漢字（篆書）は天上から下った神によって作られた同祖の文字であるとする。しかし、インドや中国が固有の文字を有していたが、日本には、漢字を遡る固有の文字がない点で、二国に対し劣等意識を抱いていたのだという。これに対し、平安時代中期の僧によって梵語・漢語の音が五十音に包摂された。このことから、インド・中国・日本のコトバが三国に相通する言語として捉えられるようになった。それを受け、慈円は、表音文字である和字と梵字を結びつけ、表意文字である漢字と対峙するものとして位置づけた。そうすることで、日本固有の文字がないという三国間における劣等性を克服する論理を展開したという。それが突き進められると神国思想が登場するが、この思想は、伊藤氏が指摘するように、インドや中国という対外的な国家観念があったからこそ展開した日本の優越意識であった。

以上のような仏教東漸に基づく三国をとおした文化伝播は、仏教のみならず、コトバをとおして運ばれる文学や絵画の制作にも影響を与えた。漢語をとおして日本に流入した和語と漢語という言語の二重性は、コトバが運んだ文化的イデオロギーをも日本に普及させた[12]。この三国のコトバをとおして作られた日本から中国、そしてインドにまで及ぶ世界認識は、「広大な地理空間を日本語の

世界に移した⁽¹³⁾」と評されている。
　このような仏教東漸の三国における日本の世界認識は、他の二国の存在によって形成されたといえる。日本国内におけるその影響は、天皇を中心とする仏教的世界観にまで及ぶものであった。それは、平安京を密教的に解釈した宇宙観として提示された。このような世界認識の登場は、この時期における思考の枠組みが仏教的世界観に依存していた点と深く関わっている。その一端は「国土観」とも言い換えられるが、思考が及んだ範囲は国土のみならず、観念によって補われる都の権威や天皇権力の在り方があったと思われる。

2　「四海」を領掌する方法

(1)　「四海」の用法

　中世日本において世界を端的に表す言葉の一つに「四海」がある。この用語は、もともと中国を中心とする天下や四方の地域や海域を示す⁽¹⁴⁾。漢代に成立した『大戴礼記』五帝徳には、四海をそれぞれ、北方幽陵（現：河北省密雲県の東北部）・南方交趾（現：ベトナム南部）・西方流沙（現：ゴビ砂漠およびタクラマカン砂漠）・東方蟠木（東海中にある山で神荼・鬱壘二神の居所）と説明しているほか⁽¹⁵⁾、漢代初頭に編さんされた中国最古の古辞書『爾雅』釈地には九夷・八狄・七戎・六蛮とあるなど、いずれも異民族や周辺地域を指している。この意味から漢字における「四海」とは、中心に対する周縁性を必然的に含んだ用語として理解できる。

　日本の中世文書における「四海」の用法は、願文や宣命、寄進状などに「四海静謐」や「四海安寧」「四海安全」「四海清平」という表現とともに登場している。これらの用法は、いずれも国土と同じ意味として機能している。この他、慶長8年（1603）に日本イエズス会によって刊行された『日葡辞書』には「Xicai. シカイ（四海）Yotçuno vmi.（四つの海）」という項目があり、「都（*Miaco*）から言って四つの方角にある四つの海。Itten xicai.（一天四海）全世界」とあり⁽¹⁶⁾、京都を中心とする東西南北を意識した意味で解釈されている。

　その一方で、「四海」は、仏教用語としても展開した。たとえば、「後七日御修法由緒作法」には、「夫正月後七日御修法者。聖朝地久之御願。四海安寧之祈

祷。万菓成就五穀豊饒修法也[17]」(以下、資料引用の下線部は引用者による) と登場するなど、密教修法にも国土を含む周辺地域を意味する用語として登場する。総じて四海とは、仏教的世界観における全世界を意味した。

　仏教的世界観における「世界」の構成は、第1章第1節で説明したように、須弥山の周囲に浮かぶ四大洲の陸地の間には水が湛えられていた。この水が「四海」であるとされ、「世界」を支える水を意味する用語として機能していた。

　4世紀頃にインドで成立した法顕訳の『大般涅槃経』には、「即立太子而以為王。集余大臣及婆羅門長者居士。以四海水灌太子頂[18]」とあり、王となる太子の頭頂に「四海」の水を灌ぐとある。この場合の「四海」とは、地理的空間である地域や海域の概念と異なり、灌頂水の源泉を意味する。灌頂とは、もともと、悟りの境地に至ったことを証明する宗教的儀式を指し、五智を象徴する水を頭頂に灌ぐことを意味した。その後、灌頂は師から弟子に対し阿闍梨位を与える儀礼となった[19]。

　転輪王が即位の際に、四海の水を頭頂に灌頂するという用法を記した聖教は多くある。転輪王とは、転輪聖王や輪王ともいい、古代インドで理想とされた国王のことである。例えば南北朝時代の東密の僧杲宝(1306〜1362)が撰した『金剛頂宗綱概』には、「譬如転輪聖王将登極時。取四海水請一明師。灌頂加持被印可已。然後登極。爾時四海敬信。萬民承奉。仏亦如是[20]」と記され、前半の「四海」は、転輪王が即位する時に灌頂する水を意味し、後半の「四海」は、「万民」や「仏」と同値される国土を意味した。

　このように、仏教における「四海」は、即位時に転輪王の頭頂に灌ぐ灌頂水の源泉を指した。しかし、古代インドの国王儀礼と、仏教における転輪王の灌頂儀礼との共通点は、水を注ぐプロセスのみであり、それ以外の部分はほとんど一致していない[21]。

(2) 即位法のなかの「四海」

　経典に登場する転輪王の灌頂と結びつくのは、近年議論が深まっている天皇の即位灌頂である。日本における天皇の即位灌頂では、実際に灌頂水を用いることはなかった。しかし寺家で伝持された天皇の即位法には、「四海」が登場し、灌頂水と同等の意味で捉えられた。次に示すのは、天台僧 澄豪(ちょうごう)(1259〜1350)が

撰述した日本の天皇即位を前提とした即位法に登場する「四海」部分の説明である[22]。

　　（中略）次四海領掌印。外五古印　自淡路國西海道。次南海道。次東海道。次山陽道。次山陰道。是名四海印（以下略）。
　　　　　　　　　　　　　　　　（『総持抄』「御即位之時奉授帝王事」）

この記述には「四海領掌印」の内容として、東西南北の道筋にそった地域が示されている。すなわち西海道・南海道・東海道・山陽道・山陰道を指し、それを「四海印」と称すという。「印」とは、造形化された仏像などの指を屈伸させて作る手印を指し、仏菩薩など尊格の性質を象徴的に表現したものも含む。ここに示された「四海印」とは、この「四海」の性質を表現したもので、日本全土を示す用語として用いられている。そして「四海印」の理念は、同資料の以下の説明により明確になる。

　　帝王御即位時。令即大極殿高御蔵（座）。御接録臣（摂籙）。令授帝王。給フ印明也。持十善治天下也。仍以十指懸肩之心。持物荷背負懸肩也。持十善重位。四海七道領掌心也。

すなわち、天皇が即位する際は、大極殿の高御座において、摂関家が天皇に印と明を授けるという。それにより天皇が「十善[23]」を持ち、天下を治めるという。インドでは、世の中に十善を実現すべき存在を帝王とする思想があった。それ故に、天皇の印明のかたちは、十指を肩に懸けるのであり、持物の荷を背負い肩に懸けることで、「十善重位」（天皇の位）を持つことであるという。それが「四海七道領掌心」であるとされ、「十善」を持つ天皇が天下を治めるという意味で用いられている。

天皇が即位する際に修した即位灌頂では、即位法が修された。即位法とは、天皇が修す即位灌頂の次第内容を説明したものであり、即位灌頂とは灌頂の行為そのものを指した。この即位法は、寺家で伝持され「四海領掌法」とも称された[24]。そこでは、天皇の支配領域として「四海」が位置づけられた。つまり、

「四海」の「領掌」とは、仏教的世界観における天皇に付属する理念的な支配領域が、天皇即位を契機に掌握されることを意味した。
　そもそも即位灌頂は、天皇が密教王としての身体を獲得するとともに、天皇自身が修すことで大日如来の擬態となる儀礼として知られている。その歴史は、平安時代後期の治暦４年（1068）に即位した後三条天皇といわれ、この時は小野流の護持僧成尊が即位法の伝授に関わったと推測されている。その後、鎌倉時代中期に成立した二条摂関家が家職として天皇に印明を伝授し、天皇が即位灌頂を恒常的に修すようになったのは、鎌倉時代後期の弘安10年（1287）伏見天皇の即位以降である。
　即位灌頂は、中世仏教と王権の関係を象徴的に表しており、天皇が密教化する点に着目が集まるが、同時に天皇の支配領域をも提示されていた。換言すれば、即位灌頂によって、天皇の支配領域が天皇の身体同様に、密教的世界観によって読み替えられたのである。
　中国の古辞書『爾雅』では「四海」が辺境の蛮夷を意味したように、漢民族が保持した伝統的な世界観では、大地を囲繞する環海が「四海」として認識された。そして、この四海の範囲は、漢民族の居住領域の拡大にともない、次第に現実的な地域へと変わった[25]。

(3) 天皇の「四海」

　天皇即位法における「四海」の領域とは、前節で論じたように西海道・南海道・東海道・山陽道・山陰道を指す。行基図に代表される日本図では、大和から東西南北に延びる道が線で示されており、これが放射線状に広がっている。中世における日本図の地理は、道線によって把握されることが多く、道は、大和とのつながりや関係を領域的に把握する認識方法でもあった[26]。次に示す南北朝時代の天台僧光宗（1276～1350）が撰述した『溪嵐拾葉集』には、即位法のなかの四海と地理上の道線とが、結びつけられている叙述がある[27]。

　一、国土衆生皆曼荼羅界会聖衣也。国ニ有五畿七道。五畿ト者胎藏ノ五大法界ヲ表シ。七道ト者悉地ノ七識和合ヲ表ス。都ニ有九重。金界ノ九表ス。天子即位ノ時<u>四海領掌</u>ノ印結ヒ金輪王ノ位ニ居シ給也。故ニ以金輪ノ法名

四海統領灌頂ト事深可思合之ヲ。又此外ニ覚大師弘法大師ノ秘決等二十五巻有之口伝ト云云。

　この叙述は、日本国土の道である五畿七道や内裏を曼荼羅に比定したものである。すなわち、「五畿」が「胎蔵」であり、「七道」が「悉地」を表すという。そして、都には「九重」＝内裏があり、それは「金界」であるという。そして、天子即位の時は、四海領掌の印を結び、金輪王の位に即くという。それを「四海統領灌頂」といい、慈覚大師や弘法大師の口伝があるという。いわば、この「四海統領」の「四海」とは、曼荼羅世界に位置づけられた五畿七道と都の内裏であり、天皇の支配領域を意味している。

　それは次に示す近世以前に成立したと考えられる『日本略記』の記述からも明らかである[28]。（句読点は引用者が適宜付した）

　一、内裏は忝も十善の御位なれば、日本の主にて一天四海にかしづかれ給ひ、六十余州より崇敬申は、王土に住居する故也。又、公方様は帝王の御代官として、天下の将軍として日本の政所と号し、又、御所と申す。

　すなわち、「内裏」＝天皇は、日本の主として「一天四海」を治め、日本全土から崇敬されるのは、「王土」に居住するからであるという。そして、公方は帝王の代官であり将軍として政治を司り、御所と表す旨が記されている。この一文は、前節で示した四海領掌法の理念と天皇の支配領域が一致する記述に加え、公方である将軍が位置づけられている。すなわち、仏教的世界観における「王土」を支配する権力者の姿が描写されており、「四海」もその表現方法の一つとして存在していた。

3　大地としての「平安京」

(1) 両部曼荼羅の都

　第2章で論じたように、「四海」とは天皇の支配領域を示す用語として登場していた。さらに、中世日本には、天皇が京都と一体になって観想する仏教儀礼

があった。本章では、密教的世界観に天皇のみならず、都も解釈された点について論じる。

　以下に示す聖教は上島享氏によって平安時代の密教的な国土観を提示する史料として紹介された『護持僧作法』である[29]。本聖教は、勝覚（1057〜1129）が永久3年（1115）に師の口決を筆写したものである。引用は平安京を観想した部分である。

　　観想、自一条至九条、配当八葉九尊、又自西大宮至東京極、観十三大院、
　　四方四角可配分護世八天、九重中上下人民悉想胎蔵界四重曼荼羅之聖衆、

　これによると、平安京の一条から九条までを、胎蔵界曼荼羅の中央の空間を意味する「八葉九尊」に比定し、さらに南北の道を同じく曼荼羅の空間を区分けした「十三大院」に見立てている。そして、曼荼羅に見立てた平安京の四隅にあたる部分に方位を守護する「八天」の配置を構想し、この平安京に住む人々を胎蔵界曼荼羅に登場する「聖衆」に見立てている。さらに同聖教には、これに関する印明を結ぶことで「宮城安穏太平」や「地中穢悪皆散」となると説明されている。

表1　平安京・曼荼羅の配置図（「九重配当図」）

東城竪行図		東城横行図	
京の南北	十三大院	京の東西	八葉九尊
大宮	四大護院	一条	宝幢
猪熊	金剛部院	二条	開敷
堀川	除蓋障院	三条	無量
油小路	文殊院	四条	天鼓
西洞院	遍智院	五条	遍照如来
河原町	蘇悉地院	六条	普賢
室町	八葉院	七条	文殊
烏丸	五大院	八条	観音
東洞院	釈迦院	九条	弥勒
高倉	地蔵院		
万里小路	蓮華部院		
富小路	虚空蔵院		
京極	外部院		

※本表は、上島享「日本中世の神観念と国土観」（『日本中世社会の形成と王権』、406〜411頁）で紹介されている随心院聖教17-2号に基づき作成した。図中の「東城」とは平安京の東側（左京）を指し、「竪行」とは都の南北の道、「横行」とは東西の道を示す。

曼荼羅を平安京にたとえた構想は、密教的な平安京を理念的に演出したものであるといえ、その発想自体は密教本意のものであるといえる。また、単に都の造形が曼荼羅に比定されたのみならず、都の護持が結びつけられていた。
　【表１】は、平安京の東西（「横」）の通りを曼荼羅の仏に、南北（「竪」）の通りが、具体的に曼荼羅を構成する空間の名称に比定されたものである。
　さらに、同作法には、平安京の東（左京）と西（右京）に両部曼荼羅（金剛界と胎蔵界）を配置すべきかも知れないが、右京の条里が不足していたため、禁中を金剛界曼荼羅に見立てたと説明されている。この点は、慶滋保胤（993～1002）が天元５年（982）に著した『池亭記』に、都としての左京北部の繁栄と右京の機能が衰退した点が記されている点とも一致する[30]。そして、東の都を「胎蔵界」、内裏を「金剛界」と観想することで、「両部不二」が「深観在之（深くこれあるを観る）」とするという。
　上川通夫氏によると、平安末期における平安京は、擬似宋風的な中世仏教を政治的に装ったエキゾチックな擬似国際都市でもあり、そこに、実権力を効さない「究極擬似的存在」である「金輪聖王」としての天皇と、政治的集団を率いた「国王」としての法皇の存在を想定された。そして、これが中世仏教で正当化され、「日本国」が形成されていたと評価する[31]。

(2) 密教のなかの天皇
　平安京が密教的世界観をあらわす両部曼荼羅であるならば、天皇もやはり密教的な世界観に位置づけられていた。第２節で論じたように、天皇は仏教界のなかでインドの理想王であった転輪王の中でも金輪聖王にたとえられていた。そして、中世寺院に伝持された即位法では、金輪聖王が即位の際に頭に灌がれた「四海」の灌頂水が、天皇の即位法のなかでは、灌頂水としてではなく、天皇の支配領域として認識されていた。そして、両部曼荼羅によって天皇と平安京とが一体化していた。このような思想は、天皇の存在を密教的に見立てることによって明確化された。しかし、天皇の存在領域が密教的世界観によって表現されたとしても、天皇自身は、密教的世界観にとってどのような意味をもつ存在であったのであろうか。
　前節で言及した勝覚筆『護持僧作法』に収められている記事には、「当代国主

金輪正王也、聖王即日天子御胤子、彼是一躰無二、而更無差異、故国主玉躰御心中有万法能生㹟字」と記されている。

すなわち、国主＝金輪正王＝日天子御胤子であり、これらは「一体不二」であり、差異はないという。そのため、国主の玉体の御心中は「万法能生㹟字」であるという。つまり、密教では全宇宙がこの㹟字に集約されているとされ、天皇と㹟字を一体として観想することによって、密教的宇宙を天皇として捉えることを意味する。また、その目的は「率土人民」を利するためとあり、国土の人民支配と結びつけられていた。

しかし、このような絶対者としての天皇が位置づけられた仏教的世界は、世俗的であったが世俗権力そのものではかった。換言すれば、中世仏教によって正当化された天皇像であり、天皇が密教王として見立てられても、仏教界に唯一絶対的な権力を持つことはなかった。

おわりに

近代日本に流入した地動説という新たな世界観が、前近代におけるそれまでの仏教的世界観に打撃を与えることにより、梵暦運動が喚起された。しかし、前近代における世界観は、仏教という中世的な価値体系のなかに、天皇を中心とする世界が構築され、そこに新たな観念が増殖する形で形成された。

都における内裏は天皇を中心とする清浄な空間であり、内裏から同心円状に国土が次第に穢れていくという境界領域的な観念があった。中世に考えられていた都の限界としての四堺四境、そして四至によって取り囲まれた国土は、天皇支配の領域として考えられていた。しかし、天皇と平安京が理念的に両部曼荼羅の不二を体現すると見立てられた世界は、仏教を絶対視する価値世界においてのみ有効であった。

天皇の身体と共に密教的に観想された内裏は、すでに天徳4年（960）年の火災以降再建と火災を繰り返し、安貞元年（1227）に内裏が焼失した後は再建されなかった。中世における天皇の身体や都は、失われた内裏とともに密教的世界観のなかで観想されたのである。そして、鎌倉時代中期以降の天皇家は、持明院統と大覚寺統に分立し、さらに北朝と南朝の天皇が交互に即位するという事

態になる。それまでの「両部不二」という密教的世界観の絶対的な思想は、その前提から根本的に崩れていくのである。

　元弘元年（1331）、もともと里内裏であった土御門東洞院殿で北朝の光厳天皇が即位して以降、ここが天皇御所となり、現在の京都御所に至る。これはそれまでの都における天皇の内裏の位置関係が実際的に変化したことを意味する。それは、都の構造自体が現実的に変化する中で、中世の密教的世界観によって構築された都と天皇との関係は既に過去のものとなることを意味した。このように、中世における内裏や天皇は、仏教によって一時的に絶対的な意味を与えられても、永久に持続することはなかったのである。

　近代に登場した梵暦も、西洋の現実的な天文学の到来によって、それまでの仏教的世界観の意味が問われた。これは、中世に内裏の位置が現実的に変化したことと同様、宗教によって構築された観念的世界が、実際的な世界の登場によって、非現実的なものとして価値転換するに至ったのである。

　中世以降、仏教的世界観が構築した世界認識は、形を変えながら近代の梵暦運動を経た後に、それは現実ではないものと認識されるに至った。しかし、仏教的世界観の本質は、現実か非現実的かであるかの問題ではなく、それが一時でも時代を動かす普遍的な価値観として提示できた点にあると考えられる。

■注
(1) 上川通夫「中世仏教と日本国」（『日本中世仏教形成史論』校倉書房、2007）。
(2) 海野一隆「一漢民族の地理思想—特にその地勢観について」（『地理の思想』地人書房、1982、70頁）。青木宏夫「前近代地図研究のメソドロジー」（『前近代地図の空間と知』校倉書房、2007）。
(3) 鮎沢信太郎「鎖国時代に刊行された万国人物図」（『西川如見の世界地理研究』京成社出版部、1944）。
(4) 奈良国立博物館特別展『天竺へ〜三蔵法師3万キロの旅』（奈良国立博物館、2011）に掲載。
(5) 横浜市立大学学術情報センター所蔵。本資料は、工藤康海旧蔵。『梵暦蒐書目録』（横浜市立大学図書館、1969、No.18）。
(6) 岡田正彦「起源／本質の探究と普遍主義のディスクール—普門円通『仏国暦象論』を読む」（『忘れられた仏教天文学—十九世紀の日本における仏教世界像』ブイツーソリューション、2010、44頁）。

⑺　岡田正彦「近代日本思想史と梵暦運動─近代的自然観と宗教言説」(前掲注6書)。
⑻　岡田正彦、前掲注6論文、38頁。
⑼　井上智勝「幕末維新期の仏教天文学と社会・地域」(明治維新研究会編『明治維新と文化』吉川弘文館、2005)。
⑽　市川浩史「日本中世前夜の「内なる三国」の思想」(『日本中世の光と影─「内なる三国」の思想』ぺりかん社、1999、14頁)。
⑾　伊藤聡「梵漢和同一観の成立基盤」(『中世天照大神信仰の研究』法蔵館、2011)
⑿　高橋公明「東アジアと中世文学」(『岩波講座日本文学史』第5巻、岩波書店、1995)。
⒀　高橋公明、前掲論文、312頁。
⒁　小学館『日本国語大辞典』の「四海」の項目には、①四方の海、②国内、くにじゅう、世界、天下、③四方の外国、国のまわり、四方のえびす、④須弥山をとりまく四方の外海とある。これらは、四海の用法に伴う意味の解釈である。小稿では、中世文書における「四海」の用法をとおして、実際に認識されていた四海の範囲と、四海を掌握した人物、その意義を追究するものである。
⒂　栗原圭介『新釈漢文大系113　大戴礼記』(明治書院、1991)所収。
⒃　《VOCABVLARIO DA LINGOA DE IAPAN com a declareção em Portugs》、『邦訳日葡辞書』(岩波書店、1980、759頁)。
⒄　勝賢記・守覚輯『秘抄』(『大正新脩大蔵経』第78巻、No.2489)所収。
⒅　法顕訳『大般涅槃經』(『大正新脩大蔵経』第1巻、No.0007)所収。
⒆　森雅秀「アビシェーカ儀礼の起源と変遷」(『インド密教の儀礼世界』世界思想社、2011)参照。
⒇　『大正新脩大蔵経』第77巻、No.2451、所収。
(21)　森雅秀「アビシェーカとプラティシュター」(前掲注19書、192頁)。
(22)　澄豪撰『總持抄』(『大正新脩大蔵経』第77巻、No.2412)所収。
(23)　十善とは、身(不殺生・不偸盗・不邪婬)、語(不妄語・不両舌・不悪口・不綺語)、意(無貪欲・無瞋恚・正見)の行為のこと。
(24)　松本郁代『中世王権と即位灌頂─聖教のなかの歴史叙述』(森話社、2005)。
(25)　木村宏「十六世紀以前、中国人の南海地域に関する地理的知識」(京都大学文学部地理学教室『地理の思想』地人書房、1982、108・109頁)。
(26)　村井章介「中世日本列島の地域空間と国家」(『アジアのなかの中世日本』校倉書房、1988)。
(27)　『溪嵐拾葉集』「第四金輪法事」(『大正新脩大蔵経』第76巻、No.2410)所収。
(28)　『続々群書類従』第八、地理部、所収。この奥書には、文禄5年(1595)・慶長13年(1608)・元文5年(1740)の記録がある。成立は文禄5年以前と考えられる。
(29)　本史料は、随心院聖教17-2号。上島享「日本中世の神観念と国土観」(『日本中世

社会の形成と王権』名古屋大学出版部、2011、406〜411頁）で【史料翻刻】紹介され
　ている。
(30)　小島憲之校注『日本古典文学大系69 懐風藻 文華秀麗集 本朝文粋』（岩波書店、
　1964年）所収。
(31)　上川通夫「中世仏教と「日本国」」（前掲注1書、271頁）参照。

Chap.4 19世紀英国における円山四条派理解について
―英国人蒐集家が京都の画師に寄せた思い―

彬子女王　*Princess Akiko of Mikasa*

はじめに

　1858（安政5）年の開国以降、日本を訪れた西洋人たちによって多くの日本絵画や版画が蒐集され、海を渡ったことは広く知られている。特に大量に海外にもたらされた浮世絵版画は、後期印象派の画家たちに影響を与えたというエピソードによって、西洋人に認められた日本の美術として度々紹介をされてきた。
　しかし、「海外にもたらされたこと」と「海外で評価されたこと」とは直結しないということを忘れてはならない。19世紀に日本を訪れることのできた数少ない西洋人たちは、未知の国「日本」の情報を本国に持ち帰ると言う使命を自然と抱いていたはずである。その蒐集された品々は質の優劣に関わらず、日本という国を知るための貴重な標本になり得た[1]。つまり、在外コレクションに含まれる日本の絵画は、絵画として評価をされたからそこにあるとは言い切れないのである。
　しかし、浮世絵の例を除けば、19世紀のヨーロッパにおいて、日本の絵画がどのように評価されたかという問題に言及する先行研究は極めて少ない。そこで本論稿では、19世紀末から20世紀初頭にかけて、英国で出版された日本絵画に関する論考を基に、英国人はどのように日本の絵画を評価したかについて述べたい。日本美術史全体を検討対象とするほど紙面に余裕はないため、本論稿では特に、19世紀に日本絵画を蒐集した英国人蒐集家たちの中で比較的評価が高い、円山四条派の絵画に対する評価に注目することとする。

19世紀の英国人日本美術蒐集家たちには単にShijo School（四条派）と呼ばれ、18世紀後半から19世紀にかけて京都を中心に繁栄した画師の一派が円山四条派である。現在の美術史研究の中では円山応挙（1733-95）を祖とする円山派と、応挙に親炙した呉春（1752-1811）を祖とする四条派を合わせて円山四条派と呼ばれている。日本美術史における円山四条派は、狩野派などに代表される伝統的な粉本主義から脱却し、自然をそのままに写す写生を旨としたことから、日本絵画の近代化を進めたとして評価されている。そして、狩野派ややまと絵の古典的な様式とは異なるその近代的かつ写実的な表現は、19世紀の英国の日本美術蒐集家たちの間で高い人気を誇った。例を挙げれば、1880年には英国人挿絵画家であったフランク・ディロン（1823-1909）が日本の写生派絵画の複製集を出版している[2]。また、本論稿でも取り上げるお雇い外国人であったウィリアム・ガウランド（1842-1922）は、1892年にロンドンの日本協会において、「日本の写生美術」と題した講演を行っている[3]。そこで円山四条派は「Naturalistic School＝写生派」と呼ばれ、特に注目された画派であった。

　本論稿では、3人の英国人日本絵画蒐集家によって書かれた円山四条派についての記述を取り上げる。ウィリアム・アンダーソン（1842-1900）、ウィリアム・ガウランド、アーネスト・ハート（1835-1898）という立場も目的も違う蒐集家たちが、円山四条派の何に惹きつけられたのか、そして19世紀の英国人の日本絵画に対する理解、彼らが円山四条派に求めたものがいかなるものであったのかを明らかにしたい。

1　3人の蒐集家

　ウィリアム・アンダーソンは、1873（明治6）年に新しく設立された、帝国海軍医学校・海軍病院の解剖学と外科の教授として採用された英国人医師である。彼はいわゆる明治政府のお雇い外国人として約7年間日本に滞在し、多くの医学生を育成しただけでなく、脚気の研究やコレラ防疫運動などにも尽力し、日本の医学界の発展に大きく貢献した。しかし、その医師としての仕事の傍ら、アンダーソンが情熱的に蒐集したのが日本絵画であった。彼の3000点を超える日本絵画のコレクションは、1881年に大英博物館によって購入されている。

2人目の蒐集家、ウィリアム・ガウランドは、同じくお雇い外国人としてアンダーソンが来日する1年前に来日した人物である。アンダーソンとは同時期に日本に滞在していたことから交流があったようだ。大阪の造幣寮で16年間勤務し、化学と英国式冶金技術の指導に携わった。在職中には造幣局長官顧問や陸軍省冶金関係特別顧問にも任命されている。しかし、現在彼はその功績よりも、アマチュアの考古学者としての一面がよく知られている。日本滞在中の16年間に、近畿地方を中心に、北は福島、南は宮崎まで400余りの古墳時代の遺跡を調査した。彼が蒐集した考古学関連の遺物は、大英博物館によって1879年に購入されたが、精密な遺跡の測量図だけでも140点の現存が確認されている。彼のもう一つの興味の中心であった円山四条派の絵画コレクションは残念ながら散逸した。第一次世界大戦の折に日本で売り立てられ、それで得た売り上げをガウランドが英国国家に寄付したためである[4]。

　3人目の蒐集家はアーネスト・ハートである。ハートはもともと眼科医であったが、1858年から医療ジャーナリストとしての活動を始めた。1866年に*British Medical Journal*（『イギリス医師会雑誌』）の編集者として採用されてからは、ジャーナリストを本業とした。彼がどのように日本美術への興味を抱いたかについてははっきりしないが、仕事の関連で極東地域に出張することが多かったことと無関係ではないだろう[5]。ハートは公衆衛生問題、特にコレラ予防に関心を持っていた。医療関係の人脈を通してアンダーソンと出会い、日本絵画の蒐集に興味を持った可能性もある。ハートがアンダーソン・コレクションから数点日本絵画を購入していることからも、2人の親密な交流がうかがえる。そして、ハート・コレクションは1901年に彼の未亡人によって大英博物館に遺贈されている。

　今まで述べてきたことからもわかる通り、このバックグラウンドの異なる3人を「日本美術」という分野で結び付けたのは、ウィリアム・アンダーソンである。アンダーソンは、1886年に自身の日本美術の研究成果をまとめた*Descriptive and Historical Catalogue of a Collection of Japanese and Chinese Paintings in the British Museum*（『大英博物館所蔵日本中国絵画カタログ』）と*The Pictorial Arts of Japan*（『日本絵画芸術』）を出版している。この2冊の書籍は、西洋における日本美術書の嚆矢として高く評価された。

ロンドンの日本協会で1892年に開催された、ガウランド所蔵の日本絵画コレクションの展覧会に関連し、ガウランドが「日本の写生美術」と題した講演を行ったことは先に述べた。その際にアンダーソンの研究なくしては自分の講演は不可能であったこと、そしてアンダーソンの著作が日本美術愛好者と研究者にとっていかに重要であるかを冒頭で述べている[6]。また、ハートは美術商工業振興協会で1886年に行った講演の中で、アンダーソンから日本美術に関する多くの助言を受けたことについて触れ、アンダーソンが日本絵画研究に遺した功績を高く評価している[7]。

　彼らのアンダーソンに対する賛辞からは、彼らがアンダーソンの日本美術観を参考にしていることがよくわかる。特に画派の分類についてはアンダーソンの分類方法をそのまま踏襲している[8]。アンダーソンが絵画蒐集を行っていた時代、日本では「日本美術史」と言う概念は未だ確立していなかった。狩野派や浮世絵派の画論や画人伝はあっても、日本美術全体を通史として言及したものは、邦語でも欧語でも出版されていなかったのである。そこでアンダーソンは、多くの絵画作品を集め、自ら西洋の科学的な分類方法を日本の絵画史に応用した。煩雑でとらえにくかった日本の絵画史を、古代から近代まで、画派別、時代別に区分けしたのである[9]。ガウランドもハートも理系の経歴を持っていることから、アンダーソンの日本絵画に対する科学的な分析は理解しやすかったであろうことが想像できる。

2　科学的な視線

　アンダーソン、ガウランド、ハートはそれぞれの日本美術に関する著作の中で、各画派の代表的な作家の説明や個々の作品の詳細な解説などを行っている。概ね好意的な意見を寄せているが、時折辛辣な批判を行うことがある。
　数例をここに挙げてみたい。アンダーソンはやまと絵について、

> 純粋なやまと絵派の特徴と言うのは、集合的にみるととても独特であるが、取り立てて分析するような目立った要素はない。（中略）しかし、京都の高尚な文化を表象する貴族の男女の描写の人形のような愚かな表現は、伝統

の落ち度と言うよりは、画家の美的眼識の欠如と言えるだろう[10]

と皮肉的に述べている。

　ハートはやまと絵について、

　　何点かの例外を除いて、やまと絵の絵師の作品に共感するふりはできない。今あなた方に彼らの作品を見せているのは、純粋な美術的価値と同じように、少なくとも考古学的価値はあると思うからである[11]

と手厳しい。

　批判はやまと絵だけにとどまらない。琳派について述べる中でアンダーソンは、

　　彼（筆者註：尾形光琳）の人物や動物の描写においては、彼の大切な慣例尊重主義が、最も重要な主題を風刺画のように変えてしまっている。彼の描く男性や女性は、下手に作られた人形よりも形や表情がなく、彼の描く馬や鹿は、塗り絵のおもちゃのようである[12]

と酷評している。

　これらの指摘に共通することは、彼らの批判の対象が日本美術に特徴的ともいえる抽象的表現であるということである。特に、西洋美術を学んだ経験のあるアンダーソンは、日本美術の中の明暗法・遠近法・解剖学の知識の欠如について繰り返し批判している[13]。西洋美術とは対照的に、浮世絵のように役者の筋肉を戯画化する表現や、大きさの不整合、位置取りのつじつまがあわないことなどが理解できなかったようである。その反面、色彩表現の調和や雪の白を絵の具を用いずに塗り残しで描くと言った、非科学的ではあるが、「即妙で創意豊かな工夫」などについては、日本人の詩情をよく表しているとの理解を見せている[14]。

　このように解剖学医としての科学的な目で日本美術を見ていたアンダーソンが、最も肯定的に評価した画派が円山四条派なのである。*The Pictorial Arts of*

Japan の中で、他の画派が 1 章の中にいくつかまとめられて記載されているのに対し、円山四条派には 1 章全てが充てられている。これはいかなる理由によるものなのだろうか。後の節で検証していきたい。

3 写実的か否か―西洋美術の観点の応用―

アンダーソンは、*The Pictorial Arts of Japan* の第 4 節の冒頭で日本絵画の特徴について以下のように述べている。

> 日本の画師の理想は、あらゆる側面で我々ヨーロッパ人のそれとは異なっている。二つの民族の美的本能が現れた作品に、同じ基準の批評を行うのは不可能なのである[15]

このアンダーソンの日本絵画に対する寛容な理解は、この時代の西洋人にしてはとても革新的なものである。しかし、アンダーソンは、遠近法や明暗法の欠如と言った絵画の写実性に関わる問題については大目に見ることが出来なかったようだ。これは、ガウランドやハートにも共通する点である。彼らは常に日本絵画を写実的か、否か、という視点で判断する。そして、「写実的」(naturalistic)、もしくは「自然主義」(Naturalism) という言葉を多用しながら作品の説明を行ったり、主題は写生されたものか、粉本からのか写しであるのか、あるいはそれらに解剖学的正確さがあるか、という観点から解説する傾向がある[16]。
　例えばアンダーソンは雪舟 (1420-1508) について、

> 雪舟の自然に対する観察力は確かなものであり、特に風景画にはそれが顕著に表れているが、直接的な本質を写そうとはせず、思い出、あるいは漠然とした雰囲気を表現しようとするのみである[17]

と批判している。
　ガウランドは、このアンダーソンの意見を自身の講演の際に引用し、実際の雪舟の作品を観衆に見せながらさらに付け加えて、

> この二つの風景画の細部の解釈のほとんどは、見る人の想像力に委ねられている。我々にとっては、このように大雑把な雪舟の作品を評するのに、なぜ日本人の批評家が「自然の」(natural)、あるいは「生きているような」(lifelike) という言葉を多用するのか理解するのは困難である[18]。

と述べている。雪舟が写実的であるかという根本的な問題はさておき、西洋美術を見慣れた彼らにとって、雪舟の作品は写実的には見えないということがよくわかる。

　つまり、彼らは西洋美術を絶対的なものだと考え、常に西洋美術を基準として比較をしている。例えば、英一蝶 (1652-1724) について、一蝶作品の特徴やその機智と言うものはとても国内的なもので、日本の外ではなかなか理解されないという[19]。また、アンダーソンは日本人画師を西洋画家になぞらえて解説する。例えば、室町初期の画僧明兆 (1352-1431) をルネサンス初期の画家で修道士であったフラ・アンジェリコ (c.1390/95-1455) に例えている[20]。また、写実的な猿などの絵で名声を誇った森狙仙 (1747-1821) を、同じく動物の絵で聞こえ高いエドウィン・ランドシーア (1802-73) に例え、ランドシーアの《老羊飼いの喪主》や《事務所のジャック》と比較して、狙仙はランドシーアより才能が劣っている、と結論付けている[21]。一方、ハートは狙仙について述べる中で、日本の画師の中でも、ヨーロッパの写実的絵画の基準に最も近い絵を描くと高く評価し、ヨーロッパの市場でも多くの狙仙作品の贋作が出回っていることを指摘している[22]。

　このように多くの場合、彼らは西洋美術と照らし合わせて日本絵画を評価しているのである。

　特に西洋美術の教育を受けていたアンダーソンは、日本人の絵師が写生をせず、師匠の作品や粉本を写すことに囚われすぎていると感じていたようである。西洋においても、師匠の作品の模写をすることは、重要な教育の一部である。ルーベンス (1577-1640) はティシャン (c.1488/90-1576) を、ミケランジェロ (1475-1564) はカラヴァッジョ (1571-1610) を、ドラクロワ (1798-1863) はルーベンスの作品をそれぞれ写している。しかし、グローヴ美術事典によれば、「過去の美術の研究をすることは、美の目標基準を具体化するためのもの」であると

いう[23]。つまり、西洋の美術教育の中で、模写をすることは、学校では教えられない知識の補助という役割しかなかったのである。

以上のことから、西洋美術の知識の上に立っているアンダーソンを始めとする英国人日本美術蒐集家たちは、写生を旨とした円山四条派の作品を、最も西洋美術の基準に近い、理解しやすい絵画として評価していると考えられる。これは、ハートが「私のコレクションの中で、写生派（筆者註：円山四条派）の筆による作品以上に、日本美術についての知識の乏しい鑑賞者を惹きつけるものはないであろう」と述べていることからも明らかである[24]。

4 英国人にとっての円山四条派
　　―アンダーソン・ガウランド・ハートの場合―

円山四条派の最大の特徴は写生である。アンダーソンは、日本絵画史の中で、狩野派ややまと絵、他の画派による写生への試みを認めてはいるが、それは評価に値する水準のものではないとする。彼の言う、実際的な知識に基づく写生美術に日本絵画史で初めて近づくことができた画師が円山応挙である[25]。応挙について、アンダーソンは以下のように述べている。

> 四条派の最も重要な特徴は、優美で流れるような輪郭線、昔の大家たちに典型的な、筆致の恣意的なマンネリズムからの解放である。そして、時にはほとんど完璧に近い、かなり真に迫った動物の生活の解釈、最後に軽やかな彩色法、描く主体の基調となる色合いの暗示的な様子、豊かで繊細な色の調和やグラデーションである[26]。

またガウランドは、四条派と古い他の画派との違いは、写生と言う初期段階の指導法の問題だけではなく、その主題、技術、そしてその弟子や追従者の社会的地位にも関係があるという[27]。彼が分析する四条派の特徴は以下の4点である。

第一に、画師は作品の主題を描くとき、古い型にはまった筆遣いを強いるのではなく、自然に直接向き合うように指導されること。第二に、四条派の作品

に用いられる画題は他の画派のそれとはかなり異なっており、主に中国からもたらされるような、想像上のもの、伝説や歴史的な画題は余り用いられないこと[28]。これは四条派の画師たちが、静なる美や京都の魅力に十分なインスピレーションを見出すことができるので、中国画題に頼る必要がないと解説される。第三に、四条派の工房はすべての人々に開かれており、狩野派や土佐派のように特定の氏族に属する必要がないこと。第四に、四条派は古めかしい極彩色の色遣いを避け、快い効果を生み出す繊細な色調や水彩表現を採用したこと[29]。この4点を根拠として、四条派は間違いなく最も優秀で、価値のある画派であるとアンダーソンは結論付けたのである[30]。

ハートは、自身のコレクションである応挙の作品を見せながら、

> この作品を見ると、おそらく応挙が教育されたと思われる中国派の伝統から、彼がいかに離れているか、彼がいかに自然に忠実か、動物の姿の上品さを遠近法で出しているか、いかに洗練されて調和のとれた色遣いか、そしていかにバランスがとれているかがよくわかるだろう[31]。

と最大限の賛辞を送っている。

アンダーソン、ガウランド、ハートの意見に共通しているのは、円山四条派のとった中国の伝統的な手法から脱却した先駆的な取り組みと、主題を自然に取材して写生を行うことへの高い評価である。しかし、それと同時に、円山四条派の自然主義は十分に写実的とは言えない、とも批判しているのである。

アンダーソンは以下のように述べている。

> 応挙に寄せられた信頼にも拘わらず、彼の作品は、彼が信念に対する十分な勇気がないことを示している。彼の線描は、どんなに細かな部分であっても、その多くが自然に忠実に描かれている。しかし、彼は未だ、おそらく無意識的に、古い教義の祭壇の上で犠牲になっているのである[32]。

さらに続けて、

四条派の自然主義の根本方針は、不完全に発達したものである。明暗法の
　　効果の多くは成功として通用するものだが、作品の最も明るい部分、反射
　　した光、投影された影の表現などは、未だ認められず、遠近法や解剖学と
　　言うものは、古い画師たちがしてきたように、完全に無視されている[33]。

と批判している。
　さらにガウランドは、応挙の作品には、彼の修業時代に身についてしまった古いマンネリスムが現れているという[34]。円山四条派についての講演の中で、自身のコレクションにある応挙筆の野生の雁の絵を見せながら、鳥の動きは生き生きと描かれているのに、作品自体は中国派の因習的形式から抜け出せていない、特に波や苔の表現にそれが顕著であると述べている[35]。
　このように、3人が三者三様に、応挙、あるいは円山四条派が旨とした写生への試みを高く評価しつつも、その試みは不十分であり、西洋絵画に当たり前のようにある遠近法や解剖学的知識の欠如を厳しく批判しているのである。
　当時の西洋美術と日本美術の間にある大きな違いは、西洋では対象となるものを解剖学的に分析し、それをその通りに絵の中に表現することに重きを置くのに対し、日本ではその根本的な考え方がない、と言う点であった。それ故に、日本絵画の中の人物や動物は、西洋美術の基準に依るところの、解剖学的正確さに従って描かれているわけではない。これが、西洋美術に慣れ親しんだ英国人蒐集家たちが受け入れられなかった要素の一つである。
　しかし、円山四条派の画師たちは、粉本を通して技術を学ぶのではなく、自然そのものを学び、描こうとした。この手法が、西洋における絵画を学ぶ手法と非常に近いものであったと言える。これは、ガウランドが応挙のことを「長い歴史の中で、型にはまった絵を学ぶのではなく、自然にある主題をそのまま描こうとした最初の画師である。それ故に自然を忠実に作品の中に表現している。」と述べていることから[36]、彼らの視点が「自然をいかに忠実に写すか」にあり、それを先駆者として行った応挙に賛辞を呈したことが明らかであろう。これが、円山四条派の作品が英国人蒐集家たちによって高く評価された最も大きな理由であると考えられる。

おわりに

　これまで述べてきたように、3人の英国人蒐集家たちが円山四条派、そして円山応挙に特別な思いを寄せてきたことは明らかである。それは、彼らが絶対的とする西洋美術の規範に基づいた価値判断である。しかし、逆にいえば、極東の小国の一画派に過ぎない円山四条派が、西洋美術と比較しうる絵画として19世紀の英国において認められていたとも言うことができる。
　ウィリアム・ガウランドによる円山四条派に関する講演の後に寄せた、ウィリアム・アンダーソンのコメントには、その思いが象徴的に現れている。

　　　写生派（筆者註：円山四条派）の絵画こそ、我々にとっては、最も明確で称賛に値するという特徴の押印をすることのできるものである。（中略）応挙と彼の画派の自然主義は限定されたものではあるものの、彼らは、科学者の考え方を満足させるくらいの誠実さと正確さを持って、自然を再現しようと努力し、その線の美しさは芸術家の目にも好ましいものである[37]。

つまり、円山四条派の作品の自然主義は西洋のそれに比べると未熟ではあるものの、十分に西洋の科学者や芸術家をも満足させられるレベルに達しており、それが円山四条派を日本美術の中で最も魅力的であると結論付ける所以だと評しているのである。
　そして、アーネスト・ハートは、そのアンダーソンの言に引き続いて、以下のように述べている。

　　　我々がヨーロッパ絵画に見出すことを期待する権利のある特徴が（日本絵画に）欠如していることを批判するのはとても簡単なことである。しかし、それらは日本の古い掛け物からは意図的に欠けているものなのである。最も美しい日本絵画は、それらが持っている（筆者註：画師の）意図や美術的手法がどのようなものであるかを我々に教えてくれるのみである。しかし、我々がそれらの作品を、それらが持つ精神性と発想、伝統と限界に対して

知識と共感を持つことを前提として鑑賞すれば、最も旧態依然としたものが少しも美しくないということに気付くであろう[38]。

　ハートは、西洋美術の凝り固まった規範に依存して判断するのではなく、日本美術の伝統や精神性を理解した上で日本絵画を見ると、その旧態依然とした考え方が間違っていることに気付かされると説明している。西洋美術の概念を取り払って鑑賞することで、日本美術の本質が理解できるというのは、当時の西洋人としては革新的なものであったに違いない。

　アンダーソン、ガウランド、ハートの日本絵画、特に円山四条派に対する考え方からは、日本美術を西洋美術の理念から見つつも、彼ら独自の相対的な見方で理解しようと努力していることがうかがえる。ガウランドは自身の講演を、円山四条派が、西洋美術の中の偉大な画派の中でその名声をさらに上げ、地位を高めていくことを切望すると締めくくっている[39]。つまり、彼らは日本美術を西洋美術の中に連綿と存在するヒエラルキーの中に位置付けることのできるものとして主張しているのである。この過程の中で、西洋絵画に特徴的な写生を重んじる円山四条派の作品は、西洋の人々が日本美術は西洋美術と比較しても引けを取らないものであると理解させるために、最も適したものであったと想像できる。これが、彼らが円山四条派の作品を蒐集し、称賛し、著作の大部分をその説明にあてた理由の一つであろう。日本美術の地位を西洋美術と比較することのできる一分野として高めていく端緒となったのが、京都に生まれた一つの画塾、円山四条派だったのである。

■注

(1) 彬子女王「標本から美術へ―19世紀の日本美術蒐集、特にアンダーソン・コレクションの意義について」、『國華』1360号、2009年、28-39頁。

(2) Dillon, Frank. *Drawings by Japanese Artists; Reproduced and Coloured in Facsimile by the Autotype Process.* London: Hogarth, 1880.

(3) Gowland, William. 'The Naturalistic Art of Japan', *Transactions and Proceedings of the Japan Society*, vol. 1, London: Kegan Paul, Trench, Trübner and Co. Ltd., 1892, pp 73-110.

(4) 上田宏範「ウィリアム・ゴーランド小伝」(W. ゴーランド著　上田宏範校注『日本

古墳文化論―ゴーランド考古論集』創元社、1981、所収）352頁。
(5) *Oxford Dictionary of National Biography*, Oxford University Press, 2004-11. Available: http://www.oxforddnb.com/. Last accessed 15th Sep 2009.
(6) Gowland (1892), p.73.
(7) Ernest Hart, *Lectures on Japanese Art Works*, Society for the Encouragement of Arts, Manufactures and Commerce, London: W. Trounce, 1887, Preface.
(8) Gowland (1892) and Hart (1887).
(9) 彬子女王前掲論文、31頁。
(10) Anderson, William. *The Pictorial Arts of Japan*, London: Sampson Low, Marston, Searle & Rivington, 1886a, p.31.
(11) Hart (1887), p.29.
(12) Anderson (1886a), p.66.
(13) Anderson (1886a), p.183.
(14) Anderson (1886a), pp214-19.
(15) Anderson (1886a), p.183.
(16) Anderson (1886a).
(17) Anderson, William. *Descriptive and Historical Catalogue of a Collection of Japanese and Chinese Paintings in the British Museum*, London: Longman & Co., 1886b, p.265.
(18) Gowland (1892), p.79.
(19) Anderson (1886a), p.64.
(20) Anderson (1886b), p.21.
(21) Anderson (1886a), pp89-90.
(22) Hart (1887), p.33.
(23) *Grove Art Online*, http://www.oxfordartonline.com/, Oxford: Oxford University Press, 2007-11. Last accessed 20th March, 2011.
(24) Hart (1887), p.33.
(25) Anderson (1886a), p.87.
(26) Anderson (1886a), pp91-92.
(27) Gowland (1892), p.91.
(28) Gowland (1892), p.91.
(29) Gowland (1892), p.92.
(30) Gowland (1892), p.104.
(31) Hart (1887), p.33.
(32) Anderson (1886a), p.87.
(33) Anderson (1886a), p.92.

⑶₄ Gowland (1892), p.86.
⑶₅ Gowland (1892), p.87.
⑶₆ Gowland (1892), p.85.
⑶₇ Anderson (1886a), p.105.
⑶₈ Gowland (1892), pp107-8.
⑶₉ Gowland (1892), p104.

Chap.5 「韓国併合」を祝賀した友禅染

木立雅朗　*Masa'aki Kidachi*

はじめに

　京都の伝統工芸が文化や芸術にとって重要なものであることは誰もが認めるだろう。しかし、それと「戦争」との関わりを強調することは被害の部分を除けば、ほとんどない。今回紹介する友禅染の絵摺りは、京都や伝統工芸も社会情勢から自由ではなかった様子を教えてくれる。伝統工芸と社会との関連について、改めて考えなおしてみたい。

1　立命館大学における染織資料収集とデジタルアーカイブ作業

　立命館大学では2002年から京都の染織図案・絵摺りを収集してきた。染織産業の衰退・図案のデジタル化など、様々な社会要因のなかで近代の図案・絵摺り資料が散逸の危機に瀕しているためである。染織の研究は技術的側面と文化的側面に分けられるが、完成品としての着物に重点が置かれ、複雑な各工程にまで十分な研究が及んでいるとは言い難い。それらの工程のほとんどは様々な分野と複合してはじめて成立するものであり、そこにこそ染織文化・京都文化を研究する意義があると考えるが、そのような総合的研究はさらに不十分である。図案も純粋に染織デザインに限定することはできない。京都画壇との関係や様々な工芸品とデザインを共有していることなど、染織図案研究の視野は京都美術や工芸全体に及ばなければならない。

染織図案・絵摺りには多くの書き込みや切り取りなど、多様な使用痕跡が確認される。多くの作業工程を経るため、幾人もの人々の間を移動し、作業工程毎の符号や担当者氏名などが書き込まれている例がある。設計図や道具として図案・絵摺りが如何にして使用されたのか、それがどのように保管されてきたのかを、それらの使用痕跡は示している。こうした痕跡は染織研究や京都文化研究の新しい地平を切り拓く視点を提供してくれるだろう。

　また、収集した資料のなかに型彫りで痛んだ図案を裏打ちしたものが含まれていた。裏打ちには染織関係の書類・新聞紙・各地の行政文書など、多様な近代文書が転用されていた。これらの反古文書は従来全く知られていなかった文献資料である。

　染織図案は店舗によって保管体制が様々であり、劣悪な状態のものも認められた。図案研究を進めるためには、大量の資料を補修・記録化する必要に迫られる。衰退が著しい染織産業の現状は資料の劣化以上に深刻な問題を孕んでおり、早急な対応が望まれている。そのため現実的な試みを模索してきたが、詳細は本書山本真紗子論文を参照願いたい。そのような試みを進める中で、デザインの中に世相を反映した資料を見出した。以下にその一部を紹介するが、その前に図案と絵摺りについて概説しておく。

2　「図案」と「絵摺り」―染織の技術・工程―

　「図案」は明治時代にdesign（デザイン）の訳語として造語された言葉だと言われている。友禅染や西陣織にとって、「図案」は着物柄の設計図に相当するが、肉筆絵画であり、鑑賞にも十分に耐える。友禅染も西陣織も多くの複雑な工程をへて完成するが、その図柄を決める最初の仕事であり、この図案に基づいて様々に分業された仕事が進められてゆく。

　友禅染は大きく分けると手描き友禅と型友禅がある。そのうち、型友禅では一つの図案に対して何枚もの型を彫り込む（型彫り）。その型で布に複雑な文様を摺り写すが、型彫り後、紙に試し摺りしたものを「絵摺り」と呼ぶ。この絵摺りによって仕上がりを確認し、後の染め作業の見本とする。精錬・下染め・下ゆのし・地張りなどの各工程を経た布地に型を用いて染める「型置き」を行

い、さらに地染め・蒸し・水洗い・上ゆのし、その他の多くの工程をへて製品として仕上げられる（京友禅史編纂特別委員会編1992）。

　なお、江戸時代にも下絵はあったが、これは技術的にも現在の図案とは異なり、おおらかなものだった。生産する量や柄の繊細さが全く異なっていたためである。明治時代に欧米の技術を積極的に利用するようになってから、繊細な図案が使用されるようになる。その意味で、図案は染織産業の近代化を象徴するものだと言えよう。

　明治時代の前半には画家が図案を描いていたが、染師や職人たちがそれを着物の約束に従って加筆・訂正する必要があったという。しかし、量産化や高度化・多様化した染織に対応するため、図案に対しても専門的な要求が高まってくるようになる。そのため、明治時代の半ばには専門の図案家も出現し、明治末年には図案家の研究組織も生まれるほど発展を遂げた。

　「図案」や「絵摺り」は製品ではないため、一般の人々の目に触れることはなく、あまり知られていない。染織関係の図書の中でも取り扱われることがあるとはいえ、概して評価が高いとは言えない。しかし、デザインとして欠くことのできない上に、手仕事の技と美しさに目を奪われる優れた絵画でもある。近年では陶芸・漆芸をはじめとする様々な工芸で図案が見直されているが、染織図案も同様に重要である。

3　1910年の友禅染絵摺り―「韓国併合」を祝ったデザイン―

　着物と「戦争」とは何の関係もないように思えるが、様々な戦争柄の着物が数多く作られていた。「戦争」を銃後から応援していたのである。

　以下に紹介する絵摺りは、2009年1月に古書店より購入した資料である。明治末頃から大正年間にわたる64枚（5群6小群）の絵摺りの中に、「韓国併合」に関連した絵摺りが6枚確認された。絵摺りはデザインの設計図として使用されたため様々な書き込みがされることがあり、これらもそうした例である。

(1)　ハングル地名柄（図1）
　大きなハングル文字で「ソウル」（赤字）と「日本」（青字）、その下敷きになる

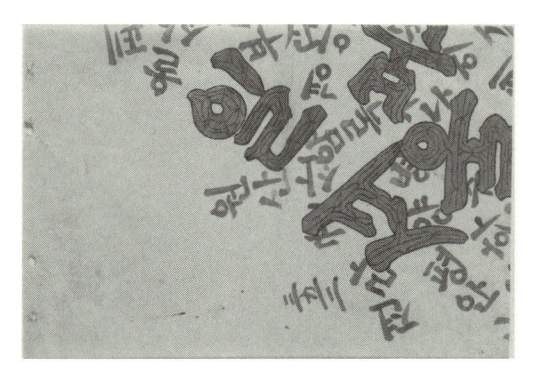

図1　ハングル地名絵摺り

ように淡い灰色の小さなハングル文字で韓国の地名（都市名）が様々な角度で書き込まれている。ソウルのハングル表記は現在と異なるが、これは戦前の古い表記法を用いているためである。ハングル表記はほぼ正確だが、1文字誤字が確認される。なお、大文字の中にはアイヌ文様の括弧文が描かれている。

「日本」が青色で描かれているのは次の「朝鮮・日本銘」と同じである。赤色の「ソウル」は青色の「日本」より目立っているが、原田敬一氏によると、当時の軍隊では味方は青色、敵は赤色で描くことがあり、そうした意識が働いた可能性もあるという。ただし、乾淑子氏によると、これは絵摺りであるため、実際に仕上がった羽裏は別の色だった可能性もある（原田氏・乾氏の意見は、2009年5月30日に立命館大学国際平和ミュージアムで開催されたGCOEシンポジウム「友禅に描かれた『韓国併合』」席上での発言から引用させて頂いた）。

ハングルの地名と混じって紛らわしいが、「三五二」もしくは「二五二」と縦書き漢数字が書かれている。こうした数字は他の絵摺りにも確認され、デザインの整理番号だと考えられる。これ以外の絵摺りには裏面に書き込みがあるが、この絵摺りには確認できない。庵逧由香氏によると、絵柄に書かれているハングル標記の地名は下記の通りである。

国名：日本、都市名：ソウル・釜山（プサン）・蔚山（ウルサン）・元山（ウォンサン）・群山（グンサン）、地方行政区（道）：全羅（チョラ）〔全羅道〕・平安（ピョンアン）〔平安道〕、河名：鴨緑（アムノク）〔鴨緑江〕

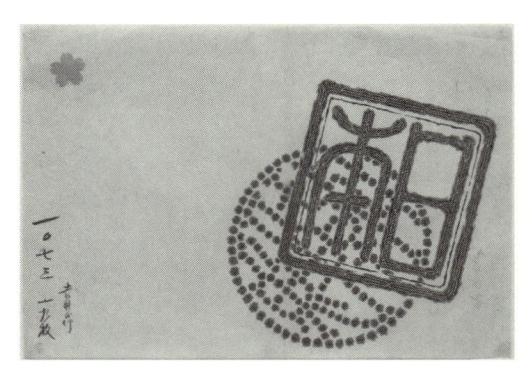

図2　朝鮮・日本銘絵摺り

(2) 朝鮮・日本銘（図2）

　絞り模様で描いた灰色の「朝鮮」という文字を覆うように、青色の「日本」という文字が上書きされている（文字はいずれも右から左）。「日本」の文字や枠にはアイヌ文様の括弧文が、左上には桜花が一つ描かれている。左下に「吉井氏行／一〇七三　⊥九枚」と書き込まれ、さらにその下に朱印「芦嶋」が押捺されている。別の絵摺りに「彫刻　芦嶋」とあるため、「芦嶋」は型彫りの業者であることがわかる。「⊥」は他の絵摺りでも確認されるが、「〆」（しめて）を示す記号だと思われる。この絵摺りのために使用された型の枚数が「しめて九枚」だったことを示している。「吉井氏行」は「工場　吉井」や「吉井」と記入された絵摺りがあることから、吉井氏の染工場行きを示す注記だと思われる。裏面に「八月廿五日（朱スタンプ）⊥（墨書）」などの書き込みが確認される。

(3) 韓半島地図（図3）

　朝鮮半島の地図と地名（京城、仁川、義州、元山、釜山）が書き込まれている。日本列島と朝鮮半島が同じ色調で描かれている。海の部分に文字や数字などが書き込まれているが、「1910・合併■■」、豊臣家の家紋と「征伐」の文字、「■（神）功皇／后征伐」の文字が確認できる。「韓国併合」を歴史的なものとして肯定的に理解しようとする意図が読みとれる。

　なお、このデザインは本州のデザインと組み合って一つになった可能性も想定されるが、本州側の絵摺りは確認できなかった。次の整理番号を与えられた

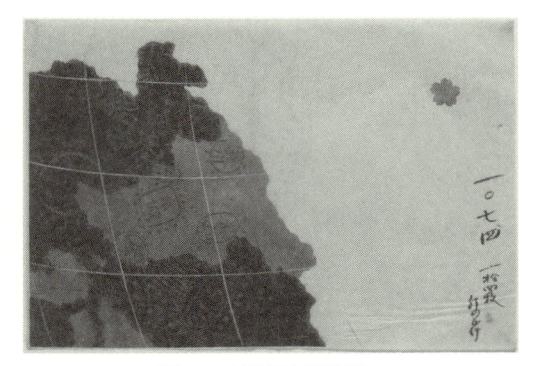

図3　韓半島地図絵摺り

「一〇七五」の絵摺りから考えて、これだけで完結していた可能性が高い。
　左上に桜の花が一つ描かれている。右上には「一〇七四　⊥拾四枚／水の氏行」と書き込まれ、その下に朱印「芦嶋」が確認される。図1は染工場などの注記が確認できなかったが、それ以外の図2・5・6は「吉井氏行」である。このデザインだけがなぜ水野氏の染工場に出されたのかは不明だが、デザインによって得手不得手があった可能性がある。このデザインだけ、青く塗りつぶした面積が大きいことに原因があるのかも知れない。裏面に「八月廿八日⊥」などの書き込みが確認される。

(4) 大日本帝国・朝鮮銘（図4）

　一部の文字が切れているが、古いハングル表記で「大日本帝国／朝鮮」（右から左へ）と書かれている。文字を区切る帯文様は、図1・2と同じく、アイヌ文様の括弧文である。右端に「一〇七五　⊥七枚　吉井氏行」という書き込みがあり、その下に朱印「芦嶋」が、裏面には「八月廿七日⊥」という書き込みが確認できる。

(5) 1910年銘（図5）

　全体は地球儀のようになっているが、中央部分は空白で模様がない。左上には、花の上に日本列島と朝鮮半島の地図が描かれている。樺太の南半分と朝鮮半島が日本列島と同じ色で描かれているのは、大日本帝国の領土を示している

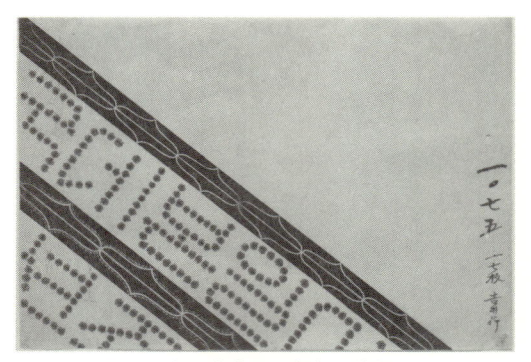

図4　大日本帝国・朝鮮銘絵摺り

のだろう。日本列島の下には五線譜が描かれている。「韓国併合」は明治43年、すなわち西暦1910年であった。「3分の4拍子」は、明治43年を、音符になぞらえた「1910」は韓国併合の年である西暦1910年を示しているのだろう。右下には桜の花がひとつ描かれている。

　下には「三四三／吉井／十枚」と書き込まれている。裏面には「八月廿七日⊥」かと思われる走り書きの書き込みが確認される。

図5　1910年銘絵摺り

(6) 檻の中の鶏柄（図6）

　檻に入れられた鶏を描いている。整理番号が「三四四」とあるため、図5の絵摺りの直後に綴られたことが分かる。酉年の干支を描いた可能性もあるが、酉年は明治42（1909）年であるから、整理番号と綴りの関係が正しければ、一年前の干支を描いたことになる。その上、檻はめでたい干支を描いたにしては不自然である。

　「鶏林」は朝鮮の異称、「秋津島・蜻蛉州」（あきづしま）は日本の異称であるから、「トンボ（蜻蛉）＝日本が、鶏＝朝鮮を捕らえた」ということを意味している可能性がある。裏面に「八月二五日（朱スタンプ）⊥（墨書）」などの書き込みが確認される。

(7) 「明治43年度秋」の袱紗（図7）

　「とんだりはねたり」と呼ばれるおもちゃに猪・象・狐などが乗っている様子を描いている。転んだ「とんだりはねたり」を象が笑顔で眺めている。左上には牡鹿のシルエット何が描かれている。なんらかの社会事象を揶揄した可能性がある。下には「水乃／十枚」と書き込まれている。整理番号は「三壱四」で図5・6より早い番号だが、裏面に「四十三年度秋／袱紗」という大きな書き込みと、「九月弐日」という朱色スタンプが確認される。

図6　檻の中の鶏絵摺り　　　　図7　とんだり跳ねたり

(8)　亥年・(9)　明治「四十四年秋勅題」の絵摺り（図8・9）

　この他に、さまざまな絵摺りがあるが、亥年を表したイノシシの絵摺り（図8）や、「四十四年秋勅題」（図9。明治44年＝1911年）の絵摺りが確認される。ちょうど明治44（1911）年が亥年にあたる。おそらく、干支は前年のうちに準備されていたのであろうから、図8は明治43年のうちに製作されたと推測される。明治44年新年の歌会始めの勅題が梅であり、図9は明治44年の歌会始め直後に製作されたと想定される。これらの絵摺りの整理番号は図8が「壱〇七七」、図9が「万一六〇四」である。図6の「三四四」以来、多量の図案が製作されたことがわかる。

　図7～9の絵摺りの年代から考えて、韓国併合に関連した図1～6の絵摺りがこれらよりも以前であることは明瞭である。「韓国併合一周年記念」や「十周年記念」などにあわせて製作されたのではないことを示している。

(10)　台紙

　これらの絵摺りを販売していた古書店では仕入れた絵摺りの冊子を外して一枚ずつ販売していた。そのため、すでに売却されていたものもある。整理番号が抜けているのはそのためであろう。この古書店からまとめて購入した図案・絵摺り（5群）は複数の小群に別れていたが、注記などから多くは「大橋商店」

図8　亥

図9　「四十四年勅題」

に関連するものだと想定される。64枚の絵摺り（5群6小群）は「大正三年秋之部（1914年）羽二重友仙摺合綴」と書かれた台紙にはさまれていた。同類の台紙に「大橋商店」と記載された冊子が数冊あったため、これも「大橋商店」のものと想定される。

なお、64枚の絵摺り（5群6小群）は綴じ穴の観察から、元来この冊子に綴じられていたのではないことが明確である（デジタル写真を重ねあわせることで、綴じ穴の同定を簡便に行うことができる）。本来の「綴」を復元するには、5群全体のを詳細に検討する必要があるが、紹介した図案に限れば、「図1」、「図2〜図4」、「図5〜図7」がそれぞれに同じ綴り穴をもっている。そのため、別々に綴じられていたと考えられる。「図2〜図4」、「図5〜図7」はデザインの整理番号も連続しており、その想定を裏付ける。また、「図5〜7」のまとまりは、複数回綴じ直された痕跡が確認される。さらに、ほぼすべての絵摺りの裏面には周囲を糊付けした痕跡が残されているため、台紙に糊付けして展示や閲覧に供した可能性がある。

このように、紹介した絵摺りは、製作・販売の様々な過程をへる中で保管状況を変更しながら使用し続けられ、最終的に依頼者である「大橋商店」においてこの台紙に綴られたと考えられる。ところで、絵摺りの裏面には「ヒシ（ン？）テ」（図2）、「ケト」（図3）、「ヒトイ」（図4）、「ヒシレ」（図5）、「ヒトテ」（図6）など、カタカナ2〜3文字程度の書き込みがなされているが、その意味は不明である。絵摺りに残された痕跡について、どの工程で記入されたものか、その意味はなにか、今後さらに検討する必要がある。

4　袱紗と羽裏のデザイン

紹介した絵摺りはいずれも着尺のものとはサイズが違うため、羽裏や袱紗など、着尺以外のものだと思われる。正方形のもののうち、僅か一枚だが「袱紗」と書かれているものがあることから、図5・6のような正方形の図案は、袱紗の絵摺りだった可能性が高い。それより小さな長方形のものにも、やはり僅か一枚だが「羽裏」と書かれたものがあるため、図1〜4は羽裏だったと思われる。袱紗はめでたい場を盛り上げるために重要な役割を果たす小道具であるし、

羽裏はおしゃれ心、あそび心を表現する重要な小道具であった。

(1) 社会を映し出したデザイン

　紹介した絵摺りのように、「韓国併合」という重要な社会変化をとり入れたのは、遊び心、おしゃれ心の現れだったと思われる。しかし、韓国人にとって、それは全く異なった意味をもつ。袱紗・羽裏のいずれにせよ、ハングルがある程度読め、絵画の意味を読み取る能力がなければ鑑賞することができない。高いレベルの絵解き能力を必要とする。そのように考えると、一般庶民のものというより、裕福で知性の高い人々をターゲットにした商品だったと考えられる。ただし、1910年を過ぎれば「旬を過ぎたデザイン」となり、あまり長期間使用され続けることはなかったと思われる。一周年記念・二周年記念などの記念の際にも持ち出されて使用した可能性があるが、それでも一過性のデザインであることにかわりはない。これらのデザインの「旬」は限られていたと思われ、その意味でも一般庶民には手の届かない贅沢品であった可能性が高い。

5　「韓国併合」当時の社会とアイヌ文様

(1) 「韓国併合」と日本人

　1910年、日本は韓国を併合して朝鮮総督府を設置した。これは征韓論以来、数十年にわたって「朝鮮」を狙い侵略し続けてきた、ひとつの帰結であった。しかし、これにとどまることなく、植民地「朝鮮」を守るために、さらに泥沼のような侵略戦争を拡大し続けることになる。人々は様々な苦しみを強いられたが、侵略の「旨み」を堪能し、積極的に加担していた。日露戦後、賠償金がとれないとわかると日比谷焼き討ち事件をおこすなど、見返りを求めていたことも確かなことである。

(2) 「韓国併合」を祝った人々―京都市・市民・呉服店―

　1910年9月2日付け『日出新聞』によると、1910年9月1日午前10時より岡崎公園平安神宮において京都市主催の「韓国併合祝賀会」が「豫定の如く」挙行されたことや、午後8時からは御苑で「何万人ゐるとも知れぬ」提灯行列の

大集合があったと伝えている。さらに翌日9月3日付けの記事では、「日韓併合を祝するの目的にて市内の呉服店その他に於いて装飾を施しつつあり」、「井上大丸呉服店は紅白の絹を以て旭日と韓国の旗を拵へ之に『祝併合』の三字を現せる絹製の額を掲げ四条室町東入る十合呉服店は絹地製の鶏に旭日を配し鶏林撫育の意味をきかせ」ていたという（水野2009、133〜134・142〜143頁）。「鶏林撫育」という言葉と図6の絵摺りのデザインが共通する。こうした記事から京都市当局・京都市民・呉服業界のいずれもが「韓国併合」を祝い、予定通りの行事を行っていたことがわかる。

(3) 公布日や祝賀行事に間に合わせた作業

「韓国併合」条約は8月22日に調印され、8月29日に公布された。公布やそれを祝う行事を想定して図1〜6までのデザインが用意されたのだろう。絵摺り裏面に記入された日付から、公布以前にその情報を入手し、公布日や祝賀行事に向け、かなり急いで作業を進めていた様子が伺える。

なお、絵摺りの裏面に記入された日付は「⊥」という「〆て（しめて）」を示すと考えられる記号を伴うことから、何らかの作業終了日を示していると考えられる。型彫り師の書き込みだと想定される絵摺り表面の文字とは異筆であるため、染工場で作業終了日や仕上げ日を記入したか、あるいは「大橋商店」で納品日を記入した可能性がある。その想定が間違っていなければ、これらのデザインの作品は公布日前日までに完成していたと考えられる。

(4) アイヌ文様

アイヌ文様にはさまざまな種類があるが、紹介した絵摺りに描かれた文様はすべて括弧文であった。これはアイヌ文様の中でもよく使われた代表的な文様である。アイヌ語では「アイウシシリキ ay-us-siriki」と読まれ、「（神の）棘がついている文様」という意味を持っている。

この括弧文様は江戸時代の終わりから明治前半期の浮世絵にも確認される。「天竺徳兵衛」という天竺（インド）に渡り、オランダ船で帰国した人物を題材とした歌舞伎で用いられた。明治前半期まではアイヌ民族の文様だという理解ではなく「外国の文様」として意識されていたようである（鈴木桂子氏のご教示によ

るところが大きい)。

(5) 日鮮同祖論とアイヌ文様

「韓国併合」当時、「日本人単一民族説」も存在したが、その理屈では台湾や韓国の支配を正当化することはできなかった。その土地に住む人々が明らかに異民族だからである。そのため、日鮮同祖論が侵略や異民族支配を肯定する理屈として広まっていった。「かつて日本の領土であった朝鮮半島を大日本帝国が復活させた。かつては同一の民族であったがゆえに、韓国の人々を同化させることは比較的容易である」というような考え方である。ただし、それらが歴史的事実に基づいていないことは明らかである。

ところで、なぜ、「韓国併合」絵摺りの中にアイヌ文様が取り入れられているのだろうか。よく理解できない部分もあるが、アイヌ民族という異民族を支配下に加えたように、大韓帝国をも同様に支配下に入れる、同化させるということを暗示している可能性がある。アイヌ文様を描くことは、異民族支配を肯定し、それによって「韓国併合」を正当化しようとしていると想定される。

当時はアイヌ民族の「人種的所属」が明らかになっておらず、ヨーロッパ系

図10　図1のアイヌ文様 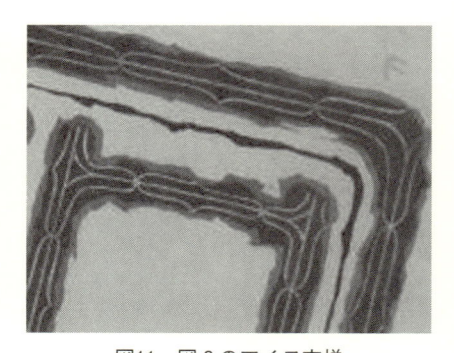　　　図11　図2のアイヌ文様

図12　図4のアイヌ文様

人種説・アジア系人種説・太平洋人種説・孤立人種説の4つの考え方があったが、いずれも、「日本人」とは異なる、先住民族だと考えられていた。そして、知識人ですら「アイヌは人間ではなく犬だという偏見」をもっていた（坂野2005、200頁）。「野蛮な民族」を支配しているという自負心、「日本版華夷思想」を示している可能性も想定できる。

(6) 「韓国併合」を記念した市販絵葉書

「韓国併合」の翌年には、韓国の少女をモチーフにした年賀葉書が現れる（2009年4月古書店より購入）。「東京図按印刷凸版部浪華屋」が発行した市販の絵葉書である。この絵葉書は、年号は不詳ながら元旦の消印が確認される。

図13 「1911」年賀葉書

年賀状として使用されているため、この絵葉書の発行は遅くとも1910年12月中のことだったと思われる。大韓帝国の民族衣裳をまとった少女が羽子板や凧という日本の遊具を手にしており、その影が「1911」に見える。後ろに見える大きな太陽は「初日の出」を示すのだろうが、「日の丸」＝日本という後ろ楯が現れること、あるいは大韓帝国が日本の支配下に入ったことを示しているのであろう。また、太陽にかかる雲によって、韓半島の地図が浮き上がっており、日本と韓国を掛け合わせていることがわかる。この絵葉書のデザインは、「韓国併合」後はじめての年を祝うために工夫されたものであり、友禅以上に分かりやすい意味が仕込まれている。

これらは当時の「国民意識」を反映していると思われる。「韓国併合」を祝うデザインは、絵葉書にせよ、袱紗にせよ、需要が十分に見込めたのであろう。

(7) 「韓国併合」百年と現代の状況

2010年、「韓国併合」百年を迎えた。友禅絵摺りや絵葉書などの当時の文物から、当時の日本人（「内地人」に限る）が「韓国併合」をお目出度いこととして喜

んで受け取っていたことが理解できる。今の私達からすれば疑問に感じることも、当時の「内地人」にとっては「当たり前」のことだったのだろう。韓国やアイヌの人々の痛みは完全に無視されている。

現代の韓国をはじめとする東アジア諸国でも「広島・長崎」の痛みは軽視されているように見える。複雑な問題であることは間違いないが、彼らにとって「広島・長崎」に投下された原爆は、日本の侵略を止めた「救い」であり、開放をもたらした「喜ばしいこと」である。「韓国併合」を祝っていた当時の人々の感覚にも違和感を抱くが、「広島・長崎」を「喜ばしいこと」と評価することにも違和感を覚える。

ところで、喜納昌吉の歌「石笛」に「沖縄、広島、長崎。ああ、忘れてはならじ」という一節がある。沖縄を広島・長崎と並列することで、被害者の連帯を喚起しているように感じる。沖縄と同じ痛みを広島・長崎に認め、同じ「人間の痛み」を共有しようという視点も感じる。その意味では、韓国の３．１独立運動や南京大虐殺も忘れてはならない、大きな「人間の痛み」に違いない。

「韓国併合」から100年を過ぎた今も、私達人類はこの痛みを共有して並列することができていない。同じ「人間の痛み」として共感することができない社会情勢が続いている。今回紹介した絵摺りは100年を過ぎた今こそ、大切なことを問いかけているように感じる。

おわりに

「韓国併合」を祝った友禅絵摺りは、当時の社会をよく現している。時代の空気を敏感に察知しつつも、その先端にあって流行を牽引しようとしている様子も理解できる。しかし、ここで紹介したデザインは、収集した大量の図案・絵摺りの中ではごく一部にすぎない。こうしたデザインそのものも消費され、次々に新しいデザインを求め、実際に大量のデザインを生み出していった。

京都の伝統工芸を評価する場合、「負」の側面を指摘することはほとんどない。しかし、長く首都であり続けた京都の歴史は、「引き続く戦争の歴史」でもあったことを忘れてはならない。戦争の歴史が長く深い京都は、社会変化や戦争に対してもっとも過敏に反応する都市であった。京都の伝統工芸が果たした役割、

あるいは歴史的な試練をみたとき、「歴史的都市」のすべてを包み込んで評価することの難しさを感じないわけにはいかない。

　最後になったが、庵逧由香氏、乾淑子氏、岡本隆明氏、金津日出美氏、喜多恵美子氏、小山俊樹氏、鈴木桂子氏、水野直樹氏、原田敬一氏、藤井健三氏、前崎信也氏をはじめとする多くの方々のご指導・ご協力を頂いた。また、朝鮮史研究会関西部会2010年11月例会で「友禅図案に描かれた「韓国併合」と裏打ち文書」と題して報告させて頂いた際にはご出席された方々から有益なご助言とご指導を頂いた。記して感謝の意を表したい。

■参考文献
乾淑子2007『図説着物柄にみる戦争』インパクト出版会
乾淑子編2008『戦争のある暮らし』水声社
小熊英二1995『単一民族神話の起源　〈日本人〉の自画像の系譜』新曜社
京友禅史編纂特別委員会編1992『京の友禅史』京都友禅協同組合
坂野徹2005『帝国日本と人類学者　一八八四―一九五二』勁草書房
比沼悟1972『近代図案ものがたり　その歴史と今後の課題』京都書院
水野直樹2009「京都の中の近代日朝関係史―長楽館と韓国合併奉告祭碑―」『二〇〇七
　年度講演録　講座・人権ゆかりの地をたずねて』財団法人世界人権問題研究センター

Chap.6 立命館大学アート・リサーチセンター所蔵友禅図案資料群の整理作業

山本真紗子　*Masako Yamamoto*

1　立命館大学アート・リサーチセンター所蔵の近代染織資料

　現在、立命館大学アート・リサーチセンターでは2002年ごろより複数回にわけて古書店より購入した西陣織の正絵、友禅染の図案・絵摺り、裂帳などの近代の染織・京都の着物に関する資料を所蔵している。文部科学省グローバルCOEプログラム「日本文化デジタル・ヒューマニティーズ拠点」（立命館大学）京都文化班木立研究室では、デジタルアーカイブを用いてこれらの資料を公開し研究を進展させるため、約3年前よりこれらの資料の本格的な整理をおこなっているが、その過程で、近代の大量資料の保存・整理作業特有の課題が浮かび上がってきた。本稿では、本学の資料の整理にかかる課題克服の方法を模索する中で構築してきた整理作業の手法、とりわけ資料の修復作業の方法を紹介することで、近代大量資料の保存、整理、活用へのひとつのありかたを提示していきたい。

(1)　京都市内の染織関連資料の残存状況と課題

　まず、京都市内の近代染織関連の資料のおかれた状況をみていきたい。
　京都市内には、近代染織（産業）に関する資料が、主に企業、公共機関、大学・研究機関に数多く残存している。しかし、近年とくに企業の所蔵資料に関しては、不況や着物離れによる転・廃業、コンピューターの使用による図案作成方法の転換などを背景に、これまで保管・伝来されてきた資料が廃棄され、ある

いは古書店への売却される等して、所蔵者の手から離れるケースも目立ってきた。こうした状況に危機感をもつ所蔵者のなかには、所蔵の図案を活用しようと、データベースの整備や図案集の刊行といった活用方法を模索しはじめている。データベースの構築に限れば、例えば企業であれば所蔵図案をビジネスのコンテンツとして利用する方法を模索しており[1]、京都市産業技術研究所繊維技術センターや社団法人日本図案家協会といった公的機関・団体がデータベースの作成をおこなっている[2]。しかし、これらは外部には原則非公開であったり、また公開されているものの利用料が発生することがあり、公開されているものであっても図案の一部のみしか表示されない、作成年代といった基礎的な情報が付与されていないなど、研究のためのツールとしては十分なものではないのも事実である[3]。

一方、資料が所蔵者の手から離れている状況は、大学や研究機関での所蔵を増加させるという結果も生んでいる。これまで服飾史や民俗学の資料として着物の現物を所蔵するコレクションがいくつか存在していたものの、近年は図案や型紙といった製造段階の資料も、相次いで寄贈・購入されるようになってきた。京都市内に限定すると、近年の動きとしては、本プロジェクトが所属する立命館大学でも、木立研究室以外に、工芸プロジェクト・染色型紙デジタルアーカイブとして伊勢型紙アーカイブ（株式会社キョーテック所蔵伊勢型紙コレクション・吉岡コレクションほか）の構築が進行している。京都工芸繊維大学では京都高等工芸学校関係資料、寺田哲朗（機械捺染図案家、日本図案家協会）関連資料[4]を所蔵しており、主として美術工芸資料館での展覧会で公開している。京都精華大学の「田中直コレクション」は、京都の染料販売会社「田中直染料店」の店主により蒐集された伊勢型紙のコレクションである。赤外線カメラでの商印と書き入れ（墨書・朱書）の調査を行い、データベースを同大学情報館ウェブサイト内で公開している。

こうした図案やそれに関する資料の特徴は、資料群として存在することに意味があるということになろう。たしかに、近代京都の染織業界では著名な日本画家が西陣織や友禅染の下絵を描く、という事例が多数あり、そうした図案にかんしてはいわゆる美術工芸品としての評価をすることも可能かもしれない。しかし、市内に残存している資料の多くは、一定数の製品を生産するための"道

具"である。一点もの、最高級品というものというよりは、庶民の晴れ着や日用着であり、当時の一般的な"趣味""流行"を反映したものと考えられる。とくに、明治期から昭和初期は、着物産業が最も興隆した時期であり、さまざまなバリエーションの図案が考案されている。これまで、明治〜昭和当時の染織、とくに着物に関する資料は、愛好者による個人コレクションや企業による収集によって進められてきた。生産（製造）業者である企業の場合は、着物や生地の現物や図案作成者などの周辺情報と同時に保管されており、学術研究としても重要なコレクションが多数あると思われる。しかし、先述の理由からその存続が危ういものも今後増加するであろう。こうしたことから、近代の着物図案や型紙資料は、一枚ずつの図案のもつ情報・意味以上に、資料群として一定量が確保されていることでより多くの情報が得られる可能性を持つといえる。今後、近代染織（産業）・着物図案の研究に向けては、とくに"大量の"資料の整理、保存、公開による活用（研究利用）がより促進されなければならない。本学の所蔵資料に関しても、こうした研究利用のための準備や活用がスムーズに行えるようなシステムを構築する必要があった。

(2) アート・リサーチセンター所蔵の資料について

現在、木立研究室で整理をおこなっている資料は明治末期から昭和前期ごろの西陣織・友禅染の図案に関するものである。複数回にわけて古書店から購入し、形状も一枚ものからアルバム状にまとめられたものまでさまざまである。現在は主に6群（2009年度〜2011年度購入）の型友禅の図案・絵摺り約1万点の資料を中心に整理作業を行っている。これらは実際に型友禅の制作に使用されたもので、この種の資料をこれほど大量に研究資料として所蔵、公開している機関は本学以外にはないと思われる。

2　立命館大学アート・リサーチセンターでの資料公開の方法

立命館大学アート・リサーチセンターでは、「21世紀COEプログラム」から文部科学省グローバルCOEプログラム「日本文化デジタル・ヒューマニティーズ拠点」（立命館大学・以下DH拠点）にかけて、多様な資料のデジタルアーカイブ化

をおこない、資料の公開と活用の促進を進めてきた[5]。本学のデジタルアーカイブ作成にあたっては、研究者による整理・調査が必ず付随しており、資料の状態によっては補修作業を行ったうえで作業を進めている。木立研究室の修復作業のポリシーも、DH拠点で行われている修復作業のポリシーと実績に基づいて行われている。

　アート・リサーチセンターでは、主にDH拠点日本文化班での浮世絵・版本類のイメージデータベース作成のため、日常的に画像の撮影をおこなっている。その準備作業の一環として、資料の修復作業もおこなわれている。センターでの修復作業は修復経験と知識を有する監督者の元、立命館大学の学部学生、院生が従事しており、手繕いと裏打ちの作業をおこなっている。糊たきなどの準備から本への綴じなおしなどの仕上げまで、全行程を学生が担当する。これは、一連の工程をしないと、各工程が理解できないためである。工房等で通常おこなわれている修復作業と同じ方法でおこなっており、資料の状態に応じた修復方法をとることはあるが、学生であるから、という理由で作業の手順や方法に改変することはおこなっていない。

　作業に従事するのは、本学で開講している資料修復に関するインターンシップの参加者を中心とした希望者である。希望者は、一か月程度でほぼすべての工程を体験し、いずれの作業でも従事できるように経験を積む。現在、アート・リサーチセンターで撮影をおこなう資料で修復が必要なものについては、特殊な場合を除き、ほぼ学生による修復をほどこされている。ここでの作業は、特に専門的な知識や訓練がない大学生であっても、一定の習熟期間を経ればある程度の修復作業を実施することが可能である、という実例である。こうした蓄積がすでにあったからこそ、型友禅資料群の整理についても、学生の参加による整理・修復という方針を採用することができた。

3　立命館大学所蔵友禅資料の整理作業

(1)　アート・リサーチセンター所蔵資料の整理作業の概況

　今回紹介する整理作業と対象となった6群（2009年〜2011年購入）は、京都市内の染屋が所蔵していたと思われる資料群である。総数は1万点以上を数え、

主に型染の技法を使用した「型友禅」の「図案」と、その試し摺りである「絵摺り」の資料で構成されている。

とくに6群の資料を整理するにあたって、問題となったのは、現在、資料が画像撮影や保存に適当な状態ではないということであった。元所蔵者もしくは古書店で保管する際、資料を二つ折以上に折り曲げた状態で段ボールにいれていたため、いずれの資料も折れ目や反りがついた状態であった。また、長年の保管のためか、埃などの汚れも目立っていた。整理や保管のために、資料一枚ずつの汚れとりや修復など、現在の状態を改善する作業を施す必要に迫られたのである。

図1　整理作業の様子
Fig. 1　Sorting

そこで、大学で所蔵している研究資料ということを活かし、学部学生による整理作業をおこなうことになった。資料収集を開始した当初（2003年～2009年まで）は日本史学専攻・学際プログラム学生有志数名による資料整理作業をおこなっていたものの、6群の購入後はあまりに数が膨大になってきたため、実習や授業の一環として位置づけられた多人数での作業に切り替えた。2008年度から歴史考古学ゼミ実習（2008年8月4日～9月23日）として開始し、これまで、2010年度博物館実習（2010年8月23日～27日、8月29日～9月3日）、2010年度冬期整理作業（2011年2月1日～11日）、2011年度京都学Cゼミ実習（2011年8月5日～12日）、同・博物館実習（2011年9月12日～9月23

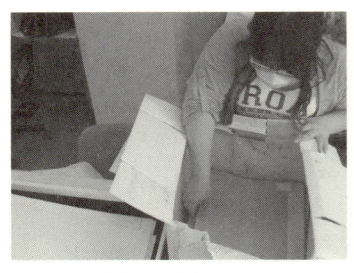

図2　箱から資料をとりだす
Fig. 2　Removing materials from boxes

図3　箱から取り出した資料
Fig. 3　Materials moved from boxes

日）を実施している。
　一回の作業で文学部の学生1～3回生約15名程度が参加し、各回とも3000～4000枚程度を撮影可能な状態にまで処置できた。作業途中で生じた修復が必要な資料については現在も継続して修復作業をおこなっている。
　学生参加による整理作業は、段ボールより資料をとりだすところから開始する。そこから、デジタル・カメラによる資料撮影をおこなう状態にするまでの作業を、実習という形で実施した。

　次に整理作業の主な内容を説明する。

(2) 台帳作成と番号付け
　保管されていた段ボールのなかから一枚ずつ資料をだすと、まず、それぞれの資料に資料番号を付与する。資料が保管されていた状態を記録するため、箱にはいっていた状態を反映する番号を付与している。
（例）6群の段ボール▲箱目内、■束内の●番目の資料→「6-▲-■-●」
　メジャーを使って資料サイズを測定し、資料番号とともに記録シートに記入する。複数枚をつづりあわせたものなど、通常と異なる資料の状況がある場合はそれも記録する。次に、鉛筆で図案の右下隅に整理番号を記入する。

(3) クリーニング
　図案の表面の埃や汚れを除去するために図案の表面に軽く刷毛をかける。その際、図案の埃を吸いこまないようにマスクの着用をしている。刷毛をかける際、弱すぎると埃や汚れの除去ができない。反対に、強すぎると図案の表面の顔料が取れてしまう危険性があるため、注意が必要である。埃や汚れは資料の痛みの原因ともなり、また埃が汚れを付けたまま水を用いる作業をおこなうと汚れが定着してしまうため、クリーニングをおこなってから修復作業にはいる。
　この段階で、修復が必要なものと、修復が必要でないものをわける。修復が

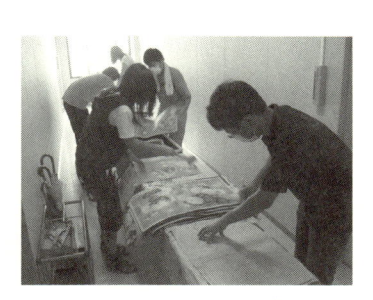

図4　クリーニングの様子
Fig. 4　Cleaning

必要でないものは、次の作業（矯正）に進む。

図5　ベニヤ板にはさんでいた資料をとりだす。
Fig. 5　Removing materials

(4)　矯正とサイズ分け

修復が必要ない資料に関しては、撮影のための準備にはいる。資料は段ボールに保管された際に二つ折以上にたたんだ状態であったことから折れ目やしわがついている。これらをすべて広げてまっすぐに伸ばす。

まず、資料の折れを指など使って伸ばした上で、ベニヤ板のあいだに和紙と資料を交互にしてはさみ入れる。ある程度の分量になったら、ベニヤ板の上に重しをのせ、半日から一晩以上放置し、折れ目を矯正する。

ベニヤ板をはずし、とりだした資料は、サイズごとにわけておく。資料の撮影は、撮影台においた資料に垂直になるよう、カメラをコピースタンドに据え付けた状態でおこなう。資料サイズに応じて、資料とカメラの距離を調整しなければならないため、なるべく調整の手間がかからないよう、あらかじめ資料のサイズをそろえておくのである。

(5)　保存と活用―微小点接着法による修復作業の実際―

本学資料の整理作業に不可欠であったのが、資料の修復作業である。本学資料は保管時の環境からか、一部の資料にはカビが生じていた。加えて、元所蔵者、もしくは古書店で保管時、段ボール箱に図案が長期間押し込められていた。また図案を型紙へカーボン転写する工程があるため、強い力で図案をなぞることにより、図案紙が図柄の輪郭線にそって弱くなり、時に切断されてしまう。そのため多数の資料に輪郭線から派生するちぎれや破れ等の破損が生じていた。このため、修復にはカビの除去作業と、破れや折れ目などからの修復が必要とされていた。

カビに対しては、アルコールの塗布や燻蒸処置によりカビ被害の進行を防止する処置をおこなうこととなった。数の上で圧倒的に多く、また、個別に手当

てが必要であったのが、図案の切れ、ちぎれ、破れの修復である。

　これらの破損に対する修復作業にあたり、課題となったのは次の点である。数千枚におよぶ大量の資料を限られた期間内で修復する必要があること。一方、専門的なスキルを持った人材の育成や外部委託、高額な修復道具や材料の使用は時間・費用の面から難しいこと。この二点である。このような課題は本学に限らず、多くの所蔵機関がかかえる悩みでもあるだろう。「安価・使いやすい道具で、短期間の研修をへれば大学生が修復に参加でき、期限内に目的（＝画像の撮影）を達成できる修復」、これが今回の修復作業での目標であり基準であった。

図6　修復作業の様子
Fig. 6　Students working on restoration

　今回、本学資料のうち、破れ・切断に対する修復にあたっては、"微小点接着法"を採用した。微小点接着法とは、ドットスタンプ

図7　修復作業の様子
Fig. 7　Students working on restoration

のような道具を用い、接着面全体に点状の糊をつけることで、資料（主に紙同士）を接着する手法である。この方法は昭和女子大学の増田勝彦教授により考案・発表された[6]。しかし、実際の大量修復の現場に採用された事例は現在まで報告されておらず、本学の取り組みが最初と思われる。

　本学資料の場合、修復の進めるにあたって、次の方針を決めたうえで作業に取り組むこととした。

■修復の程度＝本学の資料整理作業はデジタルアーカイブとして公開することを到達目標としている。そのため、デジタルアーカイブ化に欠かせない画像撮影の作業が可能になること、という基準を設け、この基準を満たす状態にすることを修復の基準とした。

　資料の修復作業では一般的に、資料を傷めない、資料の原装を損なわない、

修復前の状態に回復させることができる、といった条件があげられる。本学の作業においても、こうした条件を満たしたうえで、より簡単で失敗の少ない方法を採用したいと考えた。なぜなら、多数の学生が入れ替わりで作業に参加するため、作業の内容に熟練の必要が少ないこと、誰がやっても同じ結果を得ることができること、失敗がすくないことが重要であるからである。今回採用した微小点接着法は、一度に資料につける糊の分量が少ないため、資料への影響が少なく除去しやすい。接着に使用するメチルセルロースも、水溶性のため一度接着したあとでも水分を与えてやれば除去可能である。複数の理由から、修復した部分を修復前の状態に戻すことが比較的容易であり、今後別の修復方法を採用した場合でも対応が可能である。このような利点が本学の資料への修復作業のニーズに一致していた。

図8　修復作業の様子
Fig. 8　Students working on restoration

■修復にあたる人材＝今回、吉備国際大学の鈴木英治教授ならびに同大学大学院修士課程法寺岡宏枝氏（所属はいずれも実習実施時当時）の実演指導により、学部学生（1～3回生）の実習参加者が修復を担当した。

　参加者には鈴木教授もしくは法寺岡氏の修復の実演見学や説明を受けてもらい、二枚に分離した図案をつなげる、折り目をのばすための低温アイロンをかけるなど、簡単な作業から着手してもらう。作業中は法寺岡氏が作業を監督・指導し、作業の難易度が高いものは法寺岡氏が担当した。

■修復の道具
・メチルセルロース：通常、文書等の修復では生麩糊や膠などを採用することが多い。しかし、こうした接着剤は、鍋で煮るなど準備に手間がかかり、また熟練が必要であること、腐敗が進みやすく長期の保存が難しいことなどから、扱いに習熟が必要である。その点、メチルセルロースは、水に溶かすだ

けで作業することができ、濃度の調整も比較的容易である。水に溶けやすいという性質は、一度接着した場合でも水分を与えれば剥がせるという利点にもつながる。加えて、水に溶いたあとでも常温で長期保存が可能である。本学の整理作業では信越化学工業株式会社から販売されている「メトローズ」を水に溶かして使用している。今回の修復で用いたのは、「メトローズSM―100」の濃度8％のものである。

図9　接着用のスタンプ
Fig. 9　Stamping blocks for applying adhesion

・スタンプ：接着剤を用紙につける道具として、数センチ角の木片にマジックテープの凸面をはって作成したスタンプを用意する。
・シャーレ：シャーレに濃度を調整したメチルセルロース（8％）をいれる。シャーレには不織布をメチルセルロースに浸すように置きインクパッド状にして、スタンプにメチルセルロースが適切量つくようにする。

■修復の主な内容
A)「伸ばし」
　図案でシワやヨレが生じたり、強く折れ曲がった部分をできるだけ水平にする。指、ピンセットやヘラを使って、細かい折れをある程度水平に戻しておく。次に、図案の絵の顔料をとかさないように図案を裏にして「伸ばし」の作業をする。水が図案の損傷やカビの原因になるため、余分な水分をおとした状態の筆で、資料の折れをなぞる。濡らした箇所はペーパータオルを押しあて乾燥させる。深い折れにはペーパータオルの上から極低温のアイロンを当てる。

B)「接着」
　図案の亀裂部分・断裂部分にメチルセルロースをつけた短冊状の和紙を貼り接着する。数センチ角の短冊状にカットした薄い和紙とメチルセルロースを入れたシャーレ、前述のスタンプを用意する。スタンプにつけたマジックテープの凸部分にのみ接着剤がつき、接着面に点状に接着剤がつくようになる。

図10　微小点接着法による接着面
Fig. 10　Joining of pieces using the micro-dot adhering method

　この方法により、濃度の高い糊を少量用い、ほぼ乾燥した状態で弱い接着ができる。また接着面をなるべく小さくすることで、余分な水分が資料につくことを防ぎ、資料への負担を少なくすることができる。紙を糊で接着する場合、資料の性質や作業の内容に応じて、糊の濃度や量を調整する必要があるが、経験がないとそうした判断を下すことが難しい。水分を加えて調製する必要のない接着剤やスタンプを用いることで、接着の際の失敗を減らし、修復の専門的知識がない人であっても安全に作業を進めることが可能になる。相対的な接着面積をできるだけ小さくすることで、資料への影響をすくなくすることができるほか、万が一修復箇所を除去しなくてはならないときも、容易にはがせるようになる。
　資料の断裂部分の両端と中央を、和紙の短冊で接着させたあと、接着後剥れないようにおもしを接着部分に乗せておき、乾燥するのを待つ。

図11　アイロンをかける
Fig. 11　Ironing

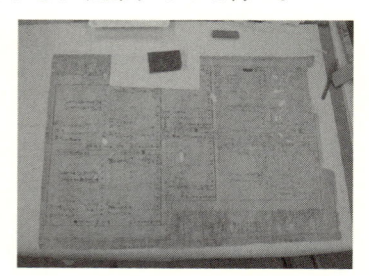

図12　おもしをおいて接着を待つ
Fig. 12　Adhesive left to dry, with a weight placed on top

4　立命館大学近代染織図案データベース（仮称）の構築

　アート・リサーチセンター所蔵資料はデジタルアーカイブとして画像を公開することを念頭においている。そのため、上記の整理作業により番号をつけ、折れ目・反り・汚れ等を除去した資料は、デジタル一眼カメラによる撮影によっ

て、高画質の画像を作成する。

撮影は、アート・リサーチセンターで運用されている撮影手法を用いている。すなわち汎用プロカメラを使用し、被写体である図案をガラス板で平面化したうえで撮影をおこなう[7]。

この画像に、整理の最初の段階で資料につけた番号や、図案に描かれた柄・模様、図案の反対面に貼り付けられた文書の種類などから検索できるよう、メタデータの作成と付与

図13 写真撮影
Fig. 13 Digital photographing

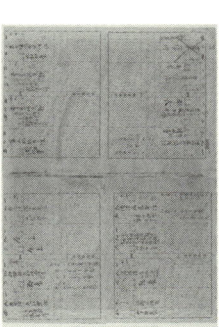

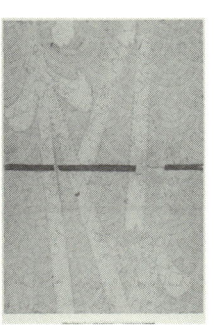

図14 撮影した資料の例
Fig. 14 Examples of photographed materials Search/List Display Details Display

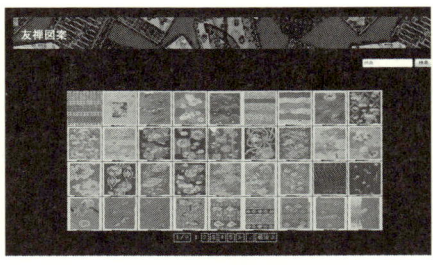

検索・一覧画面　　　　　　　詳細画面
図15 現在構築中のデータベース画面
Fig. 15 Displays of the Ritsumeikan University Modern Dyeing and Weaving Designs Database (tentative title) currently under construction

をおこなう。

　効率化された撮影により作成されたデジタル・イメージを用いてデジタルアーカイブを作成し、インターネット上で公開することで、大量の資料を一覧でき、また一般公開することで、研究利用を促す。画像を提供することで、原資料の使用を控え、資料の保全をおこなう。

おわりに

　近代資料の整理の実践のひとつとして、本学における資料整理作業の実際について述べてきた。こうした作業を継続的におこなっていくためのシステムを構築することは、予算や人員の関係上、困難な場合が多い。

　本プロジェクトによる整理作業の場合、学生参加という形で大量の資料の整理を実現することができたが、微小点接着法のような方法を用いることで、少なくとも専門的な修復にかかる費用や人員の問題については、ある程度解消することができるであろう。この修復作業は応急的な処置であるともいえるが、この方法を採用することによって、現状よりも資料の状態が悪化することを防ぎ、研究資料として活用できる道筋をつけることを可能にする、という意味では非常に現実的な方法であったのではないかと考える。

　現在、京都市内に残る他の図案資料に関しても、あるいはその他の近代文書・資料でも、大量の資料をどのように整理・活用していくか、という課題は所蔵者・管理者に大きくのしかかっていると考えられる。近代の大量資料の所蔵者・管理者は、自らの所蔵資料の性格、資料をとりまく（さまざまな意味での）環境、その資料を所蔵する意味と活用について、常に自問自答せざるを得ない。種々の要素を考え合わせて整理を進めていく必要があるが、本プロジェクトでは、所蔵機関が大学であるということから学生の力を借りることが出来るという環境が周囲にあったこと、デジタルアーカイブによる公開という整理作業の到達点が明確にあったこと、目的や我々の状況に合致する微小点接着法という方法を獲得できたこと、という三点により、整理・保管にかかわる課題についてはある程度克服しつつある。本プロジェクトの手法が直ちに他の事例に応用できるとは限らないが、近代の大量資料の整理のためのひとつの方法として提

示できれば幸いである。

　　＊本学の整理作業にあたり、吉備国際大学鈴木英治教授、法寺岡宏枝氏に指導・協力を得た。本稿の内容についても鈴木教授・法寺岡氏の教示に得るところが大きい。また本文中でも指摘したように、本学資料の整理には学生有志・博物館実習参加者の協力なしには成立しえない。末尾ではあるが記して謝する。

■注
(1) 京都新聞2009年3月10日付記事「京友禅意匠　ＩＴで守れ　1000点画像　作風情報も」・京都新聞2010年12月16日付記事「京友禅原画　世界へ発信　京と大津のネット会社」など。
(2) 早水督、北尾好隆「型友禅文様データベースの構築に関する研究」(1998〜1999)、京都市産業技術研究所・繊維技術センター。
「京都デザイン活用プロジェクト」(図案提供：社団法人日本図案家協会、ウェブサイトアドレス：http://www.kyotodesign.jp/index.html。2011年9月現在)
(3) なお、服飾史に関する先駆的なデータベースでは国立民族学博物館の服装・身装文化資料に関するデータベースがあげられる。
(4) 並木誠士・青木美保子・山田由希代 (2005)「昭和初期京都における染色産業の一側面—寺田資料の紹介と位置づけ」『人文 (京都工芸繊維大学工芸学部研究報告)』54、pp.135-145。「ここにもあった匠の技—機械捺染—」展 (京都工芸繊維大学美術工芸資料館、2010年8月9日〜10月1日)。「京都のモダンデザインと近代の縞・絣」展 (京都工芸繊維大学美術工芸資料館、2011年9月20日〜10月28日)。
(5) 赤間亮・冨田美香編集、文部科学省グローバルＣＯＥプログラム「日本文化デジタル・ヒューマニティーズ拠点」(立命館大学) 監修 (2010)『イメージデータベースと日本文化研究』ナカニシヤ出版。
(6) 増田勝彦 (2003)「微小点接着法による接着力と引き剥がし後の紙の損傷」『文化財保存修復学会第25回大会研究発表要旨集』pp.64-65。増田勝彦 (2006)「微少点接着法の実際—ドットスタンプとペーストパッド」『文化財保存修復学会第28回大会研究発表要旨集』pp.106-107。
(7) 画像撮影におけるＡＲＣモデルの詳細は前出『イメージデータベースと日本文化研究』を参照されたい。

Chap.7 俄興行がもたらした映画受容の場への影響
―京都新京極の事例―

大矢敦子　*Atsuko Oya*

はじめに

　近代以降、日本の都市部では、興行街の新設や再編が進み、特に東京、大阪、京都をはじめとする主要都市では、大小様々な劇場および映画常設館が、立地から経営に至るまで、都市の行政計画に組み込まれ、その中で新たに共存また競争関係を築こうとしていた。中でも京都は、古くから多くの芸能が生まれ、展開していった豊かな歴史を持っている。それは、すなわち多くの芸能が、人々に受容される場を、持ち続けていたということにもなるだろう。こうした豊かな興行史の側面を引きつぎ、京都は近代以降、映画という新たな興行を受け入れることになった。京都は、日活と呼ばれる当時最大の映画会社が、市内に撮影所をつくり始めた大正期以降、同じ市内の興行街で、映画が提供されていったという意味で、生産と供給が同じ地域で行われていた、当時でも数少ない都市の一つである。このように製作と興行の密接な関係を結びながら、映画はどのように提供され、興行街で広がっていったのか。映画の興行的広がりは、先行する芸能の存在、また影響なしには成立しえないものだったと考えられる。
　言い換えれば、興行場所を介して、映画が先行する芸能の、どのような側面を引き継ぎ、また土台にしながら成立していったのかという視点は、各研究分野でも重要であるが、それはあまりに明らか過ぎるため、一種暗黙の了解として認識されている部分もある。映画史では田中（1975）や佐藤（1995）が指摘するように、映画は主に作品という観点からみても、芸能との、題材、出演者、

スタッフ、演出、といった共通項とは、切り離せないものであり、また、芸能史の視点からは、倉田（2006）児玉（2001）らによって、たとえば演劇史と並走している映画史というものが、見つめられてきた。近年は、東京の浅草公園六区や、京都の新京極また西陣の事例を考察した、冨田（2004）横田（2008）上田（2009）の論考により、詳細な興行街の流行や変遷過程が浮き彫りとなりつつあり、その中での芸能と映画の、より具体的な関係性が明らかになってきている。

　本稿は、こうした先行研究を受け、1900年代末から1910年代にかけての、劇場で行われた芸能の種類の特質と、プログラム編成、に焦点を当て、明治末から大正初期にかけての、劇場から映画常設館への変遷を捉え、既存の芸能と映画の関係を考察する。特に、京都新京極の興行街の事例を取り上げ、その特徴的事例として、俄の劇場から映画常設館への推移に焦点を当て、京都という地域に存在した俄という芸能が、映画の受容の場にもたらした影響を明らかにする。

1　新京極の変遷

(1)　劇場の変遷

　京都の荒廃を防ぐため、1869（明治2）年の東京遷都以後、市は様々な政策を展開した。その一環が、寺町界隈の見世物小屋や飲食店を整備し、興行街として機能させる事であった。寺町は、安土桃山時代以降、豊臣秀吉による都市計画によって形成された寺院を中心とした区画で、その界隈には参詣者を当て込んだ、大小の見世物小屋や飲食店が立ち並んでいた。第二代京都府知事として就任した槇村正直の構想によって始められた新京極の開発は、近隣の寺院からの上地による貫通路の施工によって、道を挟んだ両側に、それぞれ小屋と飲食店を配置して行われた。こうして完成した新京極は、目抜き通りとなる新京極通を中心に、主に劇場や商店そして飲食店によって賑わい、京都の盛り場としての役割を担っていく。

　それから7年後の1876（明治9）年には、新京極に興行場として芝居3座、浄瑠璃席3軒、軍書講談落語席6軒、浄瑠璃身振狂言3軒、見世物12軒、大弓9軒、半弓3軒、楊弓15軒が存在した[1]。特に、1883（明治16）年頃までには、大歌舞

伎の上演許可が下りていた、道場演劇・東向演劇・坂井座の各劇場が、一月に1000円以上の多額の収益を挙げることもあり、歌舞伎を上演する劇場が、新京極の中心に位置していたことが分かる。一方、芝居興行だけでなく、西洋眼鏡、錦影絵、義太夫、曲ぶき、生人形、浄瑠璃、手品、昔噺といった各演芸が、他の劇場では行われており（京都府立総合資料館編1971：5）、新京極では、先に挙げた三座で行われる歌舞伎を筆頭に、多種多様な演芸が興行されていたことが伺える。

その後、1886（明治19）年に公布された「劇場興行寄席取締規則」の公布によって、各劇場の改築や改修が行われ、新京極も、京都府の規制の下、各劇場の整備が続いた。また、各劇場や寄席で行われる興行種も、先に挙げた諸演芸に加え、手踊り、玉乗り、俄、ヘラヘラ踊り、新内などの興行が行われていたことが確認できる。このように、各劇場では、興行種のある程度の固定化が行われながら、次々と生まれる演目や興行種の流行によって、番組や演目がその都度変化し、1897（明治30）年に入ると、その後の新京極を代表する、明治座（旧常盤座）・歌舞伎座が次々と開場し、興行街は第一次成熟期を迎えた。

(2) **映画の参入**

以上のような劇場変遷の過程で、とりわけ著しい変化をもたらしたものが、映画であった。1897（明治30）年、京都モスリン紡績会社監査役として渡仏していた稲畑勝太郎によって、シネマトグラフが、京都に持ち込まれたことをきっかけに、映画が劇場を中心に広がりを見せ始める。京都にもたらされた映画は、当時、新京極内の各劇場で不定期に興行が行われていたが、その後、映画上映を専門にした映画常設館での興行へと移行していった。こうした映画常設館の建設ラッシュが、1907（明治40）年に入って一つのピークを迎える。1908（明治41）年に、南電気館が京都で最初の映画常設館として開場して以降、1909（明治42）年には北電気館、1911（明治44）年にパテー館・三友倶楽部・八千代館・みかど館・中央電気館（中央館）が立て続けに新築開場した。また、たとえば、『京都日出新聞』1911年1月2日に紹介されている記事を見ると、そのほとんどが映画常設館についてであったことからも、映画がいかに当時人々の話題に上り始めていたかが伺える。同記事には、明治座と歌舞伎座と南座が劇場の情報と

して上がっているだけで、そのうち南座では横田商会活動写真会が行われており、映画常設館としては、中央電気館・南電気館・北電気館・日本館・西陣電気館の公開作品が列記されている。このように、映画が新京極内で一つの興行種としての地位を確立するに至ったことがわかる。また1912（明治45）年には、四条通より二筋北に第二新京極が開通し、新京極は映画常設館の建設ピークを受けて、興行街としての環境を更に充実させていった。

　たとえば、俄の劇場だった大虎座が帝国館に、1914（大正3）年には、義太夫節の定席だった錦座が朝日倶楽部に、1914（大正3）年には帝国館の新築時に他所へ移転していた大虎座が富士館として開場するなど、新京極内で映画常設館は、劇場や寄席から映画常設館へと次々に変貌を遂げていった（図1参照）。新京極は、常に新たな興行ジャンルを取り込みながら、柔軟性を保ちつつ、興行街としての機能を十分に備え、映画興行を通して、第二次成熟期を迎えたのである。

(3) 興行種の変更と改築による劇場の差別化

　さて、ここからは、各劇場の差別化が、どのように行われたかについて、明らかにしていきたい。たとえば、新京極内の主要な劇場の一つであった夷谷座は、1876（明治9）年9月に新京極誓願寺本堂前に開場し、当初は浄瑠璃身振を中心に興行していたが、1885（明治18）年頃から、女芝居を中心とした興行で定着した。その後、1902（明治35）年頃からは、新派と歌舞伎に重点を置いた興行形態へと移行していき、各興行期間の合間に、浄瑠璃や映画といった興行種の演目を短期間で興行するといったパターンに落ち着いていった。

　一方、1900（明治33）年12月に旧坂井座を改築して開場した歌舞伎座では、主に歌舞伎中心の興行を定期的に行っていたが、歌舞伎の一座が他の劇場へ移るなどの理由で劇場を空ける場合に限り、曾我廼家五郎十郎一座の喜劇や素浄瑠璃、女浄瑠璃、人形浄瑠璃、奇術などを提供する興行パターンが定着した。ここまでは夷谷座と同じだが、歌舞伎座は1907（明治40年）年前後から、映画をプログラムとして取り入れてき、映画興行を恒久的に可能にするため、1911（明治44）年に内装を改め、内外共に洋風に改装し、「観覧席も悉く椅子」に変化した[2]。新聞紙面では、当時興行種の幅を広げるためと記述されていたが、実際は、11

新京極の劇場寄席から映画常設館への変遷（明治大正期）

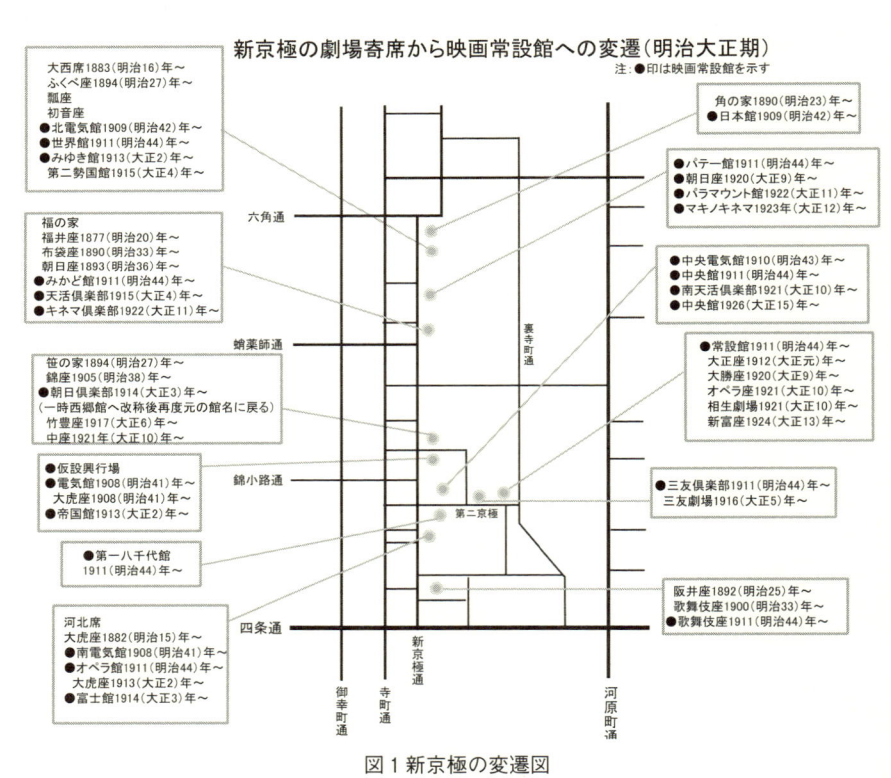

注：●印は映画常設館を示す

【大西席1883(明治16)年〜
ふくべ座1894(明治27)年〜
瓢座
初音座
●北電気館1909(明治42)年〜
●世界館1911(明治44)年〜
●みゆき館1913(大正2)年〜
第二勢国館1915(大正4)年〜】

【福の家
福井座1877(明治20)年〜
布袋座1890(明治33)年〜
朝日座1893(明治36)年〜
●みかど館1911(明治44)年〜
●天活倶楽部1915(大正4)年〜
●キネマ倶楽部1922(大正11)年〜】

【笹の家1894(明治27)年〜
錦座1905(明治38)年〜
●朝日倶楽部1914(大正3)年〜
（一時西郷館へ改称後再度元の館名に戻る）
竹豊座1917(大正6)年〜
中座1921年(大正10)年〜】

【仮設興行場
●電気館1908(明治41)年〜
大虎座1908(明治41)年〜
●帝国館1913(大正2)年〜】

【●第一八千代館
1911(明治44)年〜】

【河北席
大虎座1882(明治15)年〜
●南電気館1908(明治41)年〜
●オペラ館1911(明治44)年〜
大虎座1913(大正2)年〜
●富士館1914(大正3)年〜】

【角の家1890(明治23)年〜
●日本館1909(明治42)年〜】

【●パテー館1911(明治44)年〜
●朝日座1920(大正9)年〜
●パラマウント館1922(大正11)年〜
●マキノキネマ1923(大正12)年〜】

【●中央電気館1910(明治43)年〜
●中央館1911(明治44)年〜
●南天活倶楽部1921(大正10)年〜
●中央館1926(大正15)年〜】

【●常設館1911(明治44)年〜
大正座1912(大正元)年〜
大勝座1920(大正9)年〜
オペラ座1921(大正10)年〜
相生劇場1921(大正10)年〜
新富座1924(大正13)年〜】

【●三友倶楽部1911(明治44)年〜
三友劇場1916(大正5)年〜】

【阪井座1892(明治25)年〜
歌舞伎座1900(明治33)年〜
●歌舞伎座1911(明治44)年〜】

六角通
蛸薬師通
裏寺町通
錦小路通
第二京極
四条通
御幸町通
寺町通
新京極通
河原町通

図 1 新京極の変遷図

Fig. 1　Diagram showing the transition of Shinkyōgoku

月以降の興行を見ればわかる通り、劇場としてではなく、映画常設館として改修されたことがわかる。開場時には「物珍らしがりたがる人々」や「改築の場内見物旁々で入場する者」で賑わっていることからも、新たに映画常設館となった時、環境として洋風に整えられた内装外装の変化は、人々に強くアピールする要因の一つとなった。その後は、1913（大正2）年に松竹から日活へ賃借されたことで、日活の映画常設館として開場し、以後経営母体を変えながら、京都の代表的な映画館として認知されていったのである。

　一方、こうした劇場から映画常設館への推移の過程で、劇場の興行種やプログラム編成が、映画常設館転換後の映画プログラム編成に、影響を与えていたとは言い難い。というのも、先に触れたように、歌舞伎座は、映画常設館となる直前、歌舞伎に加え、曾我廼家五郎十郎一座の定席としても位置付けられていたが、1910（明治43）年の興行を分析すると、曾我廼家一座の喜劇の興行数は、一年間に7回と、同年の歌舞伎興行数と同じとなっている[3]。その後、歌舞伎座では契約状況は不明だが、福宝堂のフィルムが公開されており、平均して実写1作品、滑稽2～3作品、活劇または悲劇1作品といったプログラム構成で、映画興行が行われていた。たとえば、1912（大正元）年1月のプログラムを見てみると、滑稽「ビル君と電柱」、実写「海底の偉観」、西洋悲劇「金貸の息子」、日本滑稽「鳩」全3巻、滑稽「娘の行衛」、西洋史談「五十年後」、滑稽「ダム君の芝居熱」、日本悲劇「寒月」全11場[4]であった。しかし、これは当時の平均的なプログラム編成であり、取り立てて特徴的なものではない。また、明治40年代から吉沢商店また横田商会の作品を、芝居の興行の合間に興行していた夷谷座にしても、同じ様なプログラム編成となっている。夷谷座が以後、1920年代に一時期映画常設館となることからも、当時の劇場は、映画常設館となる流れの中に常に身を置いており、経営者の交代や劇場の経営状況によって、映画常設館へと変化していた。つまり、歌舞伎を中心とした主要な劇場も、常に映画常設館となる可能性があったと言える。

　以上で対象とした劇場以外の、中小の劇場や寄席は、より大きな困難を抱えていた。プログラム編成だけでなく、設備面でも到底大劇場に及ばなかったため、中小の劇場や寄席は、次々と映画常設館として改築された。たとえば、初音座としてあった寄席は、北電気館として1909（明治42）年に開場し、飄々会と

呼ばれる喜劇団の定席であった朝日座は、近隣の火事による消失後、映画常設館として改築され、1911（明治44）年には、みかど館として開場している。これら中小の寄席や劇場は、明治期の映画興行の流行を捉え、早い段階で映画常設館への興行に切り替わることによって、興行街での生存競争に打ち勝とうとしていたと言えるだろう。

　以上のように、当時の劇場は、それぞれの劇場で行われていた、興行種の性質を加味して改善が進められ、特に設備面の新しさというものが、各劇場の特徴と結びついていった。また、劇場は、歌舞伎・新派劇・喜劇といった興行種のゆるやかな固定化によって、特定の興行ジャンルを館の独自性として提示していたものの、プログラムとしての提供パターンは、主要な興行種の興行期間の合間に、諸演芸の興行を行っていた点でほぼ類似しており、しかも、その諸演芸の種類にも大きな差は無かった。特に、明治30年代は、以上に挙げた夷谷座、歌舞伎座の例からも、劇場毎の興行種またプログラム編成による独自性は、ほぼ崩れていたと言える。そこで、改築に伴う外観や設備面、また、映画常設館への移行という興行ジャンルの専門性を劇的に変化させ、なおかつその専門性を高めることで、館ごとの差別化を生み出そうとしていたと考えられる。

3　俄興行のローカル性と映画興行への影響

(1)　新京極の俄興行

　これまでに考察した、歌舞伎の劇場から映画常設館への変遷パターン以外にも、新京極では、俄の劇場から映画常設館へと転換したパターンがある。俄とは、寺院での祭礼や廓で行われた風流が元と考えられている、民間演芸の一種であり、はじめは素人の即興喜劇だったが、集団として組や連中を組織するようになった演者達が、専門的に職業として俄狂言を演じるようになっていった。江戸や大阪でも同時期に流行したが、京都では、特に廓の祭礼の練物に取り入れられ、島原で頻繁に行われた。一般的にはこうした流れから、次第に歌舞伎や浄瑠璃の趣向を元に演じられる芝居がかりの物となっていき、天保期には劇場や寄席での興行がおこなわれる様になった。明治期に入ると、関西圏では、特に大阪で組織された俄の一座が、東京で興行を行うなど、勢力を拡大しなが

表1　大虎座変遷表
Tab.1　The transition of Ōtoraza

No.	劇場	映画館	備考
1	河北席		
	大虎座(1882)		
		南電気館 (1908)	
		オペラ館 (1911)	
	大虎座(1913)		
		富士館 (1914)	
2	大虎座(1908)		南電気館開館後、場所を移して開場。
		帝国館 (1913)	
		京都日活映画劇場(1945)	

ら新派や喜劇の発生に寄与したとされている。もちろん、こうした大阪俄の進出は京都にも及び、明治30年代にはいくつかの定席が新京極に出現し地位を固めるまでになった［演博、1983］。

　その歴史を概観すると、新京極では、1885（明治18）年に大西座が俄狂言の定席として開場した。定席以外にも、ひきつづき俄狂言は寄席を中心に広く上演される興業種として新京極に広まり、明治10年代後半になると、俄狂言は新聞小説を脚色したものに人気が集中し、時事性に富んだテーマが取り入れられていった。新たに大虎座[5]が新設され、大西座と人気を二分していく存在となり、「いっぱいの見物人（中略）立見する場もない程」[6]人気を得ていた。他にも瓢座・川村座・パノラマ館・仲竹座・一六座・福栄座といった寄席や小屋でも行われた。また同時期に俄狂言から派生して、俄踊や書生俄などが現れた。

　こうした俄狂言の人気は、大虎座や大西座の俄一座によって「改良俄」または「新聞俄」と呼ばれる新たな演出を生んだ。これは、新聞紙面に掲載の小説や事件や男女の情事を、スキャンダラスに扱った雑報を脚色し、俄狂言として演じたもので、定席だけでなく、寄席や劇場でも行われた。そうした俄狂言の流行も、明治30年代後半には下火になり始め、俄狂言を含めた喜劇を上演する中小の劇場は、改築に伴い、次々と映画常設館へと姿を変えて行った。以後、新京極内での俄興行の代表格だった大虎座も、1908（明治40）年7月には、映画常設館として南電気館に改築された。しかし、すぐに"新京極錦上る"に大虎座を開場し（表1中のNo.2）、俄狂言は引き続き興行された。しかしその後再び、

大虎座は1913（大正2）年に、映画常設館に改築され、帝国館として日活の直営館となる（図1参照）。俄狂言は二度に渡って興行の場を映画に明け渡したが、さらに場所をもともと大虎座だった場所（当時は南電気館から改称し、オペラ座となっていた）に戻し、俄狂言を続けた（表1中のNo.1）。しかし、ここも最終的には映画常設館として改築され、富士館となり、新京極内での俄狂言の定席はここで消滅することとなった（表1中のNo.1参照）。

(2) 時事性と即興性

次に、映画常設館に何度も場所を明け渡しながらも、1913（大正2）年まで、場所を変えながらその座を守った大虎座の、俄興行の内容や種類を考察する。まず、明治20年〜30年代に大虎座で行われていた俄狂言の独自性として、2点の特徴を挙げることができる。それは、時事性と即興性である。

まず、大虎座が行っていた俄狂言は、主に『京都日出新聞』や『大阪朝日新聞』など、新聞紙面に掲載された連載小説や雑報を脚色したものを、俄として公演していた点に特徴がある。前項で既述の通り、これらは「新聞俄」や「改良俄」と呼ばれ、大虎座を中心に広く提供された俄狂言のジャンルであった。こうした俄のジャンルは、大虎座に出演していた、俄師の東玉や馬鹿八らによって編み出されたものである［演博、1983］[7]。

その一例として『情の分櫛』の興行がある。これは、京都の髪結いお政が惨殺された事件を俄に仕立て、『京都日出新聞』の記事掲載日と同日に興行を行ったもので、大虎座で行われた俄狂言の時事性が象徴されている[8]。こうした同時代的に事件性のあるもので、しかもスキャンダルとして扱われる一件を、たちまち俄狂言に仕立てることによって、それまで歌舞伎や浄瑠璃を脚色していただけの俄狂言に新たな広がりを持たせた。歌舞伎や新派でも、同じように時事的な事件を扱い、芝居として提示していたが、そのような場合とは違い、俄狂言では、見世物的な提示の方法、また芝居化されるほどの大きな事件でもない、いわゆるローカルな事件に注目した点が、特徴として挙げられる。特に、大虎座の出演者自身が起こした事件を、そのまま俄狂言として提示していたケースもある。例えば、1890（明治23）年には、大虎座に出演中であった馬鹿八が、彼自身に起こった騒動を俄狂言化した[9]。これは、馬鹿八と花街の芸妓の

やりとりを基にしたもので、上演時には花街の客も多く来場している。つまり、俄狂言師のセルフプロデュースとでも言える試みがなされていた点で、時事性と共に、特定の地域を対象とした話題性が、重要な要素として付加されていたと言える。

また、同時期に興行された歌舞伎劇の、同演目を俄狂言に仕立てて興行していたという点にも注目したい。例えば『日蓮記』が道場芝居（京角座）で行われた際に、大虎座でも同じ演目名で、俄狂言が行われていた[10]。また、1889（明治22）年10月『塩原多助の一代記』として、南演劇（南座）や坂井座で同時期に行われていた同演目を俄に脚色したものもあった[11]。こうした歌舞伎の人気演目を同時代的に俄に仕立てることで、話題性を持たせたと言える。プログラムとしても、1892（明治25）年頃より、歌舞伎演目を俄狂言にしたものと、新聞雑報や連載小説を俄にしたもの、この２種類の俄を上演するパターンが定着していった。つまり、主に歌舞伎の劇場を中心に、演目の流行のレベルに応じながらそれを取り込み、なおかつローカルな話題を取り込んで演目構成を行っていたことが、大虎座の俄興行の特徴として指摘できる。

次に、同座が行っていた「即席俄」を取り上げたい。これは、観客に題を提供してもらい、その場で俄狂言を仕立てて行うというもので、これも大変な人気をとったとされる。この形式はその後、相撲対戦をなぞらえた対戦形式での興行に発展した[12]。そのほか、芸子連の俄狂言の興行なども行っており、豊富な種類の俄狂言を仕立てることによって、プログラムに多様性を持たせていたと言える。

つまり、大虎座での俄狂言は、時事的で即興的な要素を、多分に発揮しえたと言えるだろう。特に、各紙に掲載された記事内容や小説の脚色によるものが多数を占めており、新聞紙面における読者層を対象としていたとも考えられ、即興性と時事性に共通した、時流に乗るスピードと多様な種類の狂言によるプログラム編成が、大虎座の俄狂言には必要不可欠な要素であったと言える。

こうした俄狂言で人気を得ていた大虎座であったが、明治40年代になると、俄狂言以外の興行演目に徐々に移行している。その一つに、映画の上映がある。大虎座は、明治期に少なくとも計４回の映画興行を行っており[13]、日活作品を上映した。これは、日活の横田永之助と、大虎座の経営者であった小林寅吉が、

帝国館の経営を共同で行うなど、経営者として密接な関係にあったことが一因であったと考えられる[14]。このような、大虎座及び日活の映画常設館経営者の結びつきにより、大虎座は日活に属すこととなったとみられる。また、大虎座跡に開場した富士館は、開館当初、尾上松之助一派の映画作品を封切っていたが、1914（大正3）年10月20日以降、新派悲劇の封切館として定着していく。こうした封切作品ジャンルの変更については、以下の理由がある。当時日活は、新京極内の7館の常設館で映画興行を行っていたが[15]、このうち、松竹との提携関係にあった、歌舞伎座（新派と活劇）・みかど館（新派と旧劇）・八千代館（新派と旧劇）の3館の契約が、6月に切れた[16]。この3館に共通しているのは、上映されていた映画が、新派作品だったことである。日活は、以上の興行場所を一気に失ってしまったため、日活の主軸であった帝国館、中央館及び富士館の3館のうち、一番新しく開場した富士館が、新たに新派の封切館になったのである。

(3) 地域への訴求力

ここからは、映画常設館となったその後を捉えるため、大虎座後に新築された富士館の興行形式、また主な上映作品と、俄の共通点を明らかにしていきたい。前述したように、富士館は後年、興行状況に応じて、日活の新派の映画封切館となったが、開館当初は、主に尾上松之助主演作、つまり旧劇の上映館であった。まず、1914（大正3）年7月に開場した、富士館の開館当初のプログラムは、「実写　コーヒの栽培」、「滑稽活劇　一目散」、「軍事大活劇　爆戦」、「怪猫退治　旧劇　安芸宮嶋大仇討」の4作品となっている（図2参照）。既に述べたように、当時、映画常設館は新築や改築の第一次ピークを終えていたが、映画興行が新京極で一般化した頃に新築された富士館は、そのプログラム内容も、同時代の他の映画常設館と同じスタイルを踏襲し、実写、滑稽、活劇、旧劇という4種類の作品を上映している。ここで注目したいのは、旧劇という映画ジャンルである。開館当初から同年9月頃まで、プログラムの最後に編成された旧劇は、富士館のメインとして位置づけられた。大虎座時代に遡ってプログラムをみてみると、大虎座では、歌舞伎を題材とした俄狂言が行われていた。中でも、1914（大正3）年9月に封切られた、映画『天保六歌仙　河内山宗俊』

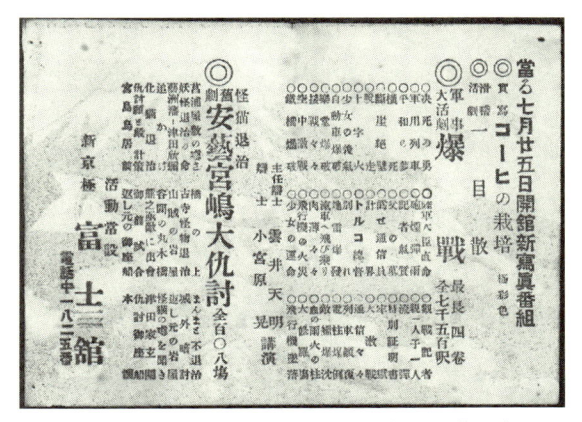

図2 大正3年富士館プログラム 立命館大学国際平和ミュージアム所蔵 h-0158
Fig. 2 Program of Fujikan in 1914
(h-0158, Kyoto Museum for World Pease, Ritsumeikan University)

は、同年6月南座で上演された『河内山宗俊』の映画化として宣伝されている[17]。つまり、かつて大虎座で行われていたように、劇場で興行されていた演目を、俄狂言に仕組むという方法を映画でも適用させ、観客にアピールしている点で、過去の劇場の宣伝や興行的な戦略をなぞっていると言えるだろう。つまり、大虎座時代に行われた俄狂言の歌舞伎への傾倒、特に同じ市内の劇場で行われた歌舞伎に当て込んだ手法というものが適用され、開館当初の映画上映のプログラムとして、機能していたと言える。

次に、新派作品を、プログラムの主軸とした後の、興行手法に目を向けてみる。例えば、1914（大正3）年11月に『カチューシャ』4巻が公開された。『カチューシャ』は、芝居として同年3月に芸術座で初演された、トルストイの『復活』を翻案したもので、松井須磨子がカチューシャを演じ、人気を博した作品である。これを、日活が同年のうちに映画化し公開した。当時、劇中で松井が歌った中山晋平作曲の「カチューシャの唄」は爆発的な人気で、その歌声と彼女の姿を映したキネトフォンの興行も、浅草で大成功を収めた。以上の人気を踏まえ、同年11月に、南座に巡業中だった芸術座に当て込んで、南座で好評だった演劇作品として告知され[18]、同作品の映画化であることが宣伝されている。

7 俄興行がもたらした映画受容の場への影響　■　99

公開後は、当時の富士館には通常は来館しない、芸術座の客筋[19]が多数足を運んだことで、『カチューシャ』は京都でも人気を得た[20]。これは、その時々の他の劇場の興行演目にも目を配り、それにあわせて興行を行い、それによって通常の観客層とは違う客層へのアピールも成功した事例の一つと言えるだろう。

おわりに

ここまでの考察を整理すると、京都の事例について言えば、劇場から映画常設館への推移に、芝居と俄のそれぞれの興行が特徴として現れていた。芝居に関しては、劇場で興行される芝居の種類によって存在しえた、各劇場の固有性の消失が要因として挙げられる。そうした状況下で、映画が興行として組み込まれ始め、劇場の中には、興行種の多様化を最大限に発揮できる場としての機能を生かし、映画常設館へと方向転換を行ったものも多くあった。俄に関しては、芝居の劇場とは違い、興行種の固有性が発揮された場であったものが、映画興行へと興行種が変化した際、俄の時事性と即興性という二つの性質が一部引き継がれ、同じ市内の劇場で行われていた演目の映画化という宣伝手法に現れていた。映画常設館は、劇場のプログラム編成や興行種の豊富さが提示されていた場として、また劇場で展開されていた興行種の性質そのものを潜在的な基盤として、成立していたのである。

■注
(1) 『郵便報知』1876年6月12日。
(2) 「演芸」『京都日出新聞』1911年10月13日。
(3) 曾我廼家の喜劇は、1月に2回、5月に3回、9月に2回の計7回。歌舞伎は2月、3月、4月、7月にそれぞれ1回、10月に2回、11月に1回の計7回。その他、演芸会や魔術、電気劇、素浄瑠璃、義太夫が計5回興行された。
(4) 「ゑんげい」『京都日出新聞』1912年1月7日。
(5) 大虎座は1882年頃に寄席だった河北席から俄の定席として解明されたとされるが、筆者は新聞記事に従って、1887年4月1日からの興行から大虎座として扱うこととする（『京都日出新聞』1887年3月31日）。なお、『中外電報』1887年3月6日では、新京極四条上る観商場跡に大虎座が新築されたことがわかる。

(6) 『京都日出新聞』1887年9月16日。
(7) 「劇場だより」『京都日出新聞』1887年8月30日、9月8日。「劇場通信」『京都日出新聞』1885年5月28日参照。
(8) 「女髪結殺しの俄狂言」『京都日出新聞』1887年9月16日。なお、大虎座に対抗した形で大西座でも同日同内容の俄興行が行われている。
(9) 「馬鹿八。馬鹿にならず」同上紙、1890年5月28日。
(10) 1888年2月1日から道場芝居（京角座）にて興行された演目。『京都日出新聞』1888年2月17日には、大虎座での同演目の俄狂言が掲載されている。
(11) 「∞かの競争」『京都日出新聞』1889年10月23日、「塩原多助は總州者にあらず」同紙、1889年10月30日。
(12) 「演芸」『京都日出新聞』1895年9月15日。
(13) 『白虎隊』(1910年8月11日)、『阪本龍馬』(1911年8月1日)、『宇都宮釣天井』(1911年8月11日)、『相馬大作』(1911年8月20日)。
(14) 帝国館は二人の共同経営であり尚且つ日活の直轄となっていた。
(15) 同年1月時点で新京極内にあった帝国館、第一八千代館、御幸館、歌舞伎座、みかど館、中央館・オペラ館の7館（「興行案内」『京都日出新聞』1914年1月1日）。
(16) 「たのしみ」『大阪朝日新聞京都附録』1914年6月20日。
(17) 「特別広告」同上紙、1914年9月20日。
(18) 「たのしみ」同上紙、1914年11月20日。
(19) 「たのしみ」同上紙、1914年11月26日。
(20) 舞台でカチューシャを演じた松井須磨子もお忍びで鑑賞したとある（「たのしみ」同上紙1914年11月24日、26日）。

■参考文献

上田学（2009）「映画常設館の出現と変容：1900年代の電気館とその観客」『アート・リサーチ』9、[Ueda, 2009]。

京都市『史料京都の歴史』5巻　社会・文化（1984）平凡社［Kyoto, 1984］

京都府立総合資料館『京都府百年の年表9芸能編』(1971)［Kyoto Prefectural Library and Archives, 1971］

倉田喜弘（2006）『芝居小屋と寄席の近代』岩波書店［Kurata, 2006］

児玉竜一（2003）「歌舞伎研究と映画—「歌舞伎と映画」その前提として」『歌舞伎研究と批評』31、6-31。[Kodama, 2003]

児玉竜一（2005）「歌舞伎から映画へ「芸能史」としての時代劇映画前史」『時代劇伝説チャンバラ映画の輝き』森話社、34-57。[Kodama, 2005]

佐藤恵里（2002）『歌舞伎・俄研究　資料編室戸市佐喜浜町俄台本集成』新典社研究叢

書139、新典社。［Sato, 2002］
佐藤忠男（1995）『日本映画史』第1巻、岩波書店。［Sato, 1995］
柴田勝「京都新京極映画常設館の変遷」(1971) 私家版［Shibata, 1971］
新京極連合会『新京極』(1972) 同朋社［Shinkyogoku rengokai, 1972］
田中純一郎（1975）『日本映画発達史』中公文庫。［Tanaka, 1975］
冨田美香「KYOTO映像フェスタ「京都映画草創期」調査報告」『アート・リサーチ』Vol.4（2004）、121-126［Tomita, 2004］
柳下毅一郎（2003）『興行師たちの映画史』青土社［Yanashita, 2003］
横田洋（2008）「連鎖劇の興行とその取り締まり─東京における事例をめぐって」『フィロカリア』No.25、31-66［Yokota, 2008］
早稲田大学坪内逍遥記念演劇博物館『演劇百科大事典』第4巻（1983）［Enpaku, 1983］

Chap.8 戦間期日本における小型映画文化の様相
―映画都市京都のもう一つの顔―

冨田美香　Mika Tomita

はじめに―小型映画が記録した京都―

　ここに1930年代から1940年にかけて、京都の映画人の活動や日常の光景を撮影した、小型映画[1]がある。いずれも反転現像による唯一のオリジナルプリントに焼き込まれた、極めて個人的なヴィジョンに基づいた、なお且つその時代と文化を鮮明に刻んだ、瞬時の記憶であり、唯一無二の映像である。

　図1と図2のフィルムは、京都の資産家で映画好きであった田中英一（1916~2007）[2]が、カメラ助手やカメラマンとして携わった映画の撮影風景をお

図1　『ロケーションの想ひ出』（監督：田中英一、1934、原版16mm）
Fig. 1　*A Memory of Location* (Dir. Tanaka Eiichi, 1934, 16mm)

図2　『カメラマンの想い出』（監督：田中英一、1934~1941、原版8mm）。左より、田中十三、田中英一、中川紫郎
Fig. 2　*Memories of Cameraman* (Dir. Tanaka Eiichi, 1934-194, 8mm) From the left, Tanaka Jūzō, Tanaka Eiichi, Nakagawa Shirō.

さめたものである。図1は、兄の田中伊助が京都の御室に設立したエトナ映画社（1934～1935）の第1回作品『神崎東下り』（1934年、監督：後藤岱山）の撮影風景であり、図2は、『慶州佛国寺と石窟庵』（1941年、中川紫郎監督、合同映画）の撮影スタッフの記念映像である。エトナ映画社設立当時、18歳の英一は、パラマウント映画をこよなく愛し、小型映画愛好者の憧憬の的であった最新鋭の16mmカメラ、シネ-コダック・スペシャル[3]を持って撮影も楽しんでいた映画ファンであった。その愛機を持参してエトナ映画社に参加した英一は、パラマウントにちなんだ田中聖峰の名前で撮影所長に就任し、と同時に岸（ギシ＝技師）雅夫の名で撮影助手として活躍し、エトナ映画社の解散後は文化映画の分野で戦時まで映画撮影にかかわった人物である。『ロケーションの想ひ出』は愛機のシネ-コダック・スペシャルで撮影されたものと思われるが、英一は複数の16mm作品に加えて、9.5mmと発売間もない8mm作品も残しており、当時の日本に流通していた小型映画のすべての規格を所持して自身の日常を撮影していたことがわかる。この英一の意向が強く作用したエトナ映画社は、小型映画部と称して、16mmによる劇映画『白い鼠』の製作も試みており、映画のスタンダード規格である35mmを主流にした劇場用映画の歩みに、サブ・スタンダードの小型映画からアプローチを果たした、ユニークな存在であった。

　図3は、9.5mmのボビンに『愛宕スキー場』と記された作品であり、旧蔵者や撮影者など、権利者が不明のオーファン・フィルムの一コマである。京都の愛

図3　『愛宕スキー場』（監督不明、1929～1930年代、原版9.5mm）
Fig. 3　*Atago Ski Resort*（Dir. Unknown, 1929-1930s, 9.5mm）

宕山スキー場は1929年から戦時まで開業しており、1930年代半ばまでに撮影された映像と推定される。積雪の少ないスキー場で、京都府民であろう人々が冬のレジャーを楽しんでいる光景が収められている。この1分半ほどの映像からは、当時存在した愛宕スキー場を確認できるだけでなく、京都市内からケーブルで気軽に訪れることのできた地元で一般の人々がスキーを楽しんでいる様子や、転んで動けなくなった子供を抱える父親の姿が甦り、時代を超えて当時の人々の感情を共有することができる。

　図4は、1937年から1941年末まで日活の社長を務めた森田佐吉（1874～1944）のプライベート・フィルムに記録されていた、日活太秦撮影所の運動会の映像から作成した画像であり、徒競走のランナーを追うパンニング・ショットのコマを重ねて、日活太秦撮影所の全景を再現したものである。1点の動画映像は、静止画像や文字にくらべて情報量がはるかに多く、研究素材としての活用度も高いことがわかる。今は失われた日活太秦撮影所の中で、紀元2600年を祝して開催された運動会に、スターや所員とその家族、地元の人々が集まり、戦時のレクリエーションを楽しんでいた光景が甦る。

　これらの小型映画が、地域や時代、歴史を、個人の視点から描き出した唯一の映像ドキュメントであり、その文化的、芸術的、学術的そして歴史的な価値は、あらためて言及するまでも無いだろう。

　このようなアマチュア映画、ホーム・ムービーへの評価は、1990年代半ばから映像アーカイブや研究者間に広まり、彼らの活動を通してこの十年間に飛躍的に高まった。例えば、国際フィルム・アーカイブ聯盟（FIAF）は、1996年に機関誌でアマチュア映画の特集を組み、翌年にはアマチュア映画をテーマにし

図4　『日活太秦撮影所運動会』（1940、原版16mm）コマより筆者作成
Fig. 4　*Nikkatsu Uzumasa Studio Athletic Festival*（1940, from 16mm）Assembled by the author.

たFIAF会議をコロンビアで開催するなど、世界各国でのアマチュア映画の発掘と保存に向けた大きな推進力となった。また、2002年には、映像アーキビスト協会（AMIA）が機関誌 The Moving Image を発行し、アマチュア映画やホーム・ムービーに関する研究とアーカイブのリーダー役を果たしている。同年には、これらの活動を推進してきた代表的なアーキビストたちによる「ホーム・ムービーの日」[4]運動が始まり、現在では日本を含めた世界14カ国以上で、埋もれているホーム・ムービーに光をあて、保存を推進する活動が毎秋展開されている。

　これらの活動と並行して、小型映画やホーム・ムービーの大国のアメリカ、イギリス、フランスの大学やアーカイブの研究者たちが、研究書[5]を続々と編纂し、それらによって、小型映画やホーム・ムービーの史的特徴が、地域や社会によって大きく異なることが明らかにされた。そして、これらのフィルムは、マイノリティも含めた個人の視点と、公的な歴史とを同時に表象しえる稀有な文化資源であることも強く認識されるようになったといってよい。日本でも、東京国立近代美術館フィルムセンターに寄贈された荻野茂二[6]コレクションを契機に、小型映画、アマチュア映画への評価が高まり[7]、「ホーム・ムービーの日」も各地で展開されているが、まだこの分野への認識が、とりわけ大学や地域映像アーカイブの分野で高まっているとはいいがたい。

　本稿では、小型映画が築いていた地域コミュニティの視点から、冒頭に提示した小型映画作品が京都で生成された文化的かつ歴史的背景を、戦間期の日本における小型映画文化の概観を通して、明らかにするものである。とくに、小型映画がサブ・スタンダードであったがゆえに、膨大な映像文化を各地で生み出しながら、戦時期の日本映画のプロパガンダ体制下に統合されていったプロセスに着目する。

1　小型映画の導入

　戦間期の日本において小型映画が普及し始めたのは、フランスで発売されたばかりのパテ・フレール社の製品、9.5mmのパテ・ベビーの映写機とフィルムが販売された、1922年[8]からである。それ以前も17.5mmなどは使用されていたが、

家庭や学校といった私的、公的空間に広く浸透するには到らなかった。翌年にアメリカのイーストマン・コダック社が発売した16mmが販売開始され、その翌1924年にはパテ・ベビーのカメラが販売された。この2系統が、1920年代から1930年代の小型映画の主流である。

　いずれも、先ず上映用のフィルムと映写機を発売し、家庭での映画上映、鑑賞を主にしたユーザー層を開拓し、その後に撮影機のカメラを販売しており、これによって小型映画のユーザー層は、従来の鑑賞者に加えて、普通写真の愛好家や、映像制作を試みる個人や団体へと広がった。20年代後半には、小型映画愛好家によるクラブ活動が活発になり、さまざまなジャンルの作品が生み出され、コンテストも頻繁に開催されるようになる。1930年代半ばには欧米のアマチュア映画祭で受賞する作品や作家を輩出する隆盛をみせ、コダックの8mmも新たに導入され、戦間期の日本における小型映画文化を形成する主流の3種類が揃った。このフランス系の9.5mm派とアメリカ系との2派が凌ぎを削っていた点が、16mm主流のアメリカや9.5mmが主流のイギリスと様相を異にする日本の特徴の一つである。

　9.5mm文化を推進する中核的な存在は、パテ社から販売権を得ていた伴野商店であり、国産の9.5mmフィルムや、カメラ、映写機の製作・販売も行っていた。9.5mmの愛好者たちは、愛着を込めて"ベビー党"と称し、「ベビーシネマ」や「ベビーキネマ」と名付けたクラブを各地で結成し、伴野の後援を受けながら機関誌も発行した。後述する京都ベビー・シネマ協会は、その代表的なクラブの一つである。ただし9.5mmは、この名称に加えて、カメラや映写機の広告にしばしば子供がユーザーとして提示されたことから、子供のおもちゃと揶揄されることが少なくなく、愛好者たちは「ベビーの冠詞を戴くことは時代錯誤」[9]として、「パテーシネマ」へと改称するようになった。

　一方、16mmの映写機やカメラは、ベル＆ハウエル社の製品を含めて種類が豊富であり、国産製品も徐々に発売されていった。初期のイーストマンの日本拠点には、大阪に開設されたシネ・コダック・サービス・ジャパンや、京都の大澤商会[10]があり、16mm愛好者は、ニューヨークを拠点としたアメリカの16mmクラブ「アマチュア・シネマ・リーグ」の日本支部を1927年に作り、本部と連絡をとりながら、日本版の機関誌『アマチュア・ムービー・メーカーズ』を発行

した。

　"小型映画"という言葉は、単純にフィルム幅の規格を示すことから、20年代から30年代にかけて、9.5mmと16mmの両規格を中立的に指し示す言葉として用いられていた。1929年から発行された『小型映画』はその代表的な媒体であり、当時は、アマチュアによって作られた映画と、家庭鑑賞用に発売されたプロの作品の双方を対象とした、いわば個人レベルで受容する小型の映画を示す用語であったといえる。ところが、この"小型映画"は、1941年から敗戦まで、敵性語の"アマチュア・ムービー"の代わりに使われるようになり、映画法やフィルムの欠乏から個人レベルでの映画受容が難しくなった状況もかかわって、戦時の文化映画、教育映画、ドキュメンタリー、ニュース映画など、35mm以下のプロの作品を示すことが多くなった。同時にこの変化は、それまで小型映画に携わっていた代表的な人々を、戦時期のプロパガンダを担う"小型映画"へと再編していくことにもなった。

2　小型映画の特色

　小型映画の特徴を大別すると、操作性、不燃性、経済性、現像サービス、多様なフィルム種、投影映像の問題、の6点といえる。これらの特徴を通して、戦間期の日本に小型映画がどのように受容されていったかを整理したい。

　第一の操作性は、ボタン一押しで撮影できるほど、カメラ、フィルム、映写機のいずれも、操作がきわめて単純で、小さくかつ軽量な点である。そのため、コダックは女性を、パテは子供を広告に用いて、機械の硬質なイメージを柔らげ、いわゆる"女子供でも出来る"イメージと同時に、家族を主にした新しいライフ・スタイルを打ち出した。これらの広告は日本でもそのまま使用され、欧米のモダンな家庭生活や女性イメージを流布し、小型映画は知的で文化的モデルともなった。

　第二の不燃性は、小型映画の普及に最も重要な要素であったものである。可燃性の35mmとは異なり、火災につながる危険性を排除できたことから、家庭や学校へと販路を広げることが出来、教育映画や文化映画への利用価値を初期から注目されることとなった。日本では当時、文部省が教育映画運動を進めてお

り、また、1928年には、大阪を中心とした大毎フィルム・ライブラリーと、東京を中心とした東日フィルム・ライブラリーが立ち上がり、道府県の小学校の教育映画会へ35㎜フィルムを貸し出す事業を開始している。同年、伴野商店は、後援するベビークラブを介して、学校教育用のパテー・ベビー・フィルムライブラリーの貸出を始めた[11]。さらに全国組織の機関誌『ベビーシネマ』に、フランスやイギリスの学校教育で経費、不燃性、作品の豊富さにおいてパテ・ベビーが用いられている報告や[12]、小型映画の映画教育作品の必要性を主張する小学校教員の記事[13]を掲載し、翌年には小学校用の教育映画を課題にしたコンテスト[14]を開催するなど、明らかにこの分野への進出を意識した活動を行っている。結果的に、大毎ライブラリーは1931年から、東日ライブラリーは1934年から、16㎜フィルムによる配給を開始し、16㎜が学校向け教育映画の大半を担うようになったが、教員が授業教材や生徒たちの記録を撮影する際には9.5㎜が使われていた[15]ようである。京都では、他府県とは異なり、独自に16㎜映写機とフィルムを購入して巡回映写する京都市小学校映画教育研究会が、1929年に京都市教育部内に設置され[16]、教材フィルムの製作[17]や普及活動[18]まで積極的に行っていた。

　第三の経済性は、35㎜との対比においてである。1930年当時の大卒者の月給平均約69円と比較すると、外国製品の値段として、9.5㎜はカメラ、映写機ともに90円、16㎜はカメラが450〜800円、映写機は540円であり、国産品や中古品は大幅に安価に購入することができた。したがって当時の小型映画の愛好者は、中流階級の上層以上の男性や、大学サークル、教員らが中心であり、国産の安価な機材が発売されると、次第にその利用者層も拡がっていった。後述するプロキノ運動や、戦時期に小型映画の活用が高まったことも、この理由が大きい。

　第四のサービスは、特にコダックの方針であり、現像やプリントのサービスを完備していたことである。コダックの宣伝文句「あなたはレバーを押しなさい。当社は其他を致します」は、利用者はボタンを押して撮影するだけで、あとはコダックのサービス・ステーションが全て作業し、プリントを渡す、という仕組みである。しかし、日本の小型映画作家たちは、自身が望む映像を得られることと露出を学ぶことも含めて自家現像を好み、その理由から、スペースも機材も電気がなくても反転現像できる9.5㎜を利用したユーザーも多かった。

とくに小型映画の初期にあたる1920年代はこの反転現像が大きな問題であり、その発達は京都の三条烏丸にある燕屋（ツバメヤ）商会に負うところが多かったといわれている[19]。

第五のフィルム種類の豊富さは、1928年に発売されたコダックのカラーフィルムとパンクロマティック・フィルム、そして1930年のトーキー（ディスク式）のことである。これによって日本では、映画館で上映される日本映画よりも、小型映画の方が早く、カラー映画やトーキー映画を作ることが可能になった。

最後は、小型映画がサブ・スタンダードの立場を変えられなかった理由でもある、映写映像が35mmに比べて劣る点である。このためコダックを初めとするメーカーは、専用スクリーンを販売したが、日本のベビー党は、専用スクリーンよりもケント紙の方が、反射率の点でどの客席からも明るい映写映像を得られると主張し、機関誌でその方法を共有[20]しながら、5百人以上の大規模上映会を各地で行うようになった。16mmについても、千人規模の上映会を開催したことが、アメリカで報道[21]されている。後述するプロキノも含め、これらの上映ノウハウを備えた小型映画人の一部は、戦時期には巡回上映のスタッフとして活動することになった。

3 小型映画文化の様相

(1) 地域コミュニティの形成とオール・ニッポン

前述したように、小型映画愛好者は、自分たちのクラブを各地域に作り、上映活動、撮影会、競技会と称したコンテスト、機関誌の発行などを実施し、地域コミュニティを形成するようになった。9.5mmの場合は、日本のクラブの多くの拠点が、カメラや映写機、フィルム、薬剤を販売する地域の写真店や薬局であり、それらが愛好者のサロンや上映会場、機関誌の発行場所にもなっていた。

日本で最も早く、盛んなクラブ活動を展開したのは、京都、大阪を中心とした京阪神の愛好者たちである。1926年に全関西ベビー・シネマ・クラブ競技会を開催し、後に大阪ベビー・キネマ・クラブや、京都ベビー・シネマ協会を構成する愛好家たちが集って作品を競いあい、その後も日活京都撮影所やマキノ

撮影所での見学会と競技会を重ねている。同年に、関東大震災からの復興を進めた東京でも、東京ベビーシネマ倶楽部が結成され、これを契機に全国パテーベビー競技大会が開催され、愛好家たちの交流の場となった。

京都のベビー・シネマ協会では、幹部として当時の日活京都撮影所脚本部の若葉馨や御子柴杜雄が参加し、顧問には村田実、森岩雄が名を連ねており、鈴木重吉やプロキノの木村荘十二も集う[22]など、プロとアマの密接な交流が多くあったようである。クラブ運営の企画や製作活動の中心的な存在として、前述の若葉や、後に童映社を結成し『煙突屋ペロー』を生み出す田中喜次や中野孝夫らがおり、反転現像で彼らを支えた三条烏丸の燕屋から、機関誌『ベビー・シネマ』を発行した。1928年には、京都スキー・ランナー倶楽部と共催で、スキーを主題にした撮影競技会を開催[23]しており、冒頭で紹介した『愛宕スキー場』の素地が形成されていたといえる。彼等の上映会場には三条の十字屋楽器店や大毎会館が利用され、1929年には、例会の参加者は50名以上、上映会の各回参加者は500人から600人という活況[24]を呈していた。日活京都から1931年に村田実監督作品で脚本家としてデビューする依田義賢も、20年代から9.5mmクラブの京都ダブル・オー・シネマ社[25]で脚本家や役者として活動しており、ベビーシネマの例会や上映会に参加していた[26]という。後述するプロキノ京都支部の活動もあわせると、この時期の京都は大小あわせて7箇所あった映画撮影所での映画製作だけでなく、小型映画の製作と上映活動が盛んな、プロ、アマ混在しての映画都市であったといえる。メンバーからは、ロンドン国際アマチュア映画人協会の1935年度コンテスト入選優秀作品として世界巡映16ミリ作品の一本に選ばれた『姉』の武内吉之助[27]を輩出した。エトナ映画社が設立されたのは、まさにこの時期である。

9.5mm、16mmのいずれも全国クラブの機関誌には、各地のクラブ活動を伝える頁があるが、なかでも京都ベビー・シネマ協会が属していた全国組織、東京ベビーシネマ倶楽部（後に日本パテーシネマ協会と改称）の機関誌『ベビーシネマ』誌は、朝鮮、満洲、台湾をはじめ、遠隔地の愛好者やクラブ活動の紹介記事を、東京や京阪神の都市圏よりも遥かに多く掲載している点で興味深い。東京ベビーシネマ倶楽部は、前述した教育映画のフィルムライブラリーと並行して、各地で開催する上映会へ、倶楽部の幹部が競技会入選作品を持参し貸与する制

度を打ち出しており、その目的を「当倶楽部と其の会合との親睦融和及小型活動写真界の党勢拡張を図りパテーベビーの威力を示したい」[28]と記している。16mmへの対抗策であることは明らかであるが、それに応えるかのように、例えば当時の朝鮮咸興のメンバーは、「今後は出来る丈け仲間を集め一の會を作り北鮮の一角からもパテーベビーの威力を示したいと思って居ります」[29]、「三人のパテー党が増したことは確かです。(筆者中略) 大切なフィルムをほんとうに有り難う御座いました」と報告しており、東京の本部から借りた入賞フィルムや、技術情報や自身の記事が掲載された雑誌を通して、本部との連帯意識をもち、地域でのコミュニティ作りを熱心にすすめている様子が伺える。投書欄には、非電化地域からの質問も確認でき、9.5mmが、16mmの六分の一の低価格や、計量カップで現像が可能な手軽さ、太陽光で反転現像も可能な特質を活かして、草の根的に拡がっていたことがわかる。彼らの活動に対して幹部は、「私共が地理的に見て考も及ばない交通不便の僻地に或は離れ小島とか、国境とか言う処にも同志の方々が立派な倶楽部を組織されていることを見て、実に小型活動写真の真の意義を其処に見出したるやの感があって誠に喜ばしい」[30]と、中央から日本の周縁までネットワークが隅々に拡がった喜びを綴っている。東京からの鉄道を介して物理的に運搬される9.5mmや機関誌が、地域と東京を結びつけ、全日本を構成する意識を形成する装置として機能していたと思われる。

(2) ジャンル：プロキノから教化、巡回へ

小型映画には、ホーム・ムービー、個人映画、実験映画、アニメーション、文化映画、教育映画、ドキュメンタリーなどさまざまなジャンルがあるが、戦間期日本の小型映画には、これらにおさまらない、日本プロレタリア映画同盟(以下、プロキノ)の作品群がある。

1929年に発足したプロキノは、日本で初めて映画を自らの武器として提唱・活動した集団である。小型映画で作品を作り、巡回映写を通してアジテーション、プロパガンダを行ったが、1934年の弾圧後、彼等のリーダーの多くが、国家体制側のプロパガンダである文化映画、教育映画等の分野で活動を展開した。例えば、武器としての映画を提唱して実践した、代表的監督の佐々元十は、プロキノ時代に植民地を題材にした映画を「資本主義国家の殖民地政策の宣伝用

としての教育映画」[31]と批判的に分析したが、1930年代半ばから国家方針の濃厚な『文化映画』誌の編集者および発行者として、その分析を実践し、プロキノ時代に培った知識とノウハウを発揮していくのである。

　京都には、プロキノ発足時からの支部があり、彼らは、右翼の暴漢に暗殺された山本宣治の葬儀の光景を16ミリで記録した『山宣労農葬』で、プロキノの幕開けを果たした。この作品は、十日間におよぶ撮影期間中、葬儀前夜に集まった人々を前に未編集で上映され、小型映画の機動性と順応性、映像の威力を、鮮明に示したものである。京都で開催されたプロキノの第三回上映会は、東京外での初上映であり、ベビー党の上映会場として小型映画観客には馴染みのある大毎会館で開催された。プロキノの『墨田川』『こども』『メーデー』『第十一回大阪メーデー』と童映社の『煙突屋ペロー』の計5作品が上映され、昼夜二回の上映は満席となり、計1000人ほどが鑑賞したという。その観客の「過半数は学生、小市民」[32]であり、労働者は約三割、残りはストライキ中の京都製紙、山谷伸銅所、友禅組合の争議団員、在日朝鮮人の人々であったという。京都ベビー・シネマ協会の代表的な小型映画作家、田中喜次の作品『煙突屋ペロー』が上映される以上、「学生、小市民」の中には、従来の小型映画上映会に通っていた観客たちが含まれていたであろうと思われる。

　戦後も独立映画で活躍する松崎啓次や北川鉄夫は、初期の代表的な京都支部メンバーであったと同時に、プロキノの中核的メンバーであった。プロキノ時代に、「全国の戦闘的アマチュア・シネアストは映画通信員に参加しろ！」[33]と呼びかけ、東京支部へ移って旺盛な制作活動を実践していた北川は、プロキノ崩壊の後、佐々と同様に体制側へ回り、小型映画の巡回映写を通した教化活動を推進していく。例えば「小型映画の闘態」[34]では、小型映画人に対し、旧作の提供とそれらを戦時下の国民精神にあわせたテーマで再編集し、関西を地盤にして翼賛会、産報、産組と関係しながら巡回映写をする運動を再び呼びかけた。その利点を、「生きた国民生活の中で共に苦しみ、共に喜んで行って何より自己の国民としての精神を鍛えてゆく」ことにあると、小型映画人自身の教化として述べている。また、「満洲から」[35]と題したエッセイでは、識字率が低く広い満洲での巡回映写活動による啓発娯楽の重要性と小型映画の活用を概説しながら、満洲では映画が「そもそもの機能を果たす最大の場を提供されている」[36]と

情熱を持って語り、満洲の農民に「明日の努力と希望を与える映画の映写が行われたならばこれこそ時局下最適最高の文化工作」[37]であると、「映画人としてのやり甲斐」[38]を語った。佐々、北川のいずれも、プロキノ時代に培ったノウハウを、資本家と労農者という二項対立から、帝国日本と殖民地におきかえて、運動を継続しているかのようである。

(3) アマチュア映画と国家目的

　プロキノ・メンバーの変節と並行して、1933年の映画国策建議案の可決から1937年のフィルムと原材料の輸入禁止へといたる間に、フィルムの使用や、映画製作の方向性と目的に対して国の統制が強くなり、小型映画といえども個人作家が自由に映画を作ることが難しくなっていた。コンテストにおいても、プロパガンダに適したテーマが掲げられるようになり、映画法の制定後は、小型映画製作者も合法的に作品を公開映写しようとする場合は、映画人としての技能審査試験をパスしなければならなくなったのである。

　小型映画界から唯一の映画人技能試験の審査員を務めたのが、小型映画作家の中で当時もっとも尊敬されていた塚本閤治である。20年代から小型映画のコンテストの一等賞をほぼ独占した塚本は、山岳映画の大家であり、登山撮影に適した9.5mmを愛用し、撮影や現像などの技術に秀で、アイリスやフェード、クランクといった機器の開発まで行った。30年代半ばには審査員を務め、国の方針にそって審査する指導的な立場となっていた。

　この時期に塚本は、小型映画人が審査員を納得させるだけの製作意図を説明できない現状を憂い、「山岳映画の製作と時局」[39]と題したエッセイで、登山行為と国家目的との合致点と、戦時下に山岳映画を作る目的と必然性を明確に記している。その合致点とは、「体育運動の中で最も精神的であると同時に最も国防に直接関係」[40]し、「銃後に於いて行い得る最も前線的な行動」[41]であり、山岳が「祖国の自然美を最も強度に最も純粋に包蔵」[42]し「守るべき国土の尊貴」[43]を感じさせるものであるという。結論として、非常時に山岳映画を作る目的と必然性は、「愛国の精神を昂揚する」[44]ことにあると記した。しかしながら、冒頭には「山岳は世の喧騒を外に沈思の場所」[45]であるという意味深長な前置きがあり、また、「自分の余技としての小型映画が幾分でも国家目的に一致すると言

う確信は如何に楽しく、又趣味を意義あらしめるものであるか」⁽⁴⁶⁾と、趣味としての小型映画を明言している。これは従来彼が開発した映画技術を誌上で開陳していたと同様の、資格審査をパスするテクニックを披露したものとも読むことができる。

　このエッセイには、プロパガンダ映画の方針指導と趣味としての小型映画製作の方法、サブ・スタンダードとしての矜持と中央からの評価への意識、というアンビバレントな二種類のメッセージを読むことが可能であり、日本の小型映画文化の特徴を端的に示していると思われる。

　戦間期の日本における小型映画の文化史的特徴には、規格ごと、ジャンルごとにさまざまなムーブメントが、個人と地域の活動を通して形成され、京都はその初期の基盤形成を担っていたといえる。それらが個々の特徴を活かしながら、体制の下で次第に一つのプロパガンダ・メディアとしての小型映画に統合されていくプロセスが浮かびあがる。そこに見えるのは、35mmのスタンダードに対するサブ・スタンダードという二項対立構図が、16mmと9.5mm、中央と辺境、という別の二項対立意識へと変転しながら、ナショナル・アイデンティティを醸成する装置として小型映画が浸透していくプロセスであり、そのダイナミズムが、戦間期日本における小型映画文化の特異性と思われるのである。

■注
（1）小型映画とは、フィルム幅を示す用語である。通常、劇場用映画が35mm幅のフィルムで撮影・上映される為、35mmがスタンダード規格とされ、それ以外はすべてサブ・スタンダードの規格となる。小型映画は、35mm幅以下のフィルムを示し、28mm、17.5mm、16mm、9.5mm、8mmなどがある。大型映画は、70mmなど、35mm以上の幅のフィルムを指す。
（2）エトナ映画社および田中英一氏については、『アート・リサーチ』5号の拙文「洛西地域映画史聴き取り調査報告4　エトナ映画の軌跡」（http://www.arc.ritsumei.ac.jp/art_coe/work/k_05.html）を参照されたい。
（3）Cine-Kodak Specialは、1933年5月発売当初より、コマ撮りを含めた多機能なプロ使用カメラとして宣伝された。直売の基本価格は375ドル（(1933) "Introducing Cine-Kodak Special", *The Movie makers*, May, 198-199.）。

(4) 「ホーム・ムービーの日」については、本部（http://www.homemovieday.com/）と日本（http://www.homemovieday.jp/index/hmd.html）のサイトを参照されたい。

(5) Patricia R.Zimmermann. (1995) *Reel Families:A Social history of Amateur Film.* Bloomington and Indianapolis: Indiana University Press. Alan Kattelle. (2000) *Home Movies: A History of the American Industry, 1897-1979.* New Hampshire: Transition Publishing. Karen L. Ishizuka and Patrisia R. Zimmermann, eds. (2008) *Mining the Home movie: Excavations in Histories and Memories.* Berkeley: University of California Press. Ian Craven, eds. (2009) *Movies on Home Ground: Explorations in Amateur Cinema.* Cambridge Scholars Publishing. を参照。

(6) 荻野茂二（1899-1991）は、1920年代後半からパテ・ベビーで創作を開始し、国内外のコンクール受賞作品を数多く生み出したアマチュア映画作家のパイオニア。

(7) 那田尚史（1995）「小型映画の技術と美的規範について（1929-1932）」『映像学』55、30-43。牧野守（1989）「戦前の日本小型映画史における主要な潮流とその特質」『映像学会会報』70。長田豊臣（2001）『科学研究費補助金（基盤研究Ｃ）研究成果報告書「芸能・演劇分野の無形文化財保存の方法に関する基礎的研究」無形文化財と記録・保存（都おどりの一六ミリ映画を題材として—）』。特定非営利活動法人映画保存協会小型映画部編（2010）「9.5ミリフィルムの調査研究　片岡コレクション調査報告」、特定非営利活動法人映画保存協会小型映画部。映画保存協会小型映画部編（2010）「戦前小型映画資料集」映画保存協会などがある。

(8) パテ・ベビーの日本での発売年には諸説あるが、(1930)「座談会記録　小型映画の沿革を語る」(『小型映画』2-1、34)の大伴喜祐「最初に輸入ったのは大正十一年です。それが震災でちょっと途切れて居りますから、先づ大正十三年から盛んになった」と倉田繁太郎の「十字屋の専務鈴木幾三郎氏が玩具みたいな機械だと一寸いじってみて之は面白いと売出したのも大正十一年です」および、三村喜作（1939）「本邦　小型映画発達漫録　その一」(『東京小型映画協会会報』27、1）を参照した。

(9) (1930)「時報　倶楽部名改称」『ベビーシネマ』3-9、12-13。

(10) "You will find Amateur Movie Makers and Progressive Dealer at each of the following addresses. Visit them!" *The Movie Makers* (Feb. 1928：136) には、日本拠点として大澤商会のみが記されている。

(11) 布施眞（1928）「パテーベビー教育用フィルムライブラリーに就いて」『アマチュアキネマ』1-3、1-2。

(12) 伴野文三郎（1928）「佛國に於ける映画教育」『ベビーシネマ』12、2。伴野文三郎（1928）「佛國の映画教育」『ベビーシネマ』14、10。

(13) 番町小学校・三星正昭「映画教授」(1928)『ベビーシネマ』12、3-4。

(14) 第六回パテーベビー撮影大競技会で募集された課題は、「小学校教科書の科目に

⑭ 依るもの又は之を題材として自己の考えをとり入れたるもの或は小学校の教授に用いられるもの」((1929)「会告」『ベビーシネマ』2-10、1）であり、一等は塚本閤治の『大自然の力』、二等は荻野茂二の『電車が軌道を走る迄』と水町程之の『伝書鳩』。

⑮ 『ベビーシネマ』には訓導からの投書も多かった。また、全国の女学校、中学校の映画設備の統計結果に、カメラは16㎜、9.5㎜の両サイズがあったが、映写機の大半は16㎜、という報告（西村正美（1938）「技術的問題の重要性」『文化映画』1-6、32-33）がある。

⑯ （1938）「全国各地　映画教育研究経営機関」『文化映画』1-6、52-53。

⑰ （1935）「クラブ・ニュース　京都市教育映画研究会」『アマチュア映画（映画と技術）』1-2、115。

⑱ 講習会は、立誠校で京都市内の1936年度師範卒業生教員と新入市教員の約200名を対象に行われた（(1936)「クラブニュース　京都市映画教育講習会」『アマチュア映画（映画と技術）』4-6、417）。

⑲ 大伴喜祐が、「顧みれば、パテーベビーが入って、反転現像の最初の発達は京都でありました、特にツバメヤさんの現像は東西の評判となって居りました、東京でも其後私共が主になって苦心研究しまして、稍完成に近いものとなり、今日では範を吾々に採って下さる方が多くなって参りました」（大伴喜祐（1928）「大競技会を通じて見たる露光及現像に就て」『ベビー・シネマ』1-2、6-7）と述べている。

⑳ 和光亮（1928）「多人数に見せる映写装置」『ベビーシネマ』2-2、13-14。

㉑ Arthur L. Gale. (1929) "Amateur Clubs: News of Group Filming," *The Movie Makers*, Oct.: 652.

㉒ 坂本為之（1939）「関西アマチュアー映画界の今昔と私」『文化映画』2-7、44-45。

㉓ （1928）「案内　全国聯合パテーベビー撮影競技大会」『ベビー・シネマ』1-2、13。

㉔ 上田寛（1929）「通信」『ベビーシネマ』2-11、2。

㉕ （1929）『D.O映画　パテー・ベビー』参照。

㉖ 坂本為之「関西アマチュアー映画界の今昔と私」前掲記事。

㉗ （1938）「クラブ・ニュース　I.A.C.世界巡映フィルムの公開」『アマチュア映画（映画と技術）』7-2、139。

㉘ （1929）「時報　巡回映写」『ベビーシネマ』2-6、2。

㉙ 鷺坂東（1929）「通信　京城便り」『ベビーシネマ』2-6、32。

㉚ 吉川速男（1930）「梅花雑信」『ベビーシネマ』3-3、14-15。

㉛ 佐々元十（1930）「殖民地映画に就て」『プロレタリア映画』2-9、16-27。

㉜ （1930）「公開闘争の記録　京都では如何に闘われて来たか」『プロレタリア映画』2-7、58。

㉝ 北川鉄夫（1930）「プロキノ映画通信員について―その草案―」『プロレタリア映

画』2-7、19-21。
(34)　北川鉄夫（1942）「小型映画の闘憊」『小型映画』2-3、3。
(35)　北川鉄夫（1943）「満洲から」『小型映画』3-3、2-3。
(36)　同上。
(37)　同上。
(38)　同上。
(39)　塚本閤治（1942）「山岳映画の製作と時局」『小型映画』2-9、5-6。
(40)　同上。
(41)　同上。
(42)　同上。
(43)　同上。
(44)　同上。
(45)　同上。
(46)　同上。

　［付記］　本稿は"A Symposium—The Makino Collection of Columbia：the Present and Future of an Archive"（2011年11月、於コロンビア大）における口頭発表を改稿したものである。

Chap. 9 *Kohitsu* and *Kiwame*-Their Historical Meanings

■Masao Kawashima

Introduction

Kohitsu, literally meaning "old brush," are masterpieces of calligraphy written during the Heian to Kamakura periods (late eighth to early fourteenth century), and have been revered in Japan. By following the activities of early modern aristocrats and Kohitsu Ryōsa, a famed calligraphy appraiser, this article aspires to discuss the historical background of how *kohitsu* came to be revered, to consider the meaning of appraising calligraphies, and to analyze the circumstances necessitating such appraisals.

Research on *kohitsu*, *kohitsu-gire* (individual works of *kohitsu*), and *kiwame* (appraisals of a *kohitsu*), has made especially remarkable progress recently, and related exhibitions have been made often[1]. In addition, libraries such as the library at Tsurumi University are keen on collecting *kohitsu-gire*.

With reference to *kohitsu-gire*, the research environment has been gradually enriched by databases, such as the National Institute of Japanese Literature's "Fragmentary Manuscripts Database of Japan[2], " which stores location information about *kohitsu-gire*, the "Waseda University Database of *Kohitsu-gire*[3], " and Nagoya University Gotō Library's "About *Kohitsu-gire* Database," being made open to the public. Moreover, it has become more or less natural for institutions to make rare materials they own (whether or not they are called *kohitsu* or *kohitsu-gire*) open to the public online. We can safely say that the open environment that the Digital Humanities Center for Japanese Arts and Cultures at GCOE program at Ritsumeikan University has advocated for in Japan is rapidly becoming a reality in the field of *kohitsu* studies.

However, the purpose of this article is not to analyze any particular *kohitsu-gire* pieces or *kiwame* appraisals, but rather to approach the matters of general applicability that I introduced at the beginning.

I have written an article entitled "*Kohitsu* juyō no shakai-teki haikei (The Social Background of the Demand for *Kohitsu*[4])" to discuss such issues from the standpoint of a historian in an attempt to analyze the historical circumstances under which *kohitsu* were in high demand. My conclusion was that the Azuchi-Momoyama Period (late sixteenth century) was the time when the demand in *kohitsu* became the most widespread, and people who specialized in appraising *kohitsu* first appeared around that time. It has thus become clear that the Azuchi-Momoyama period and the decades following, in other words, the early early-modern period, is the pivotal point in terms of the discussion of such matters. This is why this article focuses on the early early-modern period in order to discuss *kohitsu* and appraisals of *kohitsu*.

The Historical Background of the Appreciation of *Kohitsu*

Scholars like Komatsu Shigemi have already noted[5] that artistic appreciation of skillfully-made ancient calligraphy had already begun in the late Heian period (eleventh to twelfth century), and that such calligraphies were cut into pieces and appreciated as *kohitsu-gire* pieces beginning in the late Muromachi period (sixteenth century). According to Komatsu, *kohitsu* as a word meaning "ancient calligraphy" first appeared in writings in the fourteenth century.

Why did this interest arise during this period of time? Previous scholarship has pointed out that the rise of *wabi-chanoyu*, a kind of tea ceremony that values simplicity and quietness, has strong relationship with the rise of appreciation of old masterpieces of calligraphy. Takeno Jōō, a tea master, started using Japanese poetry (*waka*) and poetic treatises for ornamental scrolls at tea ceremonies, instead of the customary calligraphy by Zen priests (*bokuseki*) and Chinese paintings, which contributed to the rise of interest in *kohitsu*. I agree that such tendencies were the main cause of the appreciation of old calligraphies, but I find it equally important that, as linked verse called *renga* became popular among people of many social classes, including samurai, in the Nanbokuchō and Muromachi periods (fourteenth to fifteenth century), classical Japanese literature such as *The Tale of Genji* and *Kokin wakashū* became targets of reverence.

Knowledge of classical Japanese literature was indispensable to composing linked verse. Consequently, people of the time had stronger motivation to obtain knowledge of classical Japanese literature, both in town and in the countryside. An episode in *Nagusame-gusa* written around Ōei 25 (1415) by Shōtetsu, a priest poet, then staying in Owari province, is emblematic of such tendencies. In this scene, Lord Oda asked Shōtetsu to teach him *The Tale of Genji* because his words lacked flowery color:

I heard that you know the tale of the shining Genji well. For a long time, I was engaged in the way of *renga* linked verse. But sometimes society interrupted me, sometimes I could not engage in my hobby; the flower of my words became less colorful and the spring of my heart dried up, so I recently stopped doing this. Nevertheless, I want to listen to the story, because it is about Genji. If you have time, please tell me the story, if only a part of it.

To sum up in a quite simple way, reverence for classical Japanese literature led to reverence of the poets, which then developed into reverence for the masterpiece calligraphy that those poets wrote. Ultimately, following this trend, people started revering and collecting ancient masterpiece calligraphies.

One more thing to point out is the re-recognition of masterpieces in *jubokudō*, the way of calligraphy.

The so-called "Three Brushes" (*sanpitsu*), the three masters of calligraphy, the Emperor Saga, Kūkai, and Tachibana no Hayanari, are, needless to say, later inventions. Their prototype can be seen in the second volume of *Kōdanshō*, stating that the tablet on the gate of the Imperial Palace was written by four calligraphers, the aforementioned three and Ono no Yoshiki. However, the name "*sanpitsu*" first appears in *Wakan meisū* in the late seventeenth century. The reason for *sanpitsu* to appear in the seventeenth century is probably closely connected with the re-recognition of the court culture of the time. However, rather than delving into this issue, I would like to discuss briefly the matter of re-recognition of masterpiece calligraphy in *jubokudō*.

It is not the main purpose of this paper to discuss the entire history of Japanese calligraphy, but needless to say, the so-called "Three Master Writings" (*sanseki*) have an established status together with *sanpitsu*. These *sanseki* were also named in a later period. Although treatises on calligraphy such as *Yakaku teikin shō* and *Saiyō shō* were written at the end of the Heian period[6], and great writers like Fujiwara no Sadaie appeared, *jubokudō* itself stopped developing for a while thereafter.

Under such circumstances, *Juboku shō* was written by Prince Sonen (1298-1356), the son of the Emperor Fushimi. This is the first writing that systematically discussed Japanese *jubokudō* (the history of the way of calligraphy). The purpose of the writing was to criticize the Chinese, Song-style calligraphy, and proclaim the authenticity of the Japanese, Sesonji-style calligraphy that the prince himself had learned. The re-recognition of the masterpieces of Japanese-style calligraphy was thus promoted in this period. Emperor Fushimi's writings are known as one of the masterpieces of calligraphy among works by emperors: the twelfth volume of *Masukagami* says that "the Emperor [Fushimi]'s handwriting was quite beautiful, and contemporary people said that his writings were even better than Dainagon Yukinari of the past."

Appraisals of Kohitsu

It is conceivable that judgments were made about in whose handwriting the masterpiece calligraphies were written from a relatively early period, but we do not have enough historical materials to prove this proposition.

In the beginning of the Edo period, *kiwame-fuda*, written appraisals on a small rectangular pieces of *tanzaku* paper, were provided by expert *kohitsu* appraisers (*kohitsu-ka*). Although the use of *kiwame-fuda* gave *kohitsu-ka* certain authority, similar appraisals were performed from before *kohitsu-ka* appeared.

One example is a piece of *kaishi* paper with handwritten *waka* poems by Emperor Go-Kashiwabara in the Fujii Eikan Bunko Collection at the Art Research Center at Ritsumeikan University. Yamashina Tokitsugu's appraisal, stating "the three poems on this *kaishi* paper were handwritten by the Emperor Go-Kashiwabara. Tenbun 23, First Month. Tokushin Kōmon Togosetsu (name of the rank) Tokitsugu (red seal) (black seal)" is written on other side of the paper[7] (See Figure 1; p. 4). The entry on the twenty-fifth of the same month in Tokutsugu's *Tokitsugu-kyō ki* also states that, "This is an order to Hayase Minbu-jō. I was asked to judge the three poems on the *kaishi* paper written by the previous emperor (Emperor Go-Kashiwabara) and *Ōgimachi nendaiki*." In other words, appraisals were performed in such a manner, even though *kiwame-fuda* in the style of the rectangular piece of *tanzaku* paper issued by the expert *kohitsuka* appraisers had not been invented yet. It is simply that such action was not called "*kiwame*" at that time[8].

The entry for the twenty-fifth of the Fifth Month of Daiei 8 (1528) in *Sanetaka-kō ki* tells of an incident wherein a person named Noto Miyake acquired a calligraphy of the aforementioned Prince Sonen (the chief priest of Syōrenin temple and Tendai-zasu), who is said to have created the Syōrenin style of calligraphy, and asked Sanetaka to write a letter of appraisal in order to prove that it was actually Prince Sonen's. He then came to pick up the appraisal letter on the seventh of the Sixth Month, but Sanetaka said that he simply "added lines (*oku-gaki*) to the writing." In other words, he did not write the appraisal on a separate sheet of paper, but he wrote appraisal on the same sheet that had the prince's handwriting. This is similar to Tokitsugu's writing an appraisal on the other side of the *kaishi* paper that had Go-Kashiwabara's handwritten poetry.

According to *Sanetaka-kō ki*, such appraisals were expressed merely as "written down" and "added *oku-gaki*," and the term "*kiwame*" as in "judging if the handwriting is actually by master calligraphers" was not used. With respect to the word "*oku-gaki*," it is reported that Emperor Fushimi wrote, "This was handwritten by the Holy Master of Engi (Emperor Daigo)" in the extra space at the end of a *Hakushiku-kan* attributed to Emperor Daigo as an *oku-gaki*[9].

Details regarding Noto Miyake are largely unknown. However, according to *Sanetaka-kō ki*, the person who acted as a broker for Noto Miyake and Sanetaka was "the person from Shimo-gyō," who was probably a townsman. From this fact, it can be deduced that interest in *kohitsu* had spread even to the lower classes.

Why did a person of the Yamashina family, who did not specialize in *waka* poetry, perform appraisals of calligraphies? It is true that Tokitsugu was student of *waka* under the Sanjō-nishi family along with Sanetaka's son, and taught Oda Nobuhide and his retainers aristocratic arts such as *waka* poetry and *kemari* football in Tenbun 2 (1533). However, he was not renowned as a scholar like Sanetaka, who established his name as a scholar of *The Tale of Genji* and *Kokin wakashū*. That said, Tokitsugu owned a copy of *The Tale of Genji* and showed it to the emperor in the Sixth month of Kyōroku 2 (1529), and was ordered to hand copy *The Tale of Genji* by Emperor Go-Nara on the fourth of the Seventh Month in Kyōroku 2 (1529) and twenty-second of the Second Month in Tenbun 22 (1553). In addition, the emperor ordered Tokitsugu to hand copy the *Lotus Sutra* (*shihai*, written on the original side of double-sided paper) in the Seventh Month of Tenbun 14 (1545)[10].

In short, Tokitsugu's beautiful handwriting was highly valued by the emperor (see figure 1 for his writing style), and this made him a natural appraiser of master calligraphies. Unfortunately, it is unknown who ordered Tokitsugu to appraise Emperor Go-Kashiwabara's handwritten poetry on the *kaishi* paper or towards what ends.

Tokitsune-kyō ki (the diary of Tokitsune) records that Tokitsugu's son, Tokitsune also performed appraisals of *kohitsu* calligraphy[11]. This shows that appraisers were not necessarily from families of scholars of *waka*, or families of master calligraphers, but rather, people who were recognized as experts of judging good calligraphy.

Fujitani Tamekata and Kohitsu Ryōsa

Records in *Tokitsune-kyō ki* show that members of the Reizei family often appraised calligraphies of Fujiwara no Toshinari and Sadaie in the early Edo period. For the Reizei family, this means that they were asked to appraise the calligraphies of their ancestors, and, even though there was some sort of compensation, they did not do it for a living. In contrast, Fujitani Tamekata I (1583-1653), who diverged from the Reizei family, engaged in buying and selling *kohitsu* calligraphy, and became wealthy doing so. The Fujitani family was a family of *waka* scholars, since it diverged from Reizei family. I discussed their activities in detail elsewhere[12], but considering Tamekata's heavy engagement in the *kohitsu* market, he must have been superior in judging the value of *kohitsu* calligraphies, and his ability must have been highly recognized by others.

There are only a few historical records that show Tamekata's ability as an appraiser. One of the examples can be found in no. 638[13].

··· I had already heard about the author of the poetry treatise that the master priest was going to get, and was told that I should talk to him about the author. However, the master priest said that he could not be sure whose handwriting it was without Mr. Fujitani's letter. I would like to ask you to make sure that Mr. Fujitani's letter will reach the master priest.

This letter was written on the twenty-first of the Third Month, year unknown, from

Katō Masataka (a.k.a. Fūan) (1580-1648) to a close attendant of the master priest of Daigakuji temple. This letter, stating that the handwriting cannot be identified without Fujitani Tamekata's letter, shows that Tamekata's ability was highly regarded even outside of aristocratic society. Katō Masataka was originally a high-ranking retainer of the Katō clan in Higo, and served in important positions like the commissioner (*jōdai*) of Uchimaki. After the Katō clan was dissolved, Masakata started practicing tea ceremonies and *renga* poetry in Kyoto and Osaka. This letter was probably written after he left Higo.

Kakumei-ki, the diary of the main priest of Rokuonji temple, Hōrin Shōshō, has some entries showing that Hōrin Shōshō served as a broker for Kohitsu Ryōsa and someone else for the appraisal of a *kohitsu* of poems from *Kokin wakashū*: "Itō Kuzaemon asked me to have *Kokin wakashū* and the calligraphy of Etsukei Kajō of Mt. Ryūhō appraised, so I sent Kanbe Sōri to show these writings to Kohitsu Ryōsa." (Shōhō 3, the twenty-fifth of the Tenth Month) and "Tagenta asked me, so I sent a *kohitsu* piece of *Kokin wakashū* to Ryōsa." (Shōhō 4, fourth of the Third Month) Although Hōrin referred people in need of appraisal to Ryōsa, it does not seem like Hōrin himself was completely trusting of Kohitsu Ryōsa's appraisal ability. The following entry written on the sixteenth of the Third Month in Manji 4 (1661) shows how Hōrin regarded Ryōsa:

> In the evening, Gukei Kōseidō came. It seems like he got an apprentice; he brought a boy with him. The apprentice boy brought two fans in a box, a portrait of the superior emperor of Rokuonin (Ashikaga Yoshimitsu). The portrait is an old painting, and there are three *waka* poems written above the portrait. According to the Ryōsa *fuda*, it is the calligraphy of Asukai Eiga. But [in my opinion] it is not by Eiga.

There were three *waka* poems written above the portrait of Ashikaga Yoshimitsu, and while Kohitsu Ryōsa judged that they were written by Asukai Eiga (Masachika), who was deeply trusted by Ashikaga Yoshimasa (Yoshimitsu's grandson[14]), Hōrin disagreed, although he did not specify in the diary who he thought the writer was. It is not clear if this is a simple difference of their opinions or evidence that Hōrin does not fully trust Ryōsa in general, but this incident at least clearly shows that Hōrin does not blindly follow Kohitsu Ryōsa's judgment.

Another notable thing about this quote is the expression "Ryōsa *fuda*." Needless to say, this *fuda* is a small rectangular *kiwame-fuda* that *kohitsu* appraisers used, but Hōrin simply refers to it as *fuda* in his diary.

Tamekata also did not seem to have a good impression of Ryōsa. In a letter from Tamekata to the close attendant of the master priest of Daigakuji temple, he says: "I will give you the five poetry treatises that I told you about privately before. They are said to have been handwritten by Abutsu. It might be a good idea to show them to Ryōsa, but his reputation is not very good." (no. 236) In another letter, Tamekata says, "I present twenty-five writings including *Yamato monogatari* and poetry treatises... It is understandable that you want to show them to Ryōsa, but, you should not tell him privately that they are authentic" (no. 266) Such letters show that Tamekata did not necessarily evaluate Ryōsa highly.

Both Fujitani Tamekata and Hōrin Shōshō are from the Kajūji family, and Ryōsa must have had a delicate relationship with such aristocratic families. However, Ryōsa was also active in societal circles outside the aristocratic world. *Date-ke monjo* has a letter of appraisal provided by Ryōsa who appraised Minamoto no Yorimasa's calligraphy on *shikishi* paper[15], and Ryōsa's name often appears in records about a tea master, Sōtan. There are 246 writings including letters by Sōtan in *Shinpen Genpaku Sōtan monjo* that were published in 2007 by Ura-senke Fushinan bunko, and Ryōsa appears in twenty-two of them.

I will not introduce all of these letters, but most of them mention Ryōsa's recent activities, probably because Ryōsa was close to Sōtan. For example, Sōtan's promissory note for 2 *kan* 630 *me* worth of silver estimated to be written in Kanei 6 (1629) says that "additionally Ryōsa provided a separate guarantor's letter" (*Shinpen Genpaku Sōtan monjo* no. 239), showing Ryōsa's closeness to Sōtan to stand as guarantor for his debt.

The letter from Sōtan to Sen Sōsa and Genshitsu dated on the eighteenth of the Eleventh Month in Keian 3 (1650) (*Shinpen Genpaku Sōtan monjo* no. 182) relates a shocking incident wherein "Ryōsa's son, Kanbei, was slain." Following this, Sōtan says that, "I thought it happened because he was crooked. Both of them knew Kanbei was crooked, and thus suffered. It cannot be helped; like father, like son. It was destiny that Kanbei could not outlive his father." Sōtan's impression of Kanbei was not necessarily good, since he said Kanbei was rather "crooked in character." In spite of this, Kanbei was one of Sōtan's thirty-four apprentices[16].

Ryōsa was thus closely associated with such tea masters. Also in *Sōtan monjo*, there are records of Ryōsa's association with Konoe Nobuhiro, such as "on the twenty-seventh of this month, the great master of Konoe (Konoe Nobuhiro) came, and Ryōsa was told to accompany him." (*Shinpen Genpaku Sōtan monjo* no. 68) and "Ryōsa, Chōsuke, Konoe, and Konoe's son are very close" (*Shinpen Genpaku Sōtan monjo* no. 95). Such records appears to be trivial at the first glance, but they are actually important, since they provide actual historical proof of the legendary belief that Ryōsa "acquired skill as a *kohitsu* appraiser from Lord Konoe Kanpaku Sakihisa, and became a professional *kohitsu* appraiser," a story that is recorded in *Hosei Kohitsu Ryōhan sensei ni kyoka o e, Jōboku ni oyobu wakan shoga kohitsu kanteika inpu* (*Collection of Facsimiles of the Japanese and Chinese Paintings and Calligraphic Works of the Kohitsu Appraisers, published under the permission of Master Kohitsu Ryōhan, Revised*) that was reprinted in Keiō 3 (1867).

About Uratsuji

The buying and selling of *kohitsu* calligraphies was not necessarily unique to Fujitani Tamekata in the aristocratic society. The aforementioned *Daigakuji monjo* records another aristocratic *kohitsu* trader, Uratsuji Suetomi (1604-44). Suetomi is not very well-known, or rather, he is nearly unknown, in Japanese history, so he is not mentioned in many studies as far as I know. Suetomi was the son of Ōgimachi Sueyasu, and became an ancestor of the Uratsuji family which belonged to the Urinke clan (an aristocratic clan). He became *sangi* belatedly in Kanei 19 (1642), but died two years later at age forty, so he did not play an important role in politics. However, in terms of art trading, he brokered sales of a lot of *kohitsu* and other tea paraphernalia to Daigakuji Temple, just like Tamekata did.

The content of the fifty-three letters by Suetomi in *Daigakuji monjo* indicate that he was close to Tamekata. Not only did he often mention Tamekata in his letters but he also wrote a letter that was co-signed by Tamekata, which was pretty rare at that time (no. 417. Figure 2; p. 9).

The letters also reveal that Suetomi brokered the trade of artworks such as *The Tale of Genji* and poems on *tanzaku*, and was actively involved with the negotiation of prices. However, he does not seem to have performed appraisals of handwriting like Tamekata did. [Figure 2. A Letter Co-signed by Fujitani Tamekata and Uratsuji

Suetomi. The lower right corner has the signatures "Tamekata, Suetomi."] It is impossible to find evidence of Suetomi's appraisals in his letters or in other people's historical records.

I would like to introduce one of Suetomi's letters that reveals his activities. It is also a letter addressed to the close attendant of the master priest of Daigakuji temple, and dated on the fourteenth of the Second Month, year unknown (no. 384): "As I just said, although Mr. Fujitani has not taken a look at the art yet, please let Sōchū get it, and summon Mr. Fujitani later to discuss the matter and decide what to do." Suetomi brokers a trade of a *tanzaku* poem in this letter.

This letter names three people, Suetomi, Tamekane, and Sōchū, in relation to the trading of the *tanzaku* poem. The former two are already explained, but who is the last one, Sōchū? He also appears in Tamekane's letters quite often, and Tamekane even says that, "Sōchū is annoying, because he has a venomous tongue" (no. 277).

It is impossible to positively identify Sōchū, but one possibility is Noji Sōchū. Noji Sōchū was a master of tea ceremonies in the early Edo period, and a retainer of Kanamori Sōwa, who is known as the founder of the Sōwa style tea ceremony. In a document that he published himself, he describes his social standing as "a retainer of Kanamori Sōwa," and reveals that he brokered the trading of Sōwa's tea paraphernalia[18]. From this, we can deduce that he may be the same person as "Noji Shichirōemon" who appears in *Zuiryū saien shi no sho*[19] : "Sōtan sold [something to] Noji Shichirōemon, a retainer of Kanamori Sōwa."

Considering that Noji Sōchū had relationship with the Zen temples of the Five Mountains of Kyoto (*Kyoto gozan*), and Sōwa had close relationships with aristocratic families like the Konoe family, it is probable that the sharp-tongued Sōchū who appears in *Daigakuji monjo* is this Noji Sōchū, the retainer of Kanamori Sōwa. Another reason for this conclusion is Suetomi's letter, no. 395, that says, "against my will, I showed [the tea cup] to Sōchū, and he said that five *ryō* should be enough."

In any case, I would like to emphasize here that aristocrats actively engaged in the buying and selling of *kohitsu* calligraphies and artwork in the early Edo period, and networks of such trading were made.

Conclusion

This article analyzed the issues of the actual practice of buying and trading of *kohitsu* calligraphy and copies of classical literature, appraisals, and the popularization of such practices in the early Edo period, through following the activities of several aristocrats and Kohitsu Ryōsa. At the same time, I pointed out the possibility of a network of people engaged in such activities. It was particularly meaningful that I could provide historical evidence by finding primary sources regarding the activities of Kohitsu Ryōsa, that were mostly passed on as legend before.

It is true that there are many issues that I could only touch on in this article. I focused on aristocrats and their surroundings in this article, mainly because of the issues of available primary sources. However, the people who appreciated *kohitsu* must not have been limited to aristocrats, as can be seen in the example of "the person of Shimo-gyō," who can be speculated to be a townsman. Although the historical sources are limited, it is important to excavate more primary sources to more fully approach such issues. It is also necessary to follow and analyze other people like Fujitani Tamekata and Uratsuji Suetomi who engaged in trading in the aristocratic society. I would like to leave these for future studies.

(1) Examples of research institutes such as universities and museums that are engaged in such activities include: The Research Center of Calligraphy at Daito Bunka University sponsored the "Exhibition of *Kohitsu-gire* and *Kiwame-in*" at the Tenkoku Museum (Museum of Seal Cutting) in February, 2004 (Heisei 16). The Chadō Research Center Galleries also held an "Exhibition of *kiwame-fuda*" in December, 2008. In addition, Jakuboku Shohō Kai at Kokugakuin University publishes their institutional magazine, *Jakuboku shohō*.

(2) The database at the National Institute of Japanese Literature is not about the *kohitsu-gire* that they own, but rather, "a searching system for the location of *kohitsu-gire* whose facsimiles were published after *Kohitsu-gire teiyō* (Ii Haruki, Takada Nobutaka, ed. 1984, Tankōsha)," according to their description.

(3) Relevant articles are Kanechiku Nobuyuki's "Waseda daigaku toshokan shozō no *Kohitsu-gire* shiryō" (*Waseda daigaku toshokan kiyō*, no. 48, 2001), and Shiomura Kō's "Gotō bunko no *kohitsu-gire* dēta bēsu ni tsuite" (Nagoya daigaku fuzoku toshokan hō, no. 173, 2009). On the importance of making databases, Kanechiku said in his "Waseda daigaku zō *kohitsu-gire* dēta bēsu" on the website that, "from the standpoint of a scholar of classical Japanese literature, *kohitsu-gire* are important part of old books, and have an important meaning as primary sources. It is necessary to collect the accompanying *kohitsu-gire* that are owned separately in

different places in order to study the whole book. It would be convenient if such *kohitsu-gire* pieces were accessible online. The special collection of the main library has one collection of *kohitsu-gire* (*Kohitsu Tekagami*) and several scrolls and unbound *kohitsu-gire*. This database is being built based on such materials. Data will continue to be added."

(4) Kawashima Masao. *Muromachi bunka ronkō - Bunka-shi no naka no kōbu*. Hōsei University Press, 2008 (reprint). First published in 2006.

(5) Komatsu Shigemi. *Kohitsu*. Tankōsha, 1972. Shimosaka Mamoru, "Kohitsu to tekagami" (Catalog *Kohitsu to tekagami*. Kyoto National Museum, 1989.)

(6) For the analysis of such treatises of calligraphy, please see Miyazaki Hajime's "Chūsei shoryū no seiritsu - Sesonji-ke to Sesonji-ryū." (Kamakura ibun kenkyūkai, ed. *Kamakura-ki shakai to shiryō ron*. Tokyo-dō shuppan, 2002.) This article discusses the establishment of the Sesonji family as a family of *juboku-dō* (history of the way of calligraphy) scholars from a historical point of view.

(7) The red seal is unreadable. The black seal says "Fujiwara no Tokitsugu"

(8) Different shapes of paper were used before the time of the rectangular tanzaku style of *kiwame-fuda* that *kohitsu* appraisers used, such as *tategami* and *kirigami* styles. Early modern *Japanese-Portuguese Dictionary* (*Nippo jiten*) have entries on "Qiuame (*kiwame*)" and "Qiuwame, uru, eta (kiwame, kiwamuru, kiwameta)." However, the former is for the meaning "end, ultimate, acme," while the latter is for the meaning "do something to the ultimate degree," so the dictionary does not have "*kiwame*" in the sense of appraising *kohitsu* calligraphies.

(9) Komatsu's book. See endnote 5.

(10) From *Tokitsugu-kyō ki*.

(11) For instance, the record of the thirteenth of the Fifth Month in Eiroku 4 (1595) of *Tokitsune-kyō ki* says that Tokitsune judged if one calligraphy was by Fujiwara no Sadaie or not, and the entry of the second of the Ninth Month of Bunroku 5 (1596) records that, as a request from a master of *renga* poetry, Yūkei, Tokitsune judged that the version of *Shin chokusen shū* was in the handwriting of Ōgimachi sanjō Sanemasa when he was ranked *dainagon*.

(12) "Fujitani Tamekata shōron - Kanei Bunka ki ni okeru ichi kuge no katsudō" (in my book introduced in endnote 4). First published in 1992.

(13) *Daigakuji monjo ge* (Daigakuji, 1980). I will only mention their letter numbers when referring to letters from this collection throughout this article.

(14) Asukai Eiga was a grandson of Asukai Masayori (Sōga), a deeply trusted retainer

of Ashikaga Yoshimitsu who achieved a promotion with incredible speed, and was himself a deeply trusted retainer of Ashikaga Yoshimasa, Yoshimitsu's grandson. Lamenting the death of Yoshimitsu, Masayori wrote "Lamenting Master Rokuonin (Yoshimitsu)." This portrait is located in Sōkokuji Shōtenkaku. The temple is currently deferring the decision to declare whether the poems were written by Eiga, since the time may not match.

(15) No. 3307 of *Date-ke monjo* in *Dai nihon komonjo*, dated the Ninth Month of Shōō 2 (1653). It is unclear if this letter was created on request from the Date family, or if the Date family acquired the letter after it was written, since there is no addressee. Judging from the number of characters written in this letter, it was probably not written on *kiwame-fuda*.

(16) "Deshi-shū hikae" in Sen Sōsa, supervision, Sen Sōin, ed. *Kōshin Sōsa chasho*. Shufu no tomo sha, 1998.

(17) Such activities by Uratsuji Suetomi are recorded in documents like the letter no. 396: "Thank you for taking care of the matter of the tea cup quickly. When I told them that it is a bit too pricy, they took it back for now... Another scroll is on Princess Chūjō. It was beautifully done, and the price was one gold and five *ryō*. I showed it for the master priest's appreciation, but if he doesn't like it, please return it to me."

(18) A letter and a guarantor's letter by Noji Sōchū are in *Tōnan-ke monjo* (pictures in Kyoto-shi rekishi shiryō kan).

(19) In *Sadō koten zenshū* vol. 10.

Translated by Shiho Takai

Chap. 10 Urban Construction in Medieval *Heian-Kyō*: Analysis of Nobility Transit Routes Using GIS

■Makoto Tanaka

(Research Project: Actions and Experiences of the Heian Nobility)

Introduction

The urban construction of Heian-kyō has been examined from various angles up until now. In particular, works related to this article that deal with the transit routes of the Emperor (*tennō*), Retired Emperors (*in*) and the nobility (*kizoku*) include those authored by Kotera Takehisa (1969) and Ōmura Takuo (1990)[1], which both analyze urban construction by identifying major routes in the medieval Heian court.

The movements of the Emperor, Retired Emperors and nobility themselves were the objects of observation, and played a part in rituals (Noda 1999). Since they were not just simply movements, in old records a vast number of movement paths have been recorded.

When considering the connection between transit routes and urban construction, what is important is not just the explication of major roads but also the problems of road maintenance that accompany transit. The roads of Heian-kyō were constantly changing, for example due to the appearance of arable farmlands or residential lands (Nakamura 1968). However, when transit took place, cleaning and maintenance of the roads would be carried out by the Capital Offices (*kyōsiki*) or the Royal Police (*kebiishi*) (Nakahara 1984). Because of this, the maintenance conditions of roads with the largest number of transit instances were hypothetically good. In short, the problems of road maintenance played a part in defining the urban shape of Heian-kyō. Kotera and Ōmura's research take steps to approach the problems of transit routes and road maintenance, and are highly esteemed.

Both of these studies focus on transit routes taken during specialized rituals like royal shrine visits by the Emperor (*jinja gyōkō*) and Retired Emperors (*jinja gokō*), and concretely interrogate those changes. These methods are a valid step in pursuing changes to the rituals themselves and urban construction. However, consequentially, when used for the purpose of analyzing of transit routes, biases occur, and it becomes difficult to grasp an overall picture of transit routes among the nobility.

Up until now, it has been difficult to arrange and grasp a full picture of these types of movement routes using prevailing research methods. However, by using GIS (Geographic Information System), comprehensive research on the transit routes seen in each and every ritual has become possible through the accumulation and analysis of data found in historical records.

Thus, this paper, without bias towards specialized ritual routes, will accumulate and analyze transit routes of the Emperor, Retired Emperors and nobility found in old records from the Heian to Kamakura periods, and will aim to shed light on changes to the urban construction of Heian-kyō.

GIS Research Methodology

Before entering the main argument, I'd like to make some additional remarks about the research methodology. First, GIS (Arc Map 10.0, by ESRI, 2010) was used to make the maps that form the basis for this study. Next, I added data on movement routes collected from old records onto the map. For example, an entry in *Chūyūki* written on the 14th day of the 11th month of Eikyū 2 (1114), recording Emperor Toba's royal visit to Iwashimizu Shrine, states: "[His Majesty] left the East Gate on horse (Rokujō-dono, East Gate, Karasuma side), from Karasuma, past Rokujō, Ōmiya, Shichijō and Suzaku Boulevards, arriving at the north gate of Toba." On the occasion of transit inside and outside the capital by the Emperor, Retired Emperors and nobility, departure and arrival locations are either clearly recorded or can be extrapolated, and in this project, a database was created using those records in which transit routes inside the capital were clearly recorded. Out of convenience, these transit routes were mapped onto separate maps for the Sekkan (Fujiwara Regency) period (Tengen 5 (982)-Eihō 1 (1081)), the Insei (Retired Emperors) period (Kanji 1 (1087)-Genroku 1 (1184)), and the Kamakura period (Bunji 1 (1185)-Genkō 2 (1332))[2]. All data points total approximately 590 items[3], which means that there is great merit in using GIS for arrangement and analysis of this data. While this survey is still incomplete, I think that a reasonable trend can be grasped, so I want to move ahead with discussion.

1. Transit Routes of the Sekkan Period

During the Sekkan period, royal visits to shrines such as Iwashimizu and Kasuga would enter into the capital from various gates on the east side of the palace precincts (*daidairi*), and would often follow routes along Ōmiya, Nijō and Suzaku Boulevards (*ōji*). After the start of the Insei period, use of Suzaku Boulevard decreased, and a different route came to be often used. This route used Ōmiya, Nishinotōin or Higashinotōin Boulevards to head south to Shichijō Boulevard, then switched to Shichijō and Suzaku in order to leave the capital. Also, in order to go in the direction of Kasuga Shrine and Uji, Kujōguchi, which was near the intersection of Kujō and Higashikyōgoku Boulevards came to be used (Kotera 1969; Ōmura 1990). Ōmura indicates that Ōmiya Boulevard and Shichijō Boulevard overlap with the borders of medieval Kyōto. Ōmura's indication, when considered in regards to the formation of Heian-kyō, is a point of view that is worthy of attention. In short, the results of past research can be read anew as clearly articulating the contours of medieval Kyōto.

This paper takes as its topic an exhaustive and detailed analysis of transit routes in the left capital (*sakyō*) interior, which prior research mostly overlooks. Based on this analysis, we can posit a new construction of Heian-kyō. For transit routes during this time, a map created using GIS can be seen in Figures 1-3. Data from instances of transit by the Emperor and nobility are traced along roads within the city and routes outside the capital, with route lines becoming thicker as the number of instances becomes more numerous.

(1) **South-North Roads and Transit Routes During the Sekkan Period**

Paths with the largest amount of movement during this period were parts of Ōmiya and Tsuchimikado Boulevards at the east side of the palace precincts (Fig. 1; p. 16). Ōmiya Boulevard had a width of 12 *jō* (approx. 36 m). Among roads that ran from south to north, it was the widest after Suzaku Boulevard, and north of Nijō it touched the gate of the palace. During this time period, it was more common to conduct rituals in the palace precincts, and moreover the Emperor spent a lot of time there. As a result, for purposes of movement within and outside of the palace precincts, it was necessary to travel on Ōmiya Boulevard, and the instances of movement are numerous.

(2) East-West Roads and Transit Routes During the Sekkan Period

Tsuchimikado Boulevard is a road with a width of 10 *jō* (approx. 30 m). The part of Tsuchimikado Boulevard that runs the left capital was used frequently in its entirety. A factor in this was Fujiwara no Michinaga's mansions, which were Tsuchimikado Dono (located south of Tsuchimikado and west of Higashikyōgoku in Nanboku Ni-chō), Biwa Dono (south of Takatsukasa and west of Higashinotōin). Tsuchimikado Dono was the residence most used by Michinaga. Biwa Dono is also a residence of Michinaga's, but it was used as a palace for Emperor Sanjō (Ōta 1987).

Rituals that went back and forth between the palace precincts and either Tsuchimikado Dono or Biwa Dono include visits to the royal parents (*chōkin gyōkō*), presentation of royal brides (*judai*), movement of the Emperor to other locations (*senkō*) and funeral processions (*sōsō*). As such, these rituals were wide-ranging; however, the majority of them utilized Tsuchimikado Boulevard, and Konoe Boulevard to the south was infrequently used. We can surmise that the road used for movement was decided upon based on the nature of the ritual and the person who was doing the moving.

In this way, Michinaga's residences and temporary royal palaces were placed near Tsuchimikado Boulevard. Tsuchimikado Boulevard in turn came to be very frequently used because it tied these residences to the palace precincts and was also used for a diverse number of rituals

In this time period, it is clear that Suzaku Boulevard and Ōmiya Boulevard were used as south-north roods, and as an east-west road, Tsuchimikado Boulevard, which connected Fujiwara no Michinaga's residence and the palace precincts, was the most utilized. Ōmura (1990) indicates that there is a correlation between the residence of the Emperor and transit routes, but I want to note that a correlation can be recognized not between transit routes and the Emperor, but rather between these routes and people in positions of power, a categorization that also includes the regents.

Road maintenance during royal visits can already be seen in this time period, and Tsuchimikado Boulevard was subject to this (As noted in a record in "Shoji kuyō burui ki" of *Shōyūki*, dated the 1st day of the 7th month of Jian 2 (1022), etc.). From these records, we can think of Tsuchimikado Boulevard as not just simply a road for the usage of the nobility, but also one that had the width and good condition to withstand the throngs who would come to observe the processions accompanying royal visits. Bearing this point in mind, we might consider Tsuchimikado the main street of Heian-kyō, among the east-west roads of the time.

2. Transit Routes During the Insei Period

(1) Left Capital During the Insei Period

In the Insei period, as Figure 2 (p. 19) shows, instances of movement among the nobility increase, and their radius of movement also increases. The south part of the left capital, as well as routes towards Shirakawa and Toba has also clearly expanded. In addition to royal shrine visits by both the Emperor and Retired Emperors, an increase in the number of royal visits by both the Emperor and Retired Emperors using alternate routes (*katatagae gyōkō*, in which the procession sets off in an alternative direction to avoid inauspicious directions), visits to royal parents and congratulatory visits (*haiga*) are also tied to the increase in instances of movement. Expansion of the radius of movement can be attributed to the construction of palaces near Gojō and Rokujō Boulevards, as well as the construction of palaces for Retired Emperors in places like the south part of the left capital, Shirakawa, Toba and Hōjūji. Also, we cannot overlook the development of the area around Kujō Boulevard by the Fujiwara regents and the area around Hachijō Boulevard by the Taira regime.

(2) East-West Roads and Transit Routes During the Insei Period

The first noticeable special characteristic in the usage of roads during the Insei period is a reduction in the usage of Suzaku Boulevard and Tsuchimikado Boulevard, which were both used more often during the Sekkan period. In regards to east-west roads, Nakamikado Boulevard (10 *jō*, approx. 30 m), Ōimikado Boulevard (10 *jō*, approx 30 m), Nijō Boulevard (17 *jō*, approx. 41 m), came to be used, with Nijō Boulevard in particular being used often. During the Insei period, temporary royal palaces and mansions of the regency that were in proximity to Nijō Boulevard, such as Horikawa Dono, Kan'in, Higashi Sanjō Dono, Kaya'in and Nijō Higashinotōin Palace, were actively used. Increase in the use of Nijō may have been related to the need to connect with these residences. During this period, Nijō Boulevard was the primary east-west road, and in addition, Nakamikado and Ōimikado Boulevards followed it.

(3) **South-North Roads and Transit Routes During the Insei Period**

In regards to South-North roads, while Suzaku Boulevard declined, Higashinotōin Boulevard (8 *jō*, approx. 24 m) displayed remarkable usage. In particular, when considering routes between Nakamikado and Gojō Boulevards, passage along this road is overwhelmingly frequent compared to other South-North and East-West roads.

In addition to royal shrine visits by the Emperor to Iwashimizu and Kasuga, rituals that utilized Higashinotōin Boulevard also included royal shrine visits to Kamo by the Emperor and Retired Emperors, regent pilgrimages to shrines (*sekkan kamo mōde*), royal visits by alternate routes, visits to royal parents, royal visits to empresses, congratulatory visits and other various rituals. When thinking about the character of Higashinotōin, the following example can be used for reference: an entry in *Sankaiki* written on the 28th day of the 5th month of Jishō 3 (1179), during one of the Takakura Emperor's royal visits by alternate route, records the following as a route from Kan'in to Hōjūji: "From the East Gate, movement to the north, east at Nijō, south at Higashinotōin, east at Shichijō, the river (Previously, a route from Gojō on Kyōgoku or from Shijō was used. However, when departing, because of a flood the east side of Higashikyōgoku was damaged. As a result this path was used.)." In contrast with past precedent, due to flood damage to the east side of Higashikyōgoku, this route moved south on Higashinotōin until Shichijō, and as an alternative to Higashikyōgoku, Higashinotōin was selected. In an entry from *Chūyūki* written on the 15th day of the 7th month of Gen'ei 1 (1118), the same kind of example can be seen upon the occasion of the royal shrine visit of Retired Emperor Shirakawa. Ōmura indicates that large-scale royal shrine visits and royal visits by alternate routes should not be examined in the same way. However because Higashinotōin Boulevard was used as an alternative in extraordinary situations, we can surmise that among the roads in the left capital, Higashinotōin, which was often used for royal shrine visits by both the Emperor and Retired Emperors, was especially well-maintained.

The subjects in transit were primarily the Emperor, and after that Retired Emperors, Empresses (*chūgū*), court ladies (*nyoin*), and people related to the Regency. This trend conforms to that of other routes, as well as similar trends in the later Kamakura period. We can see manifestations of the desire of the recorder to transmit the rituals of the Emperor and Retired Emperors to later generations.

When using Higashinotōin Boulevard, points of arrival and departure were—(from each residence north of Sanjō in the left capital)—the royal palaces and palaces of Retired Emperors on Gojō and Rokujō, Hōjūji Dono, Kasuga Shrine and Iwashimizu Shrine. Ōmiya was primarily used for transit towards Kyoto's southern area, including places like Iwashimizu Shrine, Kasuga Shrine and Toba Dono. Compared to Ōmiya, Higashinotōin was used for movement from the north area of the left capital to Kamo and the south area of the left capital, in addition to Iwashimizu, Kasuga, and Toba Dono. In that way, its usefulness was multifaceted. Thus, we can surmise that Higashinotōin Boulevard had a good surface and a width that could withstand the movements of the nobility themselves as well as their observers.

As is well-known, during the Insei period, the right capital (*ukyō*) declined, and the left-right symmetry of Heian-kyō was lost. As Suzaku Boulevard declined, residences became concentrated in the left capital, and the existence of Higashinotōin became prominent among roads used for rituals. The fact that a great variety of people used Higashinotōin for a great variety of rituals was one of the special characteristics of the road, and we can consider Higashinotōin to be a main street to rival the once-great Suzaku Boulevard.

3. Transit Routes in the Kamakura Period

(1) The Left Capital and Ōmiya Boulevard During the Kamakura Period

Next, I want to examine the special characteristics of the left capital during the Kamakura period (Fig. 3; p. 22). In the Kamakura period, the locations of the residences of the Emperor, Retired Emperors and regents changed. In the early Kamakura period, their residences were centered on Kan'in Palace, and in the later Kamakura Period they were centered on the left capital and points north.

Another major change is the lessening of the functions of the palace precincts. As is well-known, following the Kamakura period the palace precincts began to decay, but it is clear that at that time, a portion of Daidairi's buildings were undergoing repair, rebuilding and preservation (Takahashi 2006). Nevertheless, compared to the Insei period (Fig. 2), the use of Ōmiya Boulevard had clearly declined, and it can be perceived as losing its role as a road used in rituals.

(2) East-West Roads and Transit Routes During the Kamakura Period

In regards to the usage conditions of east-west roads, upon first glance, the usage of Nakamikado and Shichijō Boulevards, which were frequently used during the Insei period, appear to have decreased. Usage of Nakamikado decreased due to the decline of the functional usage of the palace precincts—Usage of Shichijō decreased due to the fact that movement to Iwashimizu, Toba, and Hōjūji Dono had decreased (Fig. 3), as well as the fact that when moving to the southern part of Heian-kyō, the routes that led out to Suzaku Boulevard were no longer limited to Shichijō (Ōmura 1990).

Ōimikado Boulevard and Nijō Boulevard, however, show sustained prominent usage. Compared to the Insei period, this usage remained confined to a more local level, but as Nijō Boulevard neighbored royal palaces and palaces of Retired Emperors, we can hypothesize this type of connection.

(3) **South-North Roads and the Forms of Usage During the Kamakura Period**

In contrast to the reduction in usage of Suzaku and Ōmiya Boulevards, Higashinotōin Boulevard shows sustained prominent usage. The use of this road for royal visits by alternate routes was frequent, but other rituals such as royal visits to shrines such as Iwashimizu, Kamo and Matsuo can also be seen. There were also many palaces and palaces of Retired Emperors in the Kamakura period that did not neighbor Higashinotōin, and at the south part of Higashinotōin there are no residences designated as temporary royal palaces. Regardless, we can surmise that the reason why Higashinotōin became more prominently used is because the example of the Insei period was carried on into the Kamakura period. Ōmura (1990) states that during this time period, royal palaces cannot be used as a benchmark to measure the space of the city; that is to say, the correlation between temporary royal palaces and routes becomes insufficient. However, a reason why the usage of Ōimikado, Nijō, and Higashinotōin becomes prominent may be based on the presumption that this is an area where royal palaces and palaces of Retired Emperors are concentrated. As the decline of the right capital continues, and moreover Suzaku and Ōmiya Boulevards become less used, Higashinotōin Boulevard solidifies its position as the main street of the left capital area of Heian-kyō. As the reorganization of Heian-kyō progressed from the Insei period to the Kamakura period, perhaps Higashinotōin Boulevard acted as an axis for the reconstruction of the inner part of the left capital.

(4) Transit Routes and Their Relationship to Rokuhara Tandai

Finally, I want to touch on the relationship between movement routes and Rokuhara Tandai. Rokuhara Tandai was the authority responsible for governing the western part of Japan following the Jōkyū Incident in 1221. Before the Tandai was established, the area had Taira residences and was connected to samurai families, but I cannot find examples of movement to Rokuhara from the end of the Insei period and through the Kamakura period. Rokuhara Tandai participated in policing processions, and moreover we can see examples of them carrying the Emperor's *mikoshi*[4], but these are perhaps unusual measures. Up until now, no evidence can be seen of direct influence by Rokuhara Tandai on changes to processional routes.

Up until here, I have pursued the chronological changes in transit routes, as well as the process by which Higashinotōin came to be the main street of the left capital of Heian-kyō during the early medieval period. One thing that should be paid attention to is the existence of Nishinotōin, which shares the same width as Higashinotōin. As seen in Figures 1-3, we can see that Nishinotōin is not really used throughout all periods. Why is this? Next, I will consider this problem.

4. Higashinotōin and Nishinotōin

(1) About Nishinotōin River

Higashinotōin Boulevard and Nishinotōin Boulevard are both boulevards with a width of 8 *jō* (approx. 24 m). In the vicinity of Nishinotōin are the major residences Kan'in, Higashi Sanjō Dono, Takamatsu Dono and Kaya'in. When traversing the left capital from south to north, it should also be possible to use Nishinotōin Boulevard, but that trend cannot be detected.

In regards to the non-use of Nishinotōin, Kotera (1969) already indicates that perhaps the river running alongside Nishinotōin was the cause. Following his indications, I want to investigate the relationship between the inside of the capital and the rivers flowing through it.

In regards to the rivers flowing inside the capital, if we consult "Sakyō-zu," collected in the Kujōke-bon *Engishiki*, the entire length of Ōmiya and Horikawa Avenue (*kōji*), as well as parts of Nishinotōin, Machi Avenue, Muromachi Avenue, Karasuma Avenue, and Higashinotōin all have rivers running alongside. The existence of the problematic Nishinotōin can be seen even in the illustrations of the frontlines of Kan'in palace collected in the Ninnaji-bon Manuscript *Keizu* (Noguchi 2005), and these conforms to the rivers that can are recorded in "Sakyō-zu"

Nishinotōin River is referenced in *Chūyūki*, on the 17th day of the 5th month of Chōshō 3 (1134): "Within the capital the Hori River and Nishinotōin River flooded and there were drownings." Also, in an entry in the *Kanchūki*, dated on the 17th day of the intercalary 4th month of Kōan 7 (1284), it is recorded: "Floods overflow the capital, men and horses cannot pass Karasuma River and Nishinotōin River." It seems that from the Insei period to the Kamakura period Nishinotōin River was a river that frequently flooded.

The difference between Higashinotōin River and Nishinotōin River is the length of the river. As opposed to Nishinotōin River, which runs to the south of Nakamikado Boulevard, Higashinotōin River runs from Ichijō to Ōimikado, and at the least the south of Ōimikado can be thought of as not affected by the river.

Ōmiya River and Hori River are rivers that run alongside the entire length of their respective roads. The width of Horikawa Avenue is 8 *jō*, the same as Higashinotōin and Nishinotōin. The width of the river alongside Ōmiya Boulevard is unknown, but the width of the road is 12 *jō* (approx. 36 m), 4 *jō* wider than Higashinotōin and Nishinotōin. As Figures 1-3 show, Horikawa Avenue's instances of transit are small, but as opposed to that, the instances of usage of Ōmiya Boulevard are numerous. When conducting rituals in the palace precincts, as stated earlier, it was necessary to use this boulevard. Moreover, some historical material states that Ōmiya Boulevard and Ōmiya River do not run parallel from Yōmeimon to Ikuhōmon[5]. Thus, from the point of view of its connections to road width, Ōmiya River may not have been a large obstacle.

However, in the case of Nishinotōin Boulevard, the width of the road was narrow and flooding frequently occurred. Because of that, road maintenance might have been unable to reach there. During transit of the nobility, carriages were often used (*mikoshi* for the Emperor), and Nishinotōin Boulevard, which was not only narrow but also difficult to access for road maintenance, was difficult to pass through. Thus, it was probably excluded as a route choice.

(2) **Use of Higashinotōin Boulevard and Awareness of Precedent in Noble Society**

Apart from road conditions, we can also think that the accumulation of precedent in noble society influences this situation. I offered earlier an example where Higashinotōin Boulevard was used as an alternative road. Another example occurs in "Hyohanki," written on the 1st day of the 3rd month of Hōgen 1 (1156), on occasion of Emperor Go Shirakawa's royal visit to Iwashimizu. The royal procession set off from Takamatsu-Dono (North of Sanjō bōmon and east of Nishinotōin), and "went east from Sanjō, south from Higashinotōin, west from Shichijō, and then south like before." It continues: "In all cases, one should rely on precedent and travel on Ōmiya Boulevard. However, Lord Akisuke passed away last year in the fourth month at Rokujō and Ōmiya. During the year of mourning, it should perhaps be avoided because of that hindrance." What should be focused on is that as an alternative it is not Nishinotōin, which abuts Takamatsu-dono, but rather Higashinotōin that is selected.

As can be seen above, because Nishinotōin Boulevard was not appropriate for travel, it was excluded from possible route choices from an early stage. Moreover, instances of precedent stating "not to pass through Nishinotōin" accumulated to the point that Nishinotōin came to be thought of as a road that was not to be used. Perhaps in an almost inversely proportional fashion to the choice not to use Nishinotōin, even if its connection to the destination was illogical, Higashinotōin Boulevard was chosen and was used for transit.

Conclusion

This essay has examined road usage conditions in Heian-kyō during the medieval period based on the transit routes of the Emperor, Retired Emperors and nobility. As a result, we see clearly that from the Insei period, Suzaku Boulevard declined, and Higashinotōin Boulevard came to be frequently utilized, and this practice carried on into the Kamakura period. Furthermore, Higashinotōin came to be positioned as the main street for Heian-kyō during the early medieval period. Higashinotōin was a road used for ritual, as it were, and from the early medieval period it had a different character from Machi Avenue, which developed gradually into a thriving business district[6]. As can be seen in Figures 1-3, south of Nijō and Machi Avenue certainly has low instances of movement. We might think of this fact as an illustration of the separation of business and ritual spaces within Heian-kyō, and we can consider to be one of the special characteristics of the construction of space in Heian-kyō during the early medieval period.

Finally, in regards to my further research, there are many technical issues involving the use of GIS, as well as incomplete surveys and omissions in the recording of instances. Also, due to the length restrictions for this paper, I was unable to develop my arguments to include issues such as trends in political and economic histories, as well as connections to the samurai government. However, I believe that I was able to confirm that there are great merits to using GIS. I was unable to accomplish it this time, but because we can also use the special features of GIS to overlay these maps onto current-day roads, research on modern-day Kyōto can also pursue chronological changes as well. After this, I wish to draw out those special features and continue my research along this path.

(1) In addition to urban theory, the connection between funeral processions and movement routes has also been discussed in Maeshima (1998).

(2) When creating a map, I utilized the following resources: for the Sekkan period (Fig. 1): *Shōyūki, Midō Kanpakuki, Sakeiki, Gonki, Shunki*; for the Insei period (Fig. 2): *Chūyūki, Go Nijō Moromichiki, Hyōhanki, Sankaiki, Gyokuyō* (Prior to Genryaku 1); for the Kamakura period (Fig. 3): *Gyokuyō* (Bunji 1 onwards), *Meigetsuki* (Kenkyū 3 to Genkyū 1), *Minkeiki, Kanchūki, Fuyuhira kōki, Kinhira kōki, Hanazono-in shinki*. Division of time periods was based on the surviving conditions of old records and changes in movement routes. I define the Sekkan period as prior to the enthronement of Horikawa Emperor, the Insei period as from the enthronement of Horikawa Emperor to the fleeing of the Taira from the capital, and the Kamakura period as from the time of the fleeing of the Taira onwards. Also, the position of each residence was determined in consultation with Kawakami (1967), Kondo (1992), and Yamada (1994). Furthermore, the names of roads follow notations in Teramasu (1994).

(3) In the case that one transit route was recorded in multiple records, each was recorded separately. Due to the space limitations, I abbreviate my explanation, but because the ratio of these records to the whole is rather small in number, I believe that there are not any serious errors in my argument and I will move forward with my argument.

(4) *Minkeiki*, 1st day of the 7th month of Kangi 3 (1231). In the same year on the 6th day of the 8th month, during a royal visit by alternate route, the Emperor speaks to Hōjō Shigetoki about his "accompanying warrior," so it is clear that in the item of the 1st day of the 7th month, during that royal visit by alternate route, the warrior who

accompanied him is a Rokuhara warrior.

(5) From "Ise Monogatari Chikenshō," in *Shiryō Kyōto no rekishi*, v. 4 *Shigai, seigyō*.

(6) *Kyōto no rekishi*, v. 2, *Chūsei no meian* (Kyōto, 1971. Volume 3, Paragraph 3, written by Kawashima Masao and Yokoi Kiyoshi).

Works Consulted

Ōta, Seiroku (1987). *Shindenzukuri no kenkyū*. Yoshikawa Kōbunkan. [Ōta 1987]

Ōmura, Takuo (2006, first published 1990). "Gishikiji no hensen to toshi kūkan." *Chūsei Kyōto Shutoron*. Yoshikawa Kōbunkan. [Ōmura 1990]

Ōmura, Takuo (2006, first published 1994). "Gyōkō-Gekō no tenkai." *Chūsei Kyōto Shutoron*. Yoshikawa Kōbunkan. [Ōmura 1994]

Kawakami, Mitsugu (2002, first published 1967). "Kamakura jidai kōhanki ni okeru dairi to ingosho no kenkyū." *Nihon chūsei jūtaku no kenkyū (shintei)*. Chūō kōron bijutsu shuppan. [Kawakami 1967]

Kotera, Takehisa (1969). "Heian-kyō no kūkanteki hensen ni kansuru kōsatsu (1)(2)" *Nihon kenchiku gakkai ronbun hōkokushū*, vols. 165-166. [Kotera 1969]

Kondo, sigekazu (1992). "Dairi to ingosho." *Toshi no chūsei*, Gomi Fumihiko, ed. Yoshikawa Kōbunkan. [Kondo 1992]

Takahashi, Masaaki (2006). "Daidairi no henbō—Heian matsu kara Kamakura chūki made—" *Inseiki no dairi, daidairi to ingosho*, Takahashi Masaaki, ed. Tosho Shuppan Bunrikaku. [Takahashi 2006]

Teramasu, Hatsuyo (1994). "Heian-kyōnai gairo Kokin taishōhyō" *Heian-kyō teiyō*. Kadokawa Shoten. [Teramasu 1994]

Nakahara, Toshiaki (1984). "Kebiishi to 'kawa' to 'michi'" *Hisutoria*, v. 105. [Nakahara 1984]

Nakamura, Ken (1975, first published 1968) "Tōjiryō kōsho no sonzai keitai." *Kyōto 'machi' no kenkyū*, Akiyama Kunizō and Nakamura Ken, eds. Hōsei daigaku shuppankyoku. [Nakamura 1968]

Noguchi, Takako (2005). "Ninnaji-bon *Keizu* ni egakareta Kan'in dairi no jinchū." *Ninnaji kenkyū*, v. 5. [Noguchi 2005]

Noda, Yukiko (1999). "Heian kizoku shakai no gyōretsu—keiga gyōretsu o chūshin ni—." *Nihonshi kenkyū*, v. 447. [Noda 1999]

Maeshima, Satoshi (1998). "Chūsei zenki no sōretsu ni okeru junro to kenbutsu." *Daigakuin kenkyū nenpō*, v. 28. Chūō Bungaku. [Maeshima 1998]

Yamada, Kunikazu (1994). "Sakyō to ukyō." *Heian-kyō teiyō*, Kadokawa Shoten.

[Yamada 1994]

[Notes]

This paper is based on research findings from Ritsumeikan University's Global COE Digital Humanities Kyōto Culture Research Group. A finished version was presented in August 2011 at the 13th EAJS Conference in Estonia. The author wishes to express his gratitude towards the project representatives, Professors Sugihashi Takao and Sako Aimi, for their unfailing guidance. Survey and creation of the database of old records, as well as GIS mapping work, was carried out at Ritsumeikan with the support and cooperation of Uejima Rieko, Hanada Takuji, Tani Noboru, Namekawa Atsuko, Yoshimi Haruka and Ikematsu Naoki. Also, in regards to the creation and manipulation of the GIS maps, the cooperation of Professor Kawasumi Tatsunori, as well as Imamura Satoshi of the Department of Geography in the College of Letters at Ritsumeikan, was invaluable. The author wishes to convey his deepest gratitude to everyone involved.

Translated by Michael Chan

Chap.11 Emperor and Capital in the Buddhist Worldview: The Perception of the World in Medieval Japan

■Ikuyo Matsumoto

Introduction

During the medieval period in Japan, the mythology of the *Nihon Shoki* and *Kojiki* was absorbed into a Buddhist worldview which awarded *kami* certain qualities and assigned them hierarchical rank. In much the same way, the city space that came to be called Heian-Kyo was envisioned within an esoteric framework of the world which had the *tennō* (emperor) at its center. By referring to mythological accounts attributed to the *kami* and the buddhas, ideas about the origins of the pre-medieval world could be cemented. Such a process is also to be found in textual explanations that accorded ideological meanings to the "actual" world. Esotericism offered such ideological explanations: it understood Buddhism within a worldview that located it in actual space; the framework of the world constructed by esoteric Buddhism in medieval Japan was informed not only by Buddhist ideology but also by real geographical space.

A historical phenomenon in which ideology based on medieval Buddhism was fused to geographical space, the formation of Japanese Buddhism from the tenth century onward conformed to the East Asian Buddhist policies that centred around the Chinese emperor[1]. However, there has been a tendency to interpret this cosmic and worldview, that utilized real geographical space, as merely religious, figurative allegory or as abstract philosophy. The position of world consciousness and worldview in premodern Japan should first be understood as having derived from a system that was constructed for assumption of control over territory. The existential significance of the territory itself derived from religion and mythology. Such constructed views of the cosmos and the world present the socio-cultural changes or the "state of the world" in every period[2]. In other words, geographical space, as an object of religious ideology, embodies specific systems and specific concepts, and it can be interpreted as exhibiting a certain "world consciousness".

During the premodern period, East Asian culture, with Chinese culture at its centre, developed on the basis of the *Hua-Yi* distinction (sometimes known as the "Sino-barbarian dichotomy"). The transition from the Ming to the Qing Dynasty constituted a major turning point, and intellectuals of the Edo period (1603-1868) in Japan became aware of the change in the *Hua-Yi* distinction. Until the opening of the country at the end of the Edo period (*bakumatsu* period), China was the principle cultural civilization with which Japan compared itself. From the Age of Discovery onward - the beginning of Japan's first steps toward globalization in the 16th century- the country experienced European culture via China and South East Asia. The impact of this exposure gradually helped to open the ports. However, until the point at which Japan's consciousness of the world was one that could be measured by the attainment and production of geographically correct maps of the world, it functioned with "imaginary" descriptions, such as medieval ones that portrayed "different worlds" (*ikai*), which were based on "*Sangaikyō*", the ancient Chinese topography[3].

In this paper, I discuss the emperor and the capital as they are expressed in the worldview of medieval Japanese Buddhism. Furthermore, through examining one aspect of this worldview that was dominant before being eliminated in the modern period, I would like to offer some possibilities for understanding a "world" that had ceased to exist.

1. Japan in the Buddhist World

(1) The Buddhist Worldview and the Conflict with Modernity

At the centre of the Buddhist worldview, which was the worldview of Japan in the premodern period, was *Shumisen* (Mount Sumeru or Meru). According to this worldview, the world had emerged from a void (*kokū*). A disk-like expanse of wind (*fūrin*; Sk. vāyu-maṇḍala) supported the world within the void and it was said that the world was supported by the strength of the wind. On top of this was another expanse, this one of water - *suirin* — which was produced by the wind, and above that was the *konrin*, a metal platform, or "golden wheel", from which arose mountains, seas, and islands. This was the section that constituted the platform of the world. *Shumisen* was at the centre of this world and surrounding it were seven golden mountains, and *Tecchisen* (Sk. Cakravada) — a metal mountain range. The mountains were divided by eight seas. The entire region was called the Nine Mountains and Eight Seas (*kyūsen hakkai*). Between the mountains, the eight seas were situated like rings, and beyond this, the "four great continents" rose up out of the seas of the *konrin*. This area of sea, known as *shikai* (the "Four Seas"), will be discussed in the next section.

The *konrin* was a structure connected to *Shumisen* — the world — and the depths beneath the four great continents. Of these four continents, the one inhabited by humans was called *Nansenbushū* (Sk. Jambudvīpa). Rivers flowed in all four directions from lake *Anokudacchi* (Sk. Anavatapta) on the peak of the Himalayas (modeled on those of India). This "imaginary" landscape is shown in the "*Gotenjiku-zu*" (Map of the Five Regions of India) in the collection of Hōryuji temple, and a number of other maps[4].

The *Shitennō* (Four Heavenly Kings) were stationed on the hillsides of *Shumisen*, guarding the four great continents while lunar deity *Gatten* (Sk. Candra) and solar deity *Nitten* (Sk. Sūrya) circulated it. Upon the peak of *Shumisen* was *Tōriten* (S. Trāyastriṃśa), where lay *Zenkenjō* castle in which *Taishaku-ten* (Sk. Indra) dwelled. This world with *Shumisen* at its axis was based quite logically upon a world found within the Buddhist sutras. Figure 1 (p. 30) is a diagram from "*Shumisen zukai*" (Bunka 6; 1809) by Takai Ranzan (1762-1839), a depiction of the universe at the centre of which is *Shumisen*[5].

The *Bonreki* movement of the latter part of the Edo period made *Shumisen* not merely an aspect of the Buddhist world but an influence on people's understanding of the real world. *Bonreki*, or Buddhist astronomy (astronomy based on a Buddhist understanding of the cosmos), was the systematization by the monk Fumon Entsū (1754-1834), of sutra-based astronomy within a Copernican universe. Copernican theory had become known in Japan from the 1770s to the 1790s via books imported from Holland and translated. It was discussed in relation to physics and the other sciences grouped into the category of *Kyūrigaku* (Natural Philosophy). "*Oranda Tensetsu*" (Dutch Astronomy Explained) by Shiba Kōkan (1747-1818) which appeared in 1796 (Kansei 8), offered easy-to-understand diagrams illustrating the principles of astronomy, geography, and meteorology according to western theories. Intellectuals enthusiastic about Dutch studies (*rangaku*) upheld the superiority of western scholarship, proclaiming that they were not "describing the world symbolically, but rather portraying it just as it was[6]".

Entsū described the Buddhist world with *Shumisen* at its centre as a means of presenting an image that contrasted with that offered by Western astronomy. The universe that Buddhist astronomy provided had a "divine eye" and comprehensive, unchanging principles. Entsū argued against a Western scholarship that relied on empirical evidence (or, a "human" eye). Western scholarship stressed the importance of accounting for differences in the results attained from observation depending on the technology used. It was in such ways that western astronomy had rendered Buddhist astronomy inadequate[7].

The Buddhist astronomy movement begun by Entsū inspired lively participation from the latter part of the Edo period until 1872 (Meiji 5) when the solar calendar came into use and it was one aspect of the Buddhist view of the world that had all but disappeared by the beginning of the Shōwa period. The emergence of Buddhist astronomy was ultimately related to the issue of the relationship between Buddhist cosmology and Western astronomy, and this, further, was related to the question of belief in the transcendental third eye of the Buddha as opposed to the relative eye (or capacity for perception) of the unenlightened human. This way of thinking had not emerged suddenly during the modern period; it was the recomposition of a Buddhist form of existence that had until that time been the predominant influence on "Japanese" thought and behavior, and that was also based on new knowledge from abroad.

Buddhist astronomy scholar Okada Masahiko has stated that "if the notion of a spherical earth and the reception of Copernican theory are barometers of modern thinking, *Bonreki* descriptions of the world that present the actual existence of a flat earth might be thought of as anti-modern traditionalism. However, the influence of the modern world on people was exerted not only through concepts. More importantly, it was textual descriptions that altered peoples' perceptions of the world and its nature.[8]" In such a way, in the process of moving from a premodern to a modern world, it was historical accounts that constructed the character of the modern world.

(2) Japan's Consciousness of the Outside World

One way of understanding the Buddhist astronomy movement as an aspect of the modernization of Buddhism is by observing the changes in the outlook of the *bakufu* government, the imperial court, and the peoples of other various regions[9]. Until the time it emerged, the character of the Buddhist world had been taken to be common sense. In this section, I discuss how the world was constructed in the premodern period. Specifically, this "world" was understood as including India, China and Japan. The consciousness of this world was based on the gradual eastward movement of Buddhism to Japan from *Tenjiku* (India), and *Shintan* (China). This cultivated an awareness of, or "view of the three countries" (*sangokukan*) which was also influenced by the concept of *Mappō*, the "final age of the Dharma". *Mappō* was believed to have begun in Japan in 1052 (Eishō 7). Ichikawa Hiroshi has written that a key characteristic of Japan in its transition from the ancient to medieval periods was the emergence of its self-consciousness as a country and as a state, which was triggered by awareness of the outside "world" as represented by *Shintan* and *Tenjiku*. Additionally, there was a remarkable conceptual devaluation of the Korean Peninsula, as well as, in contrast, development of a great respect for India based on religious devotion to Shakamuni[10]. Itō Satoshi has, furthermore, pointed out the importance of the development through translations of Buddhist sutras of an idiosyncratic "view of the three countries" by Tendai monk Jien (1155-1225) from the end of the Heian period to the beginning of the Kamakura period[11].

    This view held that text, and words themselves, derived from the Buddhist sutras, as written in the *Daihan nehan gyō* (Sk. *Mahā parinirvāṇa* sutra: 8.13), and moreover, that Sanskrit characters and the *tensho* form of Chinese characters had been created by a deity descended from above. It was held that, therefore, both were of the same origin. However, in fact India and China each had their own scripts that were not derived, as Japanese was, from Chinese characters, and so this view of language revealed Japan's inferiority complex in relation to the two countries. Monks of the mid-Heian period managed to subsume Sanskrit and *kango* (Japanese words of Chinese origin) into fifty syllables. In doing so, the Japanese language could be counted alongside those of the other two countries. Jien drew on this development and not only tied phonographical Japanese characters to Sanskrit ones but also set Japanese against Chinese as an ideographical language of equal value. This enabled the Japanese language, which had no unique heritage, to be divested of its inferiority complex. The emergence of *shinkoku shisō* (the discourse on the land of the *kami*) drove this forward and, as Itō has shown, it demonstrated endeavors at establishing Japanese superiority precisely through the consciousness of India and China as foreign states.

The eastward transmission of Buddhism through three countries, described above, and the Japanese worldview that was based on this, influenced not only Buddhism itself, but also the production of text and visual culture. *Kango* and *wago* that had come into Japan with Chinese constituted two dimensions of language that helped to disseminate language-borne cultural ideology[12]. The worldview formed through the languages of the three countries, which reached from Japan to China and as far as India, has been described as "a wide geographical space that shifted into the world of the Japanese language[13]".

It was, then, in response to the existence (as it was recognized by Japan) of two other countries that the Japanese consciousness of the world formed. Within Japan, that influence had a wider impact, for it coloured the conception of the *tennō* which the Buddhist world view focused upon and it was, in turn, within an esoteric Buddhist interpretation of the Heian capital that this conception of the *tennō* became possible. The consciousness of the world that was created is profoundly related to the fact that the conceptual framework of the period depended upon a Buddhist worldview. One form of this might be described as "the view of Japanese territory", but the scope to which the conceptual framework was expanded meant that it informed not merely notions related to territory, but also those related to the political authority of the capital and the *tennō*.

2. Methods of Territorial Acquisition: The "Four Seas"

(1) The Usage of the Term "Four Seas"

One of the most direct terms used in medieval Japan to express the concept of "world" was *shikai* (literally, "four seas"). This term was originally used to signify the sea and land that surrounded China[14]. The "Goteitoku" chapter of the Han period text "*Datairaiki*" designated these seas (or regions) of the four directions in the following way: *Yūryō* in the north (present day northeast area of Miyún Prefecture in the province of Hébĕi), Kōshi in the south (present day Southern Vietnam), Ryūsa in the west (present day Gobi and Taklamakan deserts), and Hanboku in the East (described as a mountain in the middle of the Eastern Sea home to the two deities *Shinto* and *Utsuritsu*)[15]. "*Jiga*", the oldest dictionary of China, complied at the beginning of the Han period, gives as an explanation of *shikai* Kyūi, Hatsuteki, Shichijū, and Rokuban, but all these words in fact signify various tribes, and outlying areas. Accordingly, the term *shikai* can be taken to signify "surrounding areas".

In texts of medieval Japan, the word *shikai* can be found in prayer vows (*ganmon*), edicts (*senmyō*), and contracts (*kishōmon*), and in compounds such as "*shikai seihitsu*", "*shikai annei*", "*shikai anzen*", and "*shikai seihei*", all of which mean peaceful rule over, or peace and safety within the "four seas", indicating a use of the word in relation to the concept of "territory". An entry in the Christian church issued Portuguese "Nippo jisho"(Vocabvlario da Lingoa de Iapam) in 1603 (Keichou 8) for "*Xicai. Yotçuno vmi.*" ("*Shikai.* Four seas") defines *shikai* as follows: "The seas of each of the four directions from Miyako [the capital]; *Itten xicai.* The whole world[16]". Here, the meaning of *shikai* is the area north, south, east and west of the capital. In contrast, *shikai* also developed as a Buddhist term. For example, it appears in the ritual manual "*Goshichinichi misuhō yuisho sahō*" as follows:

夫正月後七日御修法者。聖朝地久之御願。四海安寧之祈祷。万菓成就五穀豊饒修法也[17]。

Here, in an esoteric rite, the term is used to mean "surrounding territory". Generally, *shikai*, within the Buddhist worldview, appears to have meant "the whole world". As discussed in the first section of the first part of this essay, the Buddhist composition of the "world" included surging waters surrounding *Shumisen*. This body of water was shikai, and it supported the "world". In around the 4th century in India, the monk Hokken (Faxian, 339?-420?) produced a translation of the *Mahā parinirvāṇa* sutra which contained the following line:

即立太子而以為王。集余大臣及婆羅門長者居士。以四海水灌太子頂[18]。

According to this, a crown prince destined to become king had water of the *shikai* poured upon his head. In this case, the use of the word *shikai* differs from that which was related to a concept of geographical space; it signified the source of the consecration water used in such initiations. Initiation (*kanjō*) was originally a religious ritual that marked, or testified to, the attainment of enlightenment, and the water poured upon the head symbolized the "five awarenesses" (*gochi*. Sk. *pañcajñānani*). Subsequently, however, the term came to mean the conferral of *ajari* (Sk. ācārya) status onto a pupil by his master[19]. There are a considerable number of sacred texts that use the term *shikai* to describe the consecration water used in the accession ceremony of a *Tenrin'ō* (Sk. *Cakravartin*). *Tenrin'ō* (the "Wheel- Turning King"), also called *Tenrin jōō* or *Rin'ō*, was the name for the ideal ruler in ancient India. Shingon Buddhist monk Gōhō (1306-1362), active in the Nanbokucho period, gave the following explanation in his "*Kongōchō shūkō gai*":

譬如転輪聖王将登極時。取四海水請一明師。灌頂加持被印可已。然後登極。爾時四海敬信。萬民承奉。仏亦如是[20]。

The *shikai* mentioned in the first half of this quotation refers to the water used in the accession ceremony of a *Tenrin'ō*. In this way, *shikai* as found in Japanese Buddhist texts means the source of water used for the accession ceremony of a Wheel-Turning King. However, the similarities Japanese rituals had with the ancient Indian ceremony of anointing a ruler upon his accession to the throne largely ended with the pouring of the water[21].

(2) **The Four Seas in the Accession Ritual**

There was a link between the initiation of a *Tenrin'ō* as it appeared in Buddhist scriptures and the accession initiation of the Japanese *tennō*. The latter subject has attracted much scholarly attention in recent years. In Japan, the accession ritual (*Sokui hō*) for an *tennō* (*Sokui kanjō*) involved no consecration water at all. However, the accession rite recorded in temple records included the word *shikai* which was taken to mean "consecration water". The following extract is an explanation of *shikai* in the accession rite from "*Sōjishō*" by the Tendai monk Chōgō (1259-1350):

次四海領掌印。外五古印。自淡路國西海道。次南海道。次東海道。次山陽道。次山陰道。是名四海印[22]。

This section explains the "*shikai ryōshō- in*", a mudra which represented roads leading North, South, East and West. Five roads are given here: the *Saikaidō*, the *Nankaidō*, the *Tōkaidō*, the *Sanyōdō* and the *San'indō*, and together they make the *shikai-in*, (or *shikai* mudra). Such mudra — the flexed finger positions one can see on Buddhist icons —represent the character and qualities of buddhas and bodhisattvas. Here, the *shikai* mudra expressed the character of the *shikai* which itself represented the entirety of Japan's land. In the same text, the concept of *shikai* is explained precisely, as follows:

帝王御即位時。令即大極殿高御蔵（座）。御接録臣（摂籙）。令授帝王。給フ印明也。持十善治天下也。仍以十指懸肩之心。持物荷背負懸肩也。持十善重位。四海七道領掌心也。

The text here relates that on the occasion of accession the *Sekkanke* (Regent) conferred a mudra and a mantra upon the *tennō*, who would be seated upon the *takamikura* seat in the *Daigokuden* (a hall within the imperial palace). The ten precepts (*jūzen*)[23] were taken by the emperor, equipping him to rule the realm. In India, there was a belief that it was the realization in the real world of the ten precepts that legitimized a ruler's authority. Therefore, the form of the *tennō*'s mudra entailed the resting of ten fingers on the shoulder, which represented objects carried, or the "heavy rank of the ten precepts" (or imperial rank). Described in the above text as *shikai shichidō ryōshō shin* (四海七道領掌心) — "the mind that holds the four seas and the seven roads" — this mudra represented the precept-bearing emperor's rule over the realm.

The accession rite was performed when the *tennō* underwent the accession initiation and the procedure of this rite is described in the manual for the initiation. Buddhist teachings refer to this accession rite as *shikai ryōshō hō*, or "Rite of Control over the Four Seas"[24]. In this case, the *shikai* designated an area controlled by the *tennō*. In other words, the "control" of the "four seas" is a conceptual attitude toward territory assigned to the *tennō* within the Buddhist world view which is conferred during the accession rite. Originally, the accession initiation was for the emperor's attainment of the "body" of an esoteric king; it is also known as a rite undertaken in order for the practitioner to achieve identification with *Dainichi Nyorai* (Mahāvairocana). It is thought that the accession initiation began with the accession of Go-sanjo *tennō* in Jishō 4 (1068), in the latter half of the Heian period and that Seison, a *goji* monk (one responsible for prayers for protecting the body of the *tennō*) of the Shingon sect Ono branch, was involved with this particular rite. In the mid-Kamakura period, the Nijō clan, regents to the *tennō*, had the specialized role of conferring the requisite mudra and mantra on the emperor. The accession initiation rite became a regular custom in the late Kamakura period after being performed for

Fushimi *tennō* in Kōan 10 (1287).

The accession initiation rite expressed the symbolic relationship between medieval Buddhism and kingship. The esotericization of the *tennō* that occurred during it is a subject that has inspired scholarly interest. However, at the same time, the rite also expressed the *tennō*'s assumption of territorial control: the land over which the emperor was to rule was absorbed into an esoteric framework just as his own body was. As previously mentioned, the *Jiga* dictionary defined *shikai* as "outlying" and "unfamiliar" territories. For the ancient Chinese, the ocean that surrounded the land was called the *shikai*, and along with the expansion of occupied land it gradually came to be perceived of as not a conceptual but a real, geographical area[25].

(3) **The Tennō's Four Seas**

The region signified by *shikai* in the imperial accession rite was, as mentioned in the previous section, one made up of the *Saikaidō*, the *Nankaidō*, the *Tōkaidō*, the *Sanyōdō* and the *San'indō*. Japanese maps, including the best-known, *Gyōki-zu* (named so because it was believed to have been made by the monk Gyōki), show a radiation of line-drawn roads leading North, South, East and West outward from the Yamato capital. The geography of the maps made in the medieval period likewise emphasised roads linking and relating to the capital and this reveals a certain type of territorial consciousness[26]. The following extract, from the Nanbokucho period work *Keiranshūyōshū* by the Tendai monk Kōshū (1276-1350) exhibits the conceptual links between the *shikai* of the accession ritual and geographical roads:[27]

一、国土衆生皆曼荼羅界会聖衣也。国ニ有五畿七道。五畿ト者胎藏ノ五大法界ヲ表シ。七道ト者悉地ノ七識和合ヲ表ス。都ニ有九重。金界ノ九表ス。天子即位ノ時四海領掌ノ印結ヒ金輪王ノ位ニ居シ給也。故ニ以金輪ノ法名四海統領灌頂ト事深可思合之ヲ。又此外ニ覚大師弘法大師ノ秘決等二十五巻有之口伝ト云云。

The text allocates the "five regions" and the "seven roads", along with the *dairi* (Imperial Palace) to sections of an esoteric Buddhist mandala. In this scheme, the "five regions" are equated with the "womb" (of the Womb World Mandala), the "seven roads" with the *shijji* (Sk. *Siddhi;* supernatural powers attained through esoteric practice), and the capital city as *kyūchō* (that is, the *dairi* in the capital city) is equated with the Diamond World (of the Diamond World Mandala). At a crown prince's accession, the *shikai ryōshō* mudra is made, and the rank of *konrinō* (Ruler of the Four Seas) is attained. This is called "*shikai tōryō kanjō*" ("Initiation of the Ruler of the Four Seas") and, it is here claimed, it was performed according to an oral transmission passed down from Jikaku Daishi (Ennin) and Kōbō Daishi (Kūkai). The "four seas" (*shikai*) of this "Ruler of the Four Seas" signified the territory to be ruled by the *tennō*: the five regions, seven roads, capital and imperial palace as they were located within a mandala. The *Nihon ryakki*, a text thought to have been produced in the premodern period, also clearly reflects such notions:[28]

一、内裏は忝も十善の御位なれば、日本の主にて<u>一天四海</u>にかしづかれ給ひ、六十余州より崇敬申は、王土に住居する故也。又、公方様は帝王の御代官として、天下の将軍として日本の政所と号し、又、御所と申す。

The *dairi*, here identified with the *tennō*, is decribed as the "lord" of Japan who governs "heaven and the four seas" (*itten shikai*), and is revered by the entirety of Japan because he lives in the "kingdom" (literally, "king's land", *ōdo*). The Shogun rules as his public representative and is also regarded as "Gosho". This text supplements the concepts explained in the previously quoted texts by adding the Shogun to the equation. It describes the authorial rulers of the "kingdom" as it appears in the Buddhist worldview, and within this appears once more the term *shikai*.

3. Heian-kyō as the World

(1) The Capital in the Mandalas of the Two Worlds

As discussed in part 2, the term *shikai* appears in texts to describe the *tennō*'s territorial control. Furthermore, in medieval Japan, there was a Buddhist ritual in which the *tennō* and the capital were identified as "one body". In this section, I address the esoteric interpretation of not only the *tennō* but also of the capital. The source I employ, a sacred text (*shōgyō*) entitled "*Gojisō sahō*" has been analysed by Uejima Susumu as a text that presents an esoteric interpretation of (state) land in the Heian period[29]. It is a textual record of oral transmissions passed to the monk Shōgaku (1057-1129) by his master in Eikyū 3 (1115), and the section quoted delineates a visualization of Heian-kyō, the capital city.

観想、自一条至九条、配当八葉九尊、又自西大宮至東京極、観十三大院、四方四角可配分護世八天、九重中上下人民悉想胎蔵界四重曼荼羅之聖衆、

In this visualization, the units in which the capital is laid out are equated to sections of a mandala: the area stretching from (street) units *ichijō* to *kujō*, is allocated to the *hachiyō kuson* ("eight petals, nine worthies") in the central section of the Womb World (Sk. Garbhadhātu) Mandala. The roads running east and west are similarly identified, but as the *jūsan daiin* (the "13 great palaces") of the mandala. Furthermore, the four corners of the capital mimic those of the mandala, and the *hatten* ("eight devas") are stationed here. The residents of the capital are seen as *seishū* (holy people). In the same text, a mudra related to this composition is explained as meaning "*kyūjō annon taihei*" (宮城安穏太平) ("safety and peace at the palace") and "*chichū oaku kaisan*" (地中穢悪皆散) ("dispersion of all impurity and wickedness in the earth").

The mandalaic composition of the capital, Heian-kyō, can be said to be an esoteric interpretation of the city, and this hermeneutic is itself a core characteristic of esoteric Buddhism. However, this was not simply a matching of the mandala form and content to that of the city; it was also a way of protecting the city. Table 1 shows how the specific allocation of elements was carried out: the streets of Heian-kyō running (horizontally) from north to south were affiliated with buddhas of the mandala, and the streets running from east to west were affiliated with various spaces in the mandala. This exercise should perhaps have logically assigned the left (east) and right (west) sides of the city to the two mandala "worlds" — the Womb World and the Diamond World (Sk. Vajradhātu). However, the spatial units into which the city was divided were too few on the west side to match spaces in the mandala so the imperial palace was made to stand for the Diamond World Mandala. This accords with the "*Chiteiki*", written by Yoshishige no Yasutane (993-1002) in Tengen 5 (982), which states that the left side of the city represented prosperity and the right, decline[30], and therefore the eastern part of the capital could be visualised as the Womb World and the imperial palace as the Diamond World. He wrote that the nonduality was to be deeply visualised ("*ryōbu funi fukaku kore aru wo miru*").

According to Kamikawa Michio, Heian-kyō at the end of the Heian period was idealized as an exotic international city with a politically-inclined Song-style

Tab. 1 Layout of Heian-Kyo and Mandala (Kyuchō layout) [This table is taken from Uejima Susumu's "Nihon chūsei no Kami kannen to Kokudo kan" in Nihon chūsei shakai no keisei to ōken]

South-North streets of the capital	The 13 Palaces of the Taizōkai Mandala	East-West streets of the capital	The Eight Petals and Nine Worthies of the Taizōkai Mandala
Ōmiya	Shidaigoin	Ichijō	Hōdō
Inokuma	Kongōbuin	Nijō	Kaishiki
Horikawa	Jogaishōin	Sanjō	Muryō
Aburanokōji	Monjuin	Shijō	Tenku
Nishinotōin	Henchiin	Gojō	Henshō Nyorai
Kawaramachi	Soshitsujiin	Rokujō	Fugen
Muromachi	Hachiyōin	Shichijō	Monju
Karasuma	Godaiin	Hachijō	Kannon
Higashinotōin	Shakain	Kujō	Miroku
Takakura	Jizōin		
Marikōji	Rengebuin		
Tomikōji	Kokūzōin		
Kyōgoku	Gaibuin		

Buddhism. In keeping with this, an idealized and perfect existence was projected onto the *tennō*, that of *konrinjōō*. In reality, the imperial figure failed to exercise any actual power. The idea of the *tennō* as *hōō* (Dharma King) was the ideal kingly head of a political group (*kokuō*). Such idealizations legitimized medieval Buddhism and helped to form the "country of Japan" (*Nihon koku*)[31].

(2) **Esoteric Buddhism and the Tennō**

If the capital city was presented as the esoteric mandalas of the two worlds, the *tennō* himself was also incorporated into that esoteric world. As discussed in the second part of this essay, the *tennō* was conceived of as ideal king of ancient India — the Wheel-Turning King, and in the accession rite as performed by Buddhist monks, the water of the "four seas" to be poured upon this monarch's head was conceptualised not as consecration water but as the territory over which the ruler was to lead. The *tennō* was identified with the capital city via the logic of the mandalas of the two worlds. These concepts clarified the esoteric interpretation of the *tennō*. If the existential territory of the *tennō* was expressed through an esoteric world view, how was the *tennō* himself represented?

Shōkaku's "*Gojisō sahō*", the text presented in the previous section, contains the following statement:

当代国主金輪正王也、聖王即日天子御胤子、彼是一躰無二、而更無差異、故国主玉躰御心中有万法能生अ字、

The ruler of the realm *kokushu* (国主) is here equated with the *konrinjōō* (金輪聖王), which is, in turn, equated with the *nittenshi goinshi* (日天子御胤子), the descendent of the sun-ruler. These together represent "the non-dual one body," *ittai funi* (一体不二); the unconditioned state. Within the mind of the jade-body (*gyokutai* 玉躰) of the ruler, the entire universe is integrated into the Sanskrit letter अ, as it is more widely in esoteric Buddhism. The *tennō* is visualized as one with the Sanskrit letter अ, and is thus he is conceived to be one with the cosmos. However, even though the Buddhist world view posited the *tennō* as this all-powerful and transcendental being, he wielded no mundane (secular) authority. In other words, this was a construction of the *tennō* that served to legitimize medieval Buddhism, and even if he was presented as an esoteric king, he had no unique transcendental power within the Buddhist world.

Conclusion

The new world view that swept into Japan with Copernican theory in the modern period dealt a blow to the previously dominant Buddhist view and galvanized the development of Buddhist astronomy. However, the premodern worldview with the *tennō* at its centre was constructed within a Buddhist system of medieval era values, and was formed in accordance with new concepts. The imperial palace in the capital was the centre of purity, and there was a notion, rooted in concepts of territorial boundaries, that impurity passed from Yamato into the rest of Japan. In the medieval period, the capital was thought to be delimited by a boundary called *shikai shikyō* (四堺四境). More widely, Japan as a whole was bordered by *shiishi* (四至). That which was contained within these boundaries was the land over which the *tennō* ruled. However, the world in which the body of the *tennō* and Heian-kyō were embodied by the non-dual Mandalas of the Two Worlds could only be effective within a world of values that regarded Buddhism as absolute.

Like the body of the *tennō*, the imperial palace was visualised esoterically. By Tentoku 4 (960) it had repeatedly burned to the ground and been rebuilt. After a fire in Antei 1 (1227) reconstruction ceased altogether. Like the lost imperial palace, the capital city and the body of the medieval *tennō* were conceived of within an esoteric framework. From the mid-Kamakura period onward, the imperial line split into the Jimyōin line and the Daikakuji line; emperors of what became the Northern and Southern Courts took turns to occupy the throne. The esoteric concept of the "non-dual two worlds" had disintegrated at its root. Buddhism in the medieval period assigned an indisputable and absolute meaning to the capital and the emperor, and the reason this was possible was that Buddhism supplemented a world in which the *tennō* and the capital exercised no real power or authority. Buddhism had given significance to his existence in each historical period. Such significance supported the people's consciousness of the outside world (that is, the conceptual "three countries") because the *tennō* was placed within the mandalaic scheme and the capital of Japan was relativized within the triad of countries. Yet in reality the *tennō* and capital were dissociated from these countries.

However, in the first year of the Genkō era (1331), Kōgon *tennō* of the Northern Court made the *Tsuchimikado higashi no tōin* Palace his imperial seat. It had originally been a substitute imperial palace and its site is where the present-day palace in Kyoto is located. The imperial palace and the *tennō*, had for but a moment in time been assigned absolute meaning, but in the real change of the city's composition, the city and emperor as constructed in a medieval esoteric view became a thing of the past.

The Buddhist worldview was irrevocably changed by *Bonreki* and the importation of Western astronomy in the modern period. Just as the location of the palacewas changed during the medieval period, the values of an imagined conceptual world constructed through religion were also altered in confrontation with the "real" world. From the medieval period onward, the consciousness of the world as constructed through the Buddhist worldview developed and changed in various ways up until the modern period. After the *Bonreki* movement had come to an end, the Buddhist worldview seemed less credible than ever as an organizational system. However, the essence of this Buddhist worldview did not depend on notions of reality and non-reality: it was an all-encompassing system that had had the power to temporarily shape society in a certain period.

(1) Kawakami Michio, Chūsei bukkyō to Nihon koku. In *Nihon chūsei bukkyō keiseishiron*. Azekura shobō, 2007.

(2) Kazutaka Unno, Ikkan minzoku no chiri shisō — toku ni sono chūsei-kan ni tsuite. In *Chiri no shisō*. Chijin shobō, 1982, p.70; Aoki Hirō, Zen kindai chizu kenkyū no mesodorojii. In *Zen kindai chizu no kūkan to chi*. Azekura shobō, 2007.

(3) Ayusawa Shintarō, Sakoku jidai ni kankō sareta bankoku jinbutsu zu. In *Nishikawa Joken no sekai chiri kenkyū*. Keiseisha shuppanbu, 1944)

(4) In *Nara kokuritsu hakubutsukan tokubetsuten: Tenjiku-e: Sanzō Hōshi san man kiro no tabi*. Nara kokuritsu hakubutsukan, 2011.

(5) In the Ayusawa Shintarō Collection (*Ayusawa Shintarō bunko*), Yokohama City University.

(6) Okada Masahiko, Kigen / honshitsu no tankyū to fuhen shugi no disukūru: Fumon Entsū "Bukkoku rekishō-ron" wo yomu. In *Wasurerareta bukkyō tenmongaku - jūkyūseiki no Nihon ni okeru bukkyō sekai-zō*. Buitsū soryūshon, 2011, p.44.

(7) Okada Masahiko, Kindai nihon shisōshi to bonreki undō: kindai-teki jinenkan to shūkyō gensetsu. In *Wasurerareta bukkyō tenmongaku - jūkyūseiki no Nihon ni okeru bukkyō sekai-zō*. (See note 6).

(8) Okada Masahiko, Ibid., note 6, p.38.

(9) Inoue Tomokatsu, Bakumatsuishin-ki no bukkyō tenmongaku to shakai chiiki. In *Meijiishin to bunka*, ed. Meijiishin kenkyūkai. Yoshikawa kōbunkan, 2005.

(10) Ichikawa Hiroshi, Nihon chūsei zen'ya no "uchinaru Sangoku" no shisō. In *Nihon chūsei no hikari to kage: "Uchinaru Sangoku" no shisō*. Perikansha, 1999, p.14.

(11) Itō Satoshi, Bon kan wa dōitsu-kan no seiritsu kiban. In *Chūsei amaterasuōkami shinkō no kenkyū*. Hōzōkan, 2010.

(12) Takahashi Kimiaki, Higashi ajia to chūsei bungaku. In *Iwanami kōza Nihon bungaku-shi* vol. 5. Iwanami shoten, 1995.

(13) Takahashi Kimiaki, Ibid., note 12, p. 312.

(14) In the entry for "Shikai" in Shōgakukan's *Nihon Kokugo Daijiten* dictionary are found the following definitions: 1) The seas in the four directions, 2) Domestic; within the country; the world; the realm, 3) Foreign countries in the four directions [of Japan]; the surroundings of the country; wild, foreign lands; the sea surrounding Shumisen. The definitions given here are interpretations of the way the word was used. This aim of this paper, however, is to clarify through an examination of the

usage of the term "*shikai*" in medieval Buddhist texts the framework of the *shikai* as is was actually understood by people.

(15) In Kurihara Keisuke, *Shinshaku kanbun taikei 113: Datairaiki*. Meiji Shoin, 1991. Please note that sections of quoted texts highlighted by underlining here and elsewhere are all by the author of this essay.

(16) VOCABVLARIO DA LINGOA DE IAPAN com a declareção em Portugs, Houyaku nichipo jisho, Iwanami shoten, 1980, p.759.

(17) In Shōken ki, Shūkaku shū, Hishō. *Taishō shinshū daizō kyō* 78:2489.

(18) In Daihan nehan kyō, (translated by Hōken).*Taishō shinshū daizō kyō* 1:0007.

(19) See Mori Masahide, Abishe-ka girei no kigen to hensen. In *Indo mikkyō no girei sekai*. Sekai shisō-sha, 2011.

(20) In *Taishō shinshū daizō kyō* 77:2451.

(21) Mori Masahide, Abishe-ka to puratishutaa. (In *Indo mikkyō no girei sekai*. Ibid. note 19, p.192.)

(22) In Sōjishō (compiled by Chōgō). *Taishō shinshū daizō kyō* 77:2412.

(23) Jūzen, the ten precepts which are divided into those concerning the body, the speech and the mind, and are as follows: to refrain from the taking of life, from stealing, from engaging in improper sexual activity, from lying, from equivocation, from slander, from misleading speech, from greed, from anger, and from wrong views.

(24) Matsumoto Ikuyo, *Chūsei ōken to sokuikanjō - shōgyō no naka no rekishi jujutsu*. Shinwasha, 2005.

(25) Kimura Hiroshi, Jūrokuseiki izen Chūgokujin no nankai chiiki ni kan suru chiriteki chishiki. In *Chiri no shisō*, ed. Kyōto Daigaku bungakubu chiri gakukyōshitsu. Chijin shobō, 1982, pp.108-109.

(26) Murai Shōsuke, Chūsei Nihon rettō no chiiki kūkan to kokka. In *Ajia no naka no chūsei Nihon*. Aekura shobō, 1988.

(27) Dai yon kinrin hō no koto. In *Keiranshūyōshū*. (*Taishō shinshū daizō kyō* 76:2410.)

(28) In *Zoku zoku gunshoruijū* 8: *chiribu*. The colophon gives the dates Bunroku 5 (1595), Keichō 13 (1608), and Genbun 5 (1740). It is thought to have been produced before 1595.

(29) This document is number 17-2 of the sacred texts of Zuishinin temple and it was first introduced in Nihon chūsei no kami kannen to kokudokan (In *Nihon chūsei shakai no keisei to ōken*) by Uejima Susumu (Nagoya Daigaku Shuppanbu, 2011, pp. 406-411).

(30) In Kojima Noriyuki, *Nihon koten bungaku taikei 69: Kaifusō bunka shūreishū honchō monzui*, Iwanami shoten, 1964.
(31) See Kawakami Michio, Chūsei bukkyō to Nihon koku (In *Nihon chūsei bukkyō keiseishiron*. Ibid., note 1), p.271.

Translated by Elizabeth Tinsley

Chap.12 The Art of the Maruyama-Shijō School in 19th century Britain: British Collectors on Kyoto Painters

■Princess Akiko of Mikasa

Introduction

It is well-known that after Japan's opening to the West in 1858 (Ansei 5), a great many Japanese paintings and prints were collected and taken overseas by visiting foreigners. Woodblock prints and paintings of the "floating world" (*ukiyo-e*) were exported in especially large numbers, and since they exerted an influence on late Impressionism they came to largely represent Japanese art to the western audience.

However, the fact that such works were exported overseas does not necessarily mean that they were highly regarded there. Most of the very few westerners who were able to travel to Japan in the nineteenth century had been dispatched in order to bring knowledge of an "unknown land" back to their own countries. The works collected were samples required for understanding an unfamiliar culture and their quality was not an issue[1]. In other words, the presence of Japanese works in foreign collections cannot be attributed to their quality.

Nonetheless, except for research that deals with the woodblock print genre, there is very little scholarly work which addresses the evaluation of Japanese art in nineteenth century Europe. This paper, therefore, discusses the British understanding of Japanese paintings from between the end of the nineteenth and the early twentieth century, based on essays on the subject published in Britain. Since the scope of this study does not allow for the examination of Japanese art in general, it focuses on the appreciation of paintings by the Maruyama-Shijō school, a relatively highly regarded school whose works were among those that made up the collections in Britain during the nineteenth century.

The Maruyama- Shijō school - known by British collectors of the time simply as the "Shijō School" - was a Kyoto-based school of painters that flourished from the second half of the eighteenth century to the nineteenth century. The Maruyama School, founded by Maruyama Ōkyo (1733-1795) and the Shijō School, founded by Go Shun (1752-1811), who was close to and influenced by Ōkyo, were as a pair called the Maruyama- Shijō School. This school rejected the traditional *funpon* practice (the use of copybooks) of which such schools as the Kano were representative, and aimed to represent objects realistically. It is known for its role in the modernization of Japanese painting. Its modern and realistic expression which differed so significantly from the classical styles favoured by the Kano School and *Yamato-e* painting was extremely popular among nineteenth century British art collectors. For example, in 1880 the British illustrator Frank Dillon (1823-1909) published a collection of autotype reproductions of Japanese "naturalistic" paintings[2]. Another figure discussed in this paper, William Gowland (1842-1922), who had been sent to Japan as an *o-yatoi gaikokujin* (a foreign employee of the Japanese government) gave a lecture in 1892 on "The Naturalistic Art of Japan" at the Japan Society in London[3]. This "naturalistic" art was the art of the Maruyama- Shijō School and as a type of Japanese art it attracted particular attention from abroad.

The paper examines the written works on the Maruyama-Shijō School by three British collectors: William Anderson (1842-1900), William Gowland, and Earnest Hart (1835-1898). Each of the three men as collectors had their own perspectives and objectives. I hope in this paper to clarify what it was that they sought in, or that drew them to, the art of the Maruyama- Shijō School.

1. The Collectors

William Anderson was an English surgeon employed as a professor of anatomy and surgery at the Imperial Naval Medical College. He lived in Japan for nearly seven years as a so-called *o-yatoi gaikokujin* and in addition to educating a great many medical students, he also conducted research on beriberi and was involved in cholera prevention work. He contributed significantly to advances in Japanese medicine. However, alongside his work as a surgeon, Anderson was a passionate collector of Japanese paintings and in 1881 he donated a collection of over three thousand pieces to the British Museum.

The second collector, William Gowland, was, like Anderson, appointed as an *o-*

yatoi gaikokujin, but had been dispatched a year before him. Since the periods of their residencies overlapped the two men likely knew each other. Gowland worked for sixteen years at the new Imperial Mint in Osaka, and dispensed advice on metallurgy and the production of new coinage. During his period of employment he was appointed advisor to the commissioner at the mint and special advisor on metallurgy to the war ministry. However, Gowland is better known as an amateur archeologist. Throughout the sixteen years he spent in Japan, he documented burial mounds of the Kofun period in the Kinki region as well as in Fukushima and Miyazaki prefectures. Artefacts he collected in relation to these activities were purchased by the British Museum in 1879, and of these the extant status of 140 detailed maps of ancient sites is confirmed. Unfortunately, his other great collection, of Maruyama-Shijo School paintings, has been dispersed. Many were sold in Japan during the First World War, and Gowland donated the proceeds to the British government[4].

Earnest Hart was another collector of Japanese art. Originally an eye doctor, Hart began working as a medical journalist after being made editor of the British Medical Journal in 1858. We do not know how he developed his interest in Japanese art, but he travelled extensively to the Far East during his profession as a journalist[5].

The key figure in bringing these three characters of very disparate backgrounds together into the field of Japanese art was William Anderson. Anderson published *Descriptive and Historical Catalogue of a Collection of Japanese and Chinese Paintings in the British Museum*, and *The Pictorial Arts of Japan*, which were both based on his own research on Japanese art. Both works were well received and became authoritative books on Japanese art in the West.

As mentioned above, in 1892 Gowland delivered a lecture at the Japan Society in London on "The Naturalistic Art of Japan" in conjunction with an exhibition of the Gowland Collection of Japanese paintings. At this time he mentioned that his lecture had been made possible by Anderson's work, and that it was of immeasurable importance to researchers and lovers of Japanese art[6]. In the preface to the reprint of lectures on Japanese art given for the Society for the Encouragement of Arts, Manufactures, and Commerce in 1886, Earnest Hart said that he had received generous encouragement from Anderson and he praised what Anderson had done for the study of Japanese painting[7]. It is clear from this that both Gowland and Hart were indebted to Anderson in terms of their understanding of Japanese art. In particular, they adopted Anderson's classification of painting schools[8].

At the time when Anderson was amassing his collection of paintings there was no such thing as "Japanese art history" in Japan. Though there were writings on the Kanō school and the makers of *ukiyo-e*, as well as biographies of artists, there were no comprehensive surveys of Japanese art in either Japanese or English. Anderson had collected a great many paintings and had applied a Western, scientific classification system to Japanese painting. To the complex history of Japanese painting he fitted a system of periodic divisions from ancient to modern. He also distinguished paintings into schools[9]. Gowland and Hart also hailed from scientific backgrounds and would no doubt have found Anderson's methodology conducive to understanding Japanese art.

2. A Scientific Eye

In their publications, Anderson, Gowland, and Hart all gave detailed explanations of the characteristics and representatives of each school and made careful observations on particular works. While they were generally fairly positive in their evaluations, they could occasionally be quite severely critical. On *Yamato-e*, for example, Anderson rather harshly wrote,

> The characteristics of the pure Yamato style are quite distinctive when taken collectively, but present no striking elements of originality upon analysis... It is probable, however, that the doll-like imbecility of their portraiture of the lords and ladies who represented the high culture of old Kioto was rather the fault of a tradition than of a lack of artistic discrimination..."[10]

Hart, also addressing *Yamato* painting, writes,

> ...with few exceptions, I cannot profess to feel myself in sympathy with the work of this [Yamato-Tosa] school of artists, and in showing you some of their productions I do so as a matter of at least as much archaeological as purely artistic merit[11].

For his part, on the Kōrin School, Anderson expressed his rather harsh opinion that,

In his delineations of the human figure and quadrupeds, however, his [Kōrin's] daring conventionality converts some of his most serious motives almost into caricature. His men and women had often little more shape or expression than indifferently-made dolls, and his horses and deer were like painted toys...[12]

The critics shared a common aversion to the somewhat abstract elements of *Yamato-e* and *Rinpa* art. Anderson, who had studied Western art, repeatedly criticised the lack of shading, perspective, and anatomical accuracy in Japanese art[13]. It seems that he simply could not comprehend an art that appeared to disregard consistency of size or composition, as exemplified in the caricature-like muscles on actors in *ukiyo-e* prints, aspects which totally contrasted with Western conventions that stressed realistic representation. On the other hand, the harmonization of colour and the effect of the white of snow that was achieved without using painting tools but simply by layering and leaving the paint was - while "unscientific" - praised as "a technique brimming with creativity and skill" and an expression of the Japanese poetic sense[14]. The scientifically-minded Anderson's most positive evaluation was reserved for the Maruyama-Shijō School: he devoted an entire chapter to it in *The Pictorial Arts of Japan*, while mentions of other schools were spread throughout the book. It is the reason for this to which I now wish to turn.

3. Naturalistic or not Naturalistic? From the perspective of Western art appreciation.

In the opening to the fourth section of *The Pictorial Arts of Japan*, Anderson describes the defining characteristics of Japanese painting as follows:

> The ideal of the Japanese painter differs in so many respects from that of his European *confrère*, that it is not possible to adopt the same standard of criticism for the works that express the aesthetic instincts of the two races[15].

Such a relativistic understanding of Japanese painting as Anderson here displays was quite rare in a Westerner of the time. However, it seems that he (along with Gowland and Hart) could not accept certain characteristics related to realistic representation that he deemed lacking, such as chiaroscuro and perspective. The evaluations of the three men constantly revolved around the question of whether a work was "naturalistic" or "not naturalistic". They explained works with frequent use of the terms "naturalism" and "naturalistic", investigating whether the subject had been rendered realistically or not, if it had been copied from a painting copybook, and if it were anatomically correct[16]. Anderson's explanation of Sesshū (1420-1506), below, is a good example of these preoccupations:

> His observation of nature was evident, especially in his landscape sketches; but he sought to produce reminiscences or general impressions rather than direct transcripts of reality[17].

Gowland quoted Anderson's comment in his lecture on the Naturalistic School and, while showing actual works by Sesshū, he added,

> In these two landscapes much of the detail is left to the imagination of the beholder, and it is difficult for us to understand how the terms "natural" or "lifelike," so frequently applied by Japanese critics to Sesshū's work, could be used for such sketchy pictures as these[18].

Regardless of whether or not Sesshū's work indeed was naturalistic, it did not appear to be so to these figures who were accustomed to Western art. In other words, Western art was for them the standard by which other art was to be measured. Anderson stated that the characteristics and "wit" of the works of Hanabusa Itchō (1652-1724), was too national in character to be fully understood or appreciated outside Japan[19]. He also tended to compare Japanese painters to European ones. The early Muromachi painter-monk Minchō (1352-1431) was compared to early Renaissance artist Fra Angelico (c.1390/5-1455);[20] Mori Sosen (1747-1821), who boasted fame for his lifelike pictures of monkeys is placed alongside Edwin Landseer (1802-1873), an artist whose paintings of animals were highly praised. From a comparison of Landseer's "Shepherd's Last Mourner" and "Jack in Office", Anderson determined that Sosen was the lesser talent[21]. On the other hand, he added that Sosen's work approached more nearly European standards than any other Japanese artist, and pointed out that many forgeries of Sosen's work had flooded the European market[22]. All this shows the tendency of the three collectors to evaluate Japanese painting based on their comparison of it with Western art.

Anderson, who had received an education in Western art, felt that Japanese artists were too concerned with copying the works of their masters or copybooks, instead of painting from life. Even in the west, copying from a master was an important part of an artist's education. Rubens (1577-1640) copied Titian (c.1488/90-1576), Michelangelo (1475-1564) copied Caravaggio (1571-1610), and Delacroix (1798-1863) copied Rubens. But according to the Grove Dictionary of Art, the study of the art of the past was a means of embodying 'an objective standard of excellence.'[23] In other words, in the Western art education system, copying was intended only to supplement what a school could not teach.

For Anderson and other British collectors, whose knowledge of art was heavily based on Western standards, the Maruyama-Shijō School's "realistic" art came closest to Western ideals, and was therefore the easiest to understand. This is indicated by Hart when he said: "I think no picture in my collection attracts more general admiration from the quite uninitiated observer than do these products of the brush of the naturalistic school".[24]

4. The Englishman's View of the Maruyama-Shijo School: the accounts of Anderson, Gowland, and Hart.

The predominant characteristic of the art of the Maruyama- Shijō school is its realism. Anderson acknowledged that the Kano School, *Yamato-e* painters and others had made some attempts at painting from life, but considered them to have failed to reach a high standard. According to him, the first artist to approach realistic representation based on actual knowledge was Maruyama Ōkyo[25]. He wrote as follows:

> The chief characteristics of the Shijō School are a graceful, flowing outline, freed from the arbitrary mannerisms of touch indulged in by many of the older masters; comparative, sometimes almost absolute, correctness in the interpretation of the forms of animal life; and lastly, a light colouring, suggestive of the prevailing tones of the objects depicted, and full of delicate harmonies and gradations[26].

Gowland explained that the differences between the Shijō School and older schools derived not only from the first principle of its teaching (*shasei*, or 'painting from life') but also from the subjects and techniques in which it specialized as well as the social positions of its students and followers[27]. He specified four characteristics of the art of the school. Firstly, students had been instructed to address nature as a model directly and had not been compelled to make use of traditional brush techniques. Secondly, the subjects of the school were quite different from those of other schools: far rarer were subjects drawn from mythology and history, that is, subject matter derived from Chinese art[28]. Because Shijō School painters found sufficient inspiration in quiet beauty and in the charms of Kyoto they had no need to rely upon Chinese subject matter. The third feature of the school was that its ateliers were open to all regardless of social status; in this respect it differed from the Kano and Tosa Schools which required its students to have certain family affiliations. Fourthly, the Shijō School avoided the use of old-fashioned, heavy body colouring and adopted delicate tones and washes to produce harmonious and satisfying effects[29]. Based on these four features, Gowland concluded that the Shijō School was unquestionably the most excellent and worthy of all the schools[30].

Referring to his own collection of paintings by Ōkyo, Hart similarly extended the highest praise:

> You will see how far he departed from the traditions of the Chinese school in which he was probably bred; how true he was to nature; how perspective of the grace of animal forms, how refined and harmonious in colour, and how just in balance[31].

Anderson, Gowland, and Hart all lauded the school's pioneering efforts to depart from Chinese traditions and paint subjects from life. However, at the same time they criticized the naturalism of the school for not being quite realistic enough. Anderson remarked:

> Notwithstanding the credit due to Ōkio, his works show that he lacked the full courage of his conviction. His drawings is often faithful to the life, even in the smallest details... but he still sacrificed, perhaps almost unconsciously, at the altar of old faith[32].

He continued:

> The naturalistic principle of the school, however, was incompletely developed: the effects of chiaroscuro were often obtained with much success, yet high lights, reflected lights, and projected shadows were still unrecognized, and both perspective and anatomy were neglected as absolutely as by the old painters...[33]

Gowland stated that old mannerisms from Ōkyo's early period of training could be detected in his work[34]. In his lecture he discussed a piece from his own collection of Ōkyo's paintings, *Wild Geese*, and concluded that while the action of the birds was filled with lively movement, the picture was not quite free of Chinese conventions, particularly in its depiction of waves and moss[35]. Each of the collectors in their own way praised the fact that the Maruyama-Shijō artists painted from life, yet the results were deemed insufficient, and the lack of perspective and chiaroscuro which were taken to be standard in Western art was the object of harsh criticism.

One of the biggest differences between Western art and Japanese art of that period was that while in the West artists tried to view their subjects according to anatomical theory and reproduce them as accurately as possible, in Japan the very idea of this did not exist. This is why the bodies of humans and animals in Japanese art were not depicted according to standards based on anatomical correctness in the Western sense. And this was an aspect of the art that the British collectors were unable to accept.

Nevertheless, painters of the Maruyama- Shijō School had attempted to study nature and paint from life rather than from copybooks. This was closer to Western painting methods. Gowland's assessment that Ōkyo was "the first artist for many centuries to study natural objects themselves, and not conventional drawings of them, and thus to represent Nature faithfully in his paintings"[36] was reflective of the collectors' opinion that the fidelity to life displayed by an artistic representation was the measure of the success of an artist: Ōkyo was, in their eyes, a pioneer. This is the main reason why the paintings of the Maruyama-Shijō School were so highly praised by the British collectors.

Conclusion

As I have shown, the three British collectors held the Maruyama- Shijō School and Maruyama Ōkyo in high regard, yet this value-laden judgment was based on the school's fulfillment of criteria set by Western art which they considered to be standard. Yet, it may also be pointed out that these opinions nonetheless reflected the acceptance in nineteenth century England of a school of painting from but a small country in the Far East as one that could be positioned within the context of Western art. William Anderson's comments after William Gowland's lecture on the Maruyama-Shijō School demonstrates this thinking:

It is the Naturalistic School of Painting that, for us, gives Japanese Pictorial Art its most distinctive and admirable stamp of character... Limited as was the naturalism of Ōkio and his school, in so far as they attempted to reproduce nature they did so with an honesty and with accuracy of observation as satisfying to the mind of the scientist as their beauty of line is acceptable to the eye of the artist[37].

The naturalism of the Maruyama-Shijō school may not have been naturalistic "enough" but it nonetheless satisfied the scientists and artists of the west, and this was grounds enough for elevating it to the highest position in the rankings of Japanese art. Earnest Hart concurred with Anderson, remarking:

It is easy to, therefore, to be critical as to the absence of characteristics which we have a right to expect in European pictures, but which are intentionally absent from the old Japanese *kakemono*. The most beautiful Japanese pictures can only give us what they have of intention and of artistic method. But if we look at them subject to knowledge and sympathy with their spirit and conception, with their tradition and limitations, we shall find...that even the most archaic are not the least beautiful."[38]

Hart did not judge Japanese art within an unyielding framework based on Western standards. He viewed it according to its own spirit and traditions, and even draws attention to the erroneous thinking underlying such judgment. To evaluate

Japanese art and comprehend it without using Western concepts was nothing short of progressive for a Westerner of the time.

The collectors' evaluations of Japanese painting, especially that of the Maruyama-Shijō School, were fundamentally based on Western ideals, but it is also evident that they nonetheless made efforts to understand it in their own individual ways. Gowland concluded his lecture by commenting that he hoped the Maruyama-Shijō School would advance its reputation and reach the position it deserved among the great art schools of the Western world. The collectors were asserting that Japanese art could take its place in the hierarchy of Western art. Because the works of the Maruyama-Shijō School exhibited a naturalism that made it palatable to Western taste it was the most appropriate for demonstrating that Japanese art did not trail behind that of the West. This is one of the reasons why the collectors amassed the school's works, praised it, and devoted much space in their publications to explaining it. And so it was that one of the beginnings of the elevation of Japanese art to compete with Western art was a single Kyoto atelier – that of the Maruyama-Shijō School.

(1) Princess Akiko of Mikasa. "From Specimen to Artwork: The Anderson Collection and the Significance of 19th Century Japanese Art Collections". *Kokka*, 1360. 2009, pp. 28-39.

(2) Dillon, Frank. *Drawings by Japanese Artists; Reproduced and Coloured in Facsimile by the Autotype Process*. London: Hogarth, 1880.

(3) Gowland, William. 'The Naturalistic Art of Japan', *Transactions and Proceedings of the Japan Society*, vol. 1, London: Kegan Paul, Trench, Trübner and Co. Ltd., 1892, pp 73-110.

(4) Ueda Hironori. William Gowland shōden. In Ueda Hironori ed. W. Gowland. *Nihon Kofun bunkaron: Gowland Kōkoronshu*. Sōgensha, 1981, p.352.

(5) *Oxford Dictionary of National Biography*, Oxford University Press, 2004-11. Available: http://www.oxforddnb.com/. Retrieved 15th Sep 2009.

(6) Gowland (1892), p.73.

(7) Ernest Hart, *Lectures on Japanese Art Works*, Society for the Encouragement of Arts, Manufactures and Commerce, London: W. Trounce, 1887, Preface.

(8) Gowland (1892) and Hart (1887).

(9) Princess Akiko of Mikasa. 2009, p.31.

(10) Anderson, William. *The Pictorial Arts of Japan*, London: Sampson Low, Marston, Searle & Rivington, 1886a, p.31.

(11) Hart (1887), p.29.
(12) Anderson (1886a), p.66.
(13) Anderson (1886a), p.183.
(14) Anderson (1886a), pp.214-19.
(15) Anderson (1886a), p.183.
(16) Anderson (1886a).
(17) Anderson, William. *Descriptive and Historical Catalogue of a Collection of Japanese and Chinese Paintings in the British Museum*, London: Longman & Co., 1886b, p.265.
(18) Gowland (1892), p.79.
(19) Anderson (1886a), p.64.
(20) Anderson (1886b), p.21.
(21) Anderson (1886a), pp.89-90.
(22) Hart (1887), p.33.
(23) *Grove Art Online*, http://www.oxfordartonline.com/ , Oxford: Oxford University Press, 2007-11. Retrieved 20th March, 2011.
(24) Hart (1887), p.33.
(25) Anderson (1886a), p.87.
(26) Anderson (1886a), pp.91-92.
(27) Gowland (1892), p.91.
(28) Gowland (1892), p.91.
(29) Gowland (1892), p.92.
(30) Gowland (1892), p.104.
(31) Hart (1887), p.33.
(32) Anderson (1886a), p.87.
(33) Anderson (1886a), p.92.
(34) Gowland (1892), p.86.
(35) Gowland (1892), p.87.
(36) Gowland (1892), p.85.
(37) Anderson (1886a), p.105.
(38) Gowland (1892), pp.107-8.

Translated by Elizabeth Tinsley

Chap.13 Yuzen Dyeing Works that Celebrated Japan's Annexation of Korea

■Masa'aki Kidachi

Introduction

It is undeniable that Kyoto's traditional crafts are important culturally and artistically. However, besides sufferings and damages, such importance is scarcely emphasized when the craft is linked to a war. The Yuzen dyeing *e-zuri* featured in this paper will demonstrate that even Kyoto and traditional crafts could not escape the grips of social conditions. Let us take this opportunity to rethink the relationship between traditional crafts and society.

1. Collecting of dyeing and weaving-related materials and creation of a digital archive at Ritsumeikan University

Ritsumeikan University has been collecting Kyoto's dyeing and weaving designs and *e-zuri* since 2002, materials related to modern design and *e-zuri* were on the verge of becoming scattered and lost due to various social factors such as the decline of the dyeing and weaving industry and the digitalization of designs. Researches on dyeing and weaving are divided into the technical aspect and the cultural aspect, while emphasis is placed on the kimono as the final product. It is hard to say if sufficient research has been conducted on each of the complex step in the production process. The majority of the production process is possible due to the combination of various production areas and I believe that is what makes a research on dyeing and weaving culture, as well as Kyoto culture meaningful, but that kind of comprehensive research is still lacking. Even designs are not limited only to dyeing and weaving purposes. Researches on dyeing and weaving designs should be broadened to cover Kyoto's art and crafts overall, such as by looking at the link between the designs and the artistic circles of Kyoto, or the fact that such designs were also used for various types of crafts.

Many dyeing and weaving designs and *e-zuri* of which have been found with traces of varied used, as evident from the notes written directly onto these materials or the fact that they were cut up. As Yuzen dyeing require many stages of production, the designs and *e-zuri* pass through many hands—in some cases we find materials marked with symbols designating each production stage and the name of the person in charge of each stage. These are traces of use that tell us how designs and *e-zuri* were used as blueprints or tools, and how they were kept. Such traces may provide a new perspective in the exploration of a new horizon for research on dyeing and weaving, as well as on Kyoto culture.

Meanwhile, materials we collected also contained designs damaged from stenciling and backed using all sorts of modern-period documents, such as dyeing and weaving-related writings, newspapers, and administration documents from various places. These types of scrap paper that had been unknown serve as reference materials.

The system used to keep dyeing and weaving designs vary depending on the shop and some were found to be in very bad condition. In order to propel research on designs along, restoring and keeping a record of large amounts of materials has become a pressing necessity. With serious issues pertaining to the deterioration of such materials with the now significant decline of the dyeing and weaving industry, measures respond to such issues are urgently needed. For this reason, we have been searching for answers through realistic trials, details of which are provided in the paper by Masako Yamamoto in this volume. It was during our search for answers that we discovered designs that reflected social conditions. Before introducing some of such designs, an overview of the Japanese design concept *zu'an* and *e-zuri* shall be given.

2. *Zu'an* and *e-zuri*: dyeing and weaving technology and process

The word *zu'an* is said to be the Japanese equivalence of the English word *design* and created during the Meiji Period. In the case of Yuzen dyeing and Nishijin textile, *zu'an* takes care of the designing of patterns and images on a kimono; it was hand drawn and it also provided visual appreciation. Both Yuzen dyeing and Nishijin textile require a process of many complex steps to finish, and the very first step of that is deciding what designs to use. Based on the chosen designs, a variety of tasks are then allocated and the process of creating the fabric would then progress along.

Yuzen dyeing can be largely divided into hand-drawn and stenciled types. In the case of stenciled Yuzen, several pieces of stencils are used to print complex patterns and images of the one single, overall design over kimono fabric (a process known as *katabori*). The test printing on paper after *katabori* is called *e-zuri*. This is used to check the final finish of the design and serves as a reference for the ensuing dyeing process. After several stages including *senren* (refining), *shitazome* (preliminary dyeing), *shitayunoshi* (preliminary steam ironing), and *jibari* (stretching), the stencil is placed over the fabric for dyeing (known as *kataoki*), before continuing on to *shitazome* (preliminary dyeing), *mushi* (steaming), *mizuarai* (washing in water), *ueyunoshi* (steam ironing finish), and many other stages to create the final product. (Kyō Yūzen-shi Hensan Tokubetsu Iinkai 1992).

Although there also existed pre-production designs (*shita-e*) during the Edo period, these were rough sketches and required different techniques than those used for the modern *zu'an* designs. This is because the production volumes and details of the designs were completely different back then. As the Meiji period began, western technologies became keenly adopted in Japan and refined designs were used. In that sense, *zu'an* designs symbolize the modernization of Japan's dyeing and weaving industry.

During the first half of the Meiji period artists painted *zu'an* designs and it was the duty of dyers and other professionals involved to add to or alter the designs according to rules set for the making of kimonos. However, in order to respond to the dyeing and weaving industry that was transitioning toward mass-, high-level and diversified production, professional designing thus became highly required. Consequently, in the latter half of the Meiji period professional designers began appearing, and by the end of the Meiji period there was even a research organization founded by such professional *zu'an* designers.

Since *zu'an* and *e-zuri* are not products, people in general have no chance in seeing these and thus did not know much about them. These items are also scarcely mentioned in books on dyeing and weaving, making them less evaluated in general.

However, as designs required in the making of the kimono fabric, these works can be considered as excellent paintings created from skilled hands and finished with breathtaking beauty. In the same way that designs used in various crafts, such as ceramics and lacquer ware, have begun drawing attention in recent years, it is also equally important for dyeing and weaving design to be given such attention.

3. Yuzen dyeing *e-zuri* from 1910: designs that celebrated Japan's annexation of Korea

Kimonos may appear to be unrelated to *wars*, but in fact many of them were created with various war-related designs. These were created to support a war at the home front.

The *e-zuri* introduced below are materials we purchased from secondhand bookstores in January 2009. Of the sixty-four pieces (five sets and six subsets) of *e-zuri* ranging from the end of the Meiji period to the Taisho period, six were related to Japan's annexation of Korea in 1910. These examples also came with all kinds of notes written on them, as is typical with *e-zuri* used as drafts for the final design.

i . Design using place names in Hangul (Fig. 1)

In this example, the Korean words for 'Seoul' and 'Japan' (*ilbon*) are each printed in large Hangul writing (in red and blue, respectively), while underneath are other Korea place names (cities) in light grey laid out in various angles. The Hangul for

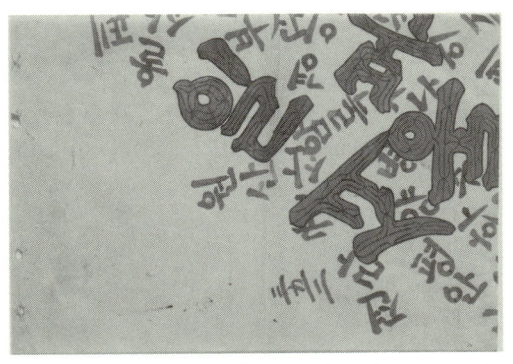

Fig. 1   *E-zuri* with a design showing place names in Hangul

'Seoul' is slightly different from present-day representation due to the old Hangul system used before World War II. All other Hangul writings are correct, except one character. In addition, the design also includes Ainu decorative bracket patterns.

The word for 'Japan' is printed in blue, as is the same in the next example with a design showing the names 'Chōsen' (Korea) and 'Nihon' (Japan). Although the red used for the name 'Seoul' stands out more than the blue for 'Japan', according to Keiichi Harada, at the time blue was a color used in the military to denote an ally, while red was used to indicate an enemy. The use of the two colours may have been due to that. However, according to Professor Inui, as this is an *e-zuri*, the actual finish colours on the *haura* (lining of *haori* kimono coat) may also have been different (from their opinions given during the GCOE 'Yuzen ni egakareta Kankoku heigō (The Annexation of Korea as depicted in Yuzen Designs)' Symposium held at Kyoto Museum for World Peace, Ritsumeikan University on May 30, 2009).

Among the names of places in Hangul are also hardly distinguishable numbers '352' and '252' written vertically in Chinese characters (*kanji*). We believe these may be serial numbers given to the design, as similar numbers have also been confirmed in other *e-zuri*. While other *e-zuri* in this collection have notes written on the back, there is none on the back of this particular piece. The place names in Hangul in this design, according to Associate Professor Anzako, are as follows:

Country: Japan

Cities: Seoul, Busan, Ulsan, Wonsan, Gunsan

Local administrative districts (*do* or 'provinces'): Jeolla, Pyongan

River: Amnok

ii. Design with the names *Chōsen* (Korea) and *Nihon* (Japan) (Fig. 2)

In this design, the Japanese for 'Japan' is printed in blue, covering the grey, tie-dyed design of the Japanese words *chōsen* (Korea), both reading from right to left. Ainu decorative bracket patterns are applied to the characters for 'Japan' and the square frame, while a single cherry blossom is printed at the top left-hand corner. In the bottom left-hand side of the design we find the characters '*Yoshii-shi yuki* (to be sent to Yoshii)' to the right of '1073' and '⊥9 sheets', as well as a red seal with the characters '' below that. From the fact that the words '*chōkoku Ashijima*' (stencil by Ashijima) were found on other *e-zuri*, we know that the characters 'Ashi-jima' indicate the workshop that handled the stencil making. The character '⊥' has also been found

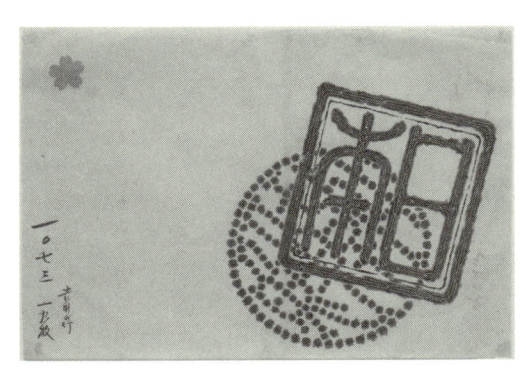

Fig. 2 Design with the names of Korea and Japan

on other *e-zuri*, but is believed to be a varied use of the common '✗' (denoting *shimete*, or ending mark). What this tells us is that the number of stencils used for this *e-zuri* '9 sheets in the end'. The series of characters to the right ('*Yoshii-shi yuki*') is believed to denote that the print was to be sent to the dyeing factory of a certain person called Yoshii, as there are other *e-zuri* marked also with the characters '*kōjō* (factory) *Yoshii*' or 'Yoshii'. On the reverse side of this print were the characters that read 'August 25 (followed by a red seal) ⊥ (in black ink).

iii. Design with the Korean Peninsula (Fig. 3)

In this design a map of the Korean Peninsula and place names in *kanji* (Keijō—former name of Seoul, Incheon, Uiju, Wonsan and Busan) are printed. Part of the Japanese archipelago is also shown and given the same colour as that of the Korean Peninsula. Characters and numbers can also be seen in the area indicating the ocean, such as '1910-merge-[?]', the Toyotomi family crest and the word meaning 'conquest', as well as 'Empress [Jin?]kō conquest'. From these we can clearly see the intention of this design was to try and see the annexation of Korea as an affirmative historical event.

Furthermore, it is possible that this design may have been part of a larger design that showed the Honshu Island. Unfortunately, no *e-zuri* with Honshu Island was found. From the fact that the serial number for this *e-zuri* was '1074' and the serial number for the next print in the same set (shown next) was '1075', it is highly likely that this was the entire design.

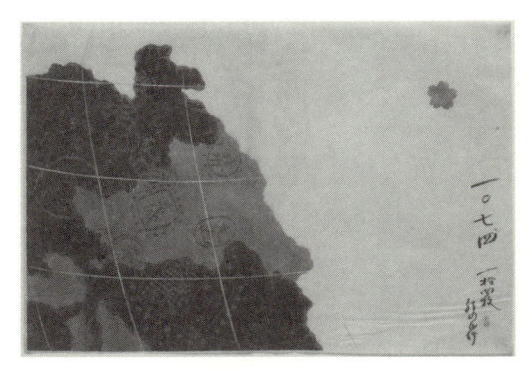

Fig. 3   *E-zuri* design with the Korean Peninsula

At the top right-hand side is a single cherry blossom. Meanwhile, the words '1074', '⊥15 sheets' and 'Mizuno-shi yuki (to be sent to Mizuno)' are written in the lower right-hand side, with the red seal 'Ashijima' underneath. While no indication of the dyeing factory was found in the first design (Fig. 1), designs 2, 5 and 6 (Fig. 2, 5 and 6) all have the words 'Yoshii-shi yuki'. It is unclear why only this design (Fig. 3) was sent to the dyeing factory of a certain person named Mizuno, but it is possible that this may have been due to nature of the designs—this design is the only one of the collection with a large area of blue, which may have been the reason for the different dyeing factory. On the reverse side of this print are the written words 'August 28 ⊥'.

ⅳ. Design with the Hangul characters for 'Great Japanese Empire' and 'Korea' (Fig. 4)

In this example, part of the names Great Japanese Empire and Korea in Korean are printed in old Hangul (from right to left). In the bands that separate the characters are the same Ainu decorative bracket patterns seen in examples 1 and 2. To the right of the print are the writings '1075', '⊥7 sheets' and 'Yoshii-shi yuki (to be sent to Yoshii)', below which is the red seal 'Ashijima'. On the reverse side are the characters that read 'August 27.'

ⅴ. Design with the year '1910' (Fig. 5)

In this print the overall design looks like a globe, with the middle part left empty. At top-left of the design is a map of Japan and the Korean Peninsula, placed over a

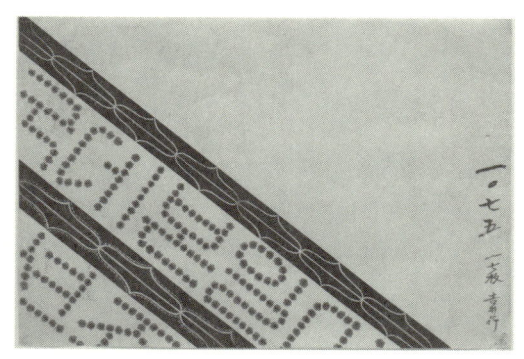

Fig. 4 *E-zuri* with Hangul characters for 'Great Japanese Empire' and 'Korea'

couple of flowers. The fact that the southern part of Sakhalin and the Korean Peninsula are given the same colour as that of the Japanese archipelago may be an indication that these were territories of the Great Japanese Empire. Below the Japanese archipelago is a staff notation. As the annexation of Korea took place in the 43rd year of Meiji (1910), the 4/3 tempo may have been used to refer to that year, while the number '1910' shown as musical notes may also have been used in the same way to indicate the year of the annexation. At the lower right-hand corner is a single cherry blossom.

Fig. 5 *E-zuri* showing design with the year '1910'

13 Yuzen Dyeing Works that Celebrated Japan's Annexation of Korea

At the centre-bottom of the design are the characters for '343' and to the left the words 'Yoshii' and '10 sheets'. On the reverse side we found cursive writings that appear to be 'August 27 ⊥'.

vi. 'Hens in cage' design (Fig. 6)

Hens in a cage are depicted in this design. From the serial number '344' written on the right-hand side we know that this print was made immediately after the previous *e-zuri* shown in Fig. 5. This may have been designed for the year of the rooster, although judging from the fact that the closest year of the rooster at the time was in 1909 (42nd year of Meiji) and if the serial number is correct, then this would have been a design made for the Chinese zodiac from the previous year. Not only that, it is unnatural to depict the auspicious zodiac animal with a cage.

It is likely that the hens were used to indicate Korea, as the same Chinese character for 'hen' is used in a different name for Korea, while Japan also had a different name using the characters for 'dragonfly'—in other words, it is possible that the dragonfly symbolized Japan and the hen was used to indicate Korea. On the reverse side we found the written words 'August 25 (a red seal) ⊥ (black ink)'.

Fig. 6 *E-zuri* with design of hens in a cage

Fig. 7　Tondari-hanedari

vii. *Fukusa* (silk wrapping cloth) from autumn of the 43rd year of Meiji (Fig. 7)

This design depicts animals like a boar, an elephant and a fox hopping on a toy known as *tondari-hanedari* ('hop and jump'). The elephant smiles and looks at one of the *tondari-hanedari* torys rolled on its side. At the top-left is a silhouette of a stag-like shape. It is likely that this design may have been made to poke fun at some social phenomenon. At the bottom-right are the characters 'Mizuno' and '10 sheets'. The serial number on the side reads '314', which is an earlier number than that of the prints in Figs. 5 and 6. However, on the reverse side there are the characters 'Year 43 Autumn / Fukusa' in large writing and a red seal that reads 'September 20'.

viii. Year of the boar and Meiji '44th Year Autumn *Chokudai*' *e-zuri* (Figs. 8, 9)

There were also many other *e-zuri*, among which we found one with a design of a boar for the year of the boar (Fig. 8) and one for the '44th Year (of Meiji) Autumn *Chokudai* (subject of the New Year's Imperial Poetry Contest)'. (Fig. 9. The 44th year of Meiji was 1911.) It just so happened that the 44th year of Meiji (1911) was the year of the boar. Since it is likely that Chinese zodiac designs were created in preparation in the year before, the design shown in Fig. 8 may have been made sometime in the 43rd year of Meiji. The *chokudai* or subject of the New Year's Imperial Poetry Contest for

Fig. 8   Year of the boar design

Fig. 9   The 44th Year *Chokudai* subject

the following year was *ume* (Japanese apricot or commonly known as plum) and the print shown in Fig. 9 may have been created immediately after the contest began that year. The serial number for the print in Fig. 8 was '1077' and '11604' for the print in Fig. 9. This indicates that *e-zuri* were produced in proliferation since the serial number '344' of the print in Fig. 6.

If we take into consideration the years the *e-zuri* in Figs. 7 to 9 were created, we can see clearly that the *e-zuri* in Figs. 1 to 6 related to the annexation of Korea were made before these prints, which indicate that these prints were not created to coincide with such commemorative events as the 'first anniversary' or the 'tenth anniversary' of the annexation of Korea.

ix. Print mount

The secondhand bookstore that sold these *e-zuri* had taken the prints apart from the booklets they were bound in and sold them individually. For that reason, there were prints that were already sold prior to our acquisition of this collection, which may explain some skipped serial numbers. The designs and *e-zuri* (5 sets) we purchased in bulk from this bookstore were divided into small bundles, with many carrying notes indicating these may have been related to a certain *Ōhashi Shōten* store. The 64-sheet *e-zuri* set (5 groups of 6 smaller groups) came between a mount with the writing 'Taishō 3rd year autumn part (1914) *Habutae Yuzen suriawase tuzuri* ('habue' being a type of Japanese silk and 'suriawae' is book of bound e-zuri pieces)'. Since several booklets were found to have a similar mount with the name *Ōhashi Shōten* written on it, it is possible that these were also related to the Ōhashi *Shōten* store.

Furthermore, from our observation of the binding holes of these 64 *e-zuri* (5 groups of 6 smaller groups), we know that these were not originally bound together in this tome (we can easily identify prints with the same binding holes by overlapping digitized images of these prints). In order to restore the original binding of these prints, it is necessary to study the entire 5 groups in detail. In regard to the designs introduced in this paper, however, we know that the print in Fig. 1, the prints in Figs. 2 to 4, and the prints in Figs. 5 to 7 have unique binding holes, respectively. Thus, it is possible that these three groups of prints were bound separately. In addition to that, the fact that the serial numbers are consecutively given to the prints in Figs. 2 to 4 and Figs. 5 to 7 provides evidence of separate binding. We have also confirmed traces of repeated re-binding of the prints in Figs. 5 to 7. Also, from the traces of glue around the edges of nearly all the prints on the reverse side we can conclude that these may have been mounted for the purpose of displaying or browsing.

In this way, the *e-zuri* introduced in this paper may have been continuously used whilst their storage conditions changed through various manufacturing and selling processes, before finally ending up being mounted and bound by the client *Ōhashi Shōten* store. Incidentally, we have discovered that several *katakana* characters were written on the reverse side of these prints, such as 'hi-shi-(n?)-te' (Fig. 2), 'ke-to' (Fig. 3), 'hi-to-i' (Fig. 4), 'hi-shi-re' (Fig. 5), and 'hi-to-te' (Fig. 6), but their meaning is unclear. Our next task will be to further examine during which part of the making of these prints were the traces of marking and writing added and what they signify.

4. *Fukusa* and *haura* designs

The size of the *e-zuri* introduced in this paper are all different from that for *kijakumono* (material used in kimono), for that reason we believe the designs were meant for other items, such as *haura* (*haori* (kimono coat) lining) and *fukusa*. Of all the square designs only one had the word 'fukusa' written on it, but it is also highly likely that other square designs such as those in Figs. 5 and 6 may have been *e-zuri* for printing on fukusa. For that same reason, of all the rectangular designs smaller than these square designs, there is only one piece with the word 'haori' written on it, hence the designs in Figs. 1 to 4 may have been for the *haori*. The *fukusa* was a small item with an important role in enlivening an auspicious occasion, while the *haori* was an important piece of garment for expressing one's trendiness and playfulness.

Designs reflecting the society

As shown by the *e-zuri* introduced in this paper, the use of the theme of the 'annexation of Korea', an important social change, reflects the playfulness and trendiness of the Japanese people at the time. However, to the Koreans it had a completely different significance. Regardless of whether the designs were meant for a *fukusa* or a *haura*, they cannot be appreciated unless the viewer can read Hangul to some extent and understand the significance of the pictures depicted. These designs required a high-level ability in deciphering the meaning of the pictures. Considering this, we can imagine that the products with these designs printed on them were targeted at the rich with higher intelligence, than for the ordinary commoners. However, these designs would have become old fashioned once the year 1910 passed, and likely not have been continuously used for a very long time. While it is possible that they may have been used again during commemorative events, such as to celebrate the first or second anniversary of the annexation, the ephemeral nature of the designs still remained unchanged. As these designs are likely to have been limited by their 'seasonal' nature, it would also mean the great possibility that the items with these designs printed on them were luxury items ordinary commoners were unable to afford.

5. The society at the time of the annexation of Korea and Ainu patterns

The annexation of Korea and the Japanese

In 1910 Japan annexed Korea and established the Korean Government-General Office there. This marked an end to the relentless attempts over several decades to invade Korea since the *seikanron* (policy of conquering Korea by military force). Japan, however, did not stop at simply annexing the peninsula; it continued to further expand its muddy invasion war on Korea, in the name of protecting this new territory known back then as *Chōsen*. Despite the many hardships forced upon the people, they were able to enjoy the 'benefits' of the invasion and actively supported it. When the Koreans realized after the Russo-Japanese War that they were not going to receive any compensation, they sought revenge, as evident in incidents like the Hibiya Incendiary Incident.

The public that celebrated the annexation of Korea: the city of Kyoto, its citizens and kimono stores

An article in Kyoto's Hinode Shimbun newspaper dated September 2, 1910 reported that the celebration party for the annexation of Korea held at Okazaki Park and Heian Jingu shrine by the city of Kyoto from ten in the morning on September 1 went as planned; meanwhile, from eight in the evening there was a big gathering of thousands of people participating in a lantern procession at the Imperial Gardens. Another article dated on the following day, September 3, reported that "kimono stores and other shops in Kyoto city are putting up decorations to celebrate Japan's annexation of Korea", while "Inoue-Daimaru Kimono Store put up a silk banner in red and white showing the rising sun and the Korean flag, with the three characters *shuku hei-gō* (celebrating the annexation)', and the Sogō Kimono Store at Kyoto's Shijō Muromachi Higashi-iru made a silk fabric showing a hen and the rising sun to signify *kirin fuyoku*—Japan's tending of Korea." (Mizuno 2009: 133-134 and 142-143) The term *kirin fuyoku* shares the idea behind the design for the *e-zuri* we saw in Fig. 6. Such articles tell us that everyone in Kyoto—be it the city officials, the citizens or the kimono industry—celebrated the annexation of Korea and related events went ahead as scheduled.

Printing process scheduled to be ready for the announcement of the annexation and celebration events

The Treaty on annexation of Korea by Japan was signed on August 22 and announced on August 29, 1910. It is possible that the designs shown in Figs. 1 to 6 were made beforehand in preparation for the announcement and ensuing celebratory events. From the date provided on the reverse side of the *e-zuri* we can see that information about the annexation would have been obtained prior to the announcement and printing of the designs rather hurried to prepare for the day of announcement and celebratory events.

Furthermore, the mark '⊥' found on the reverse side of the these prints believed to signify another commonly used symbol '✕ (read as *shimete*, meaning 'end' or 'close')' could have been used to indicate the date a certain job was finished. Since the handwriting differs to the writing believed to be that of the stencil master found on the front, it is likely that someone at the dye factory may have written these to indicate the job finish or the final finish date, or by *Ōhashi Shōten* store to record the date these prints were obtained. If this hypothesis is correct, then these designs would most certainly have been completed prior to the date of the announcement of the annexation.

Ainu design

There are many types of Ainu designs, but only the bracket pattern is used on all of the *e-zuri* shown in this paper. This bracket pattern is typical of Ainu patterns and commonly used in Ainu designs. In the Ainu language this pattern is known as *ay-ussiriki*, meaning 'pattern with (divine) thorns'.

This bracket pattern has also been found in the ukiyo-e woodblock prints from the end of the Edo period to the early years of the Meiji period. It was used to depict a kabuki story about a character called Tenjiku Tokubei who traveled to India (*Tenjiku*) and returned home on a Dutch ship. Until the first half of the Meiji period, this pattern was not seen as an Ainu folk design pattern but recognized as a foreign pattern (owing greatly to the instructions by Ms. Keiko Suzuki).

The Japan-Korea single ancestry theory and Ainu designs

When Japan annexed Korea, there was also the theory concerning the homogeneity of the Japanese race, but such belief was unable to justify Japan's rule over Taiwan and Korea. This is because people living in these places were clearly of different races. For that reason, the Japan-Korea single ancestry theory was disseminated and served as a pretext for Japan's invasion of Korea and rule over the different race there. According to this belief, it was legitimate for the Great Japan Empire to revive the Korean Peninsula that was once Japan's territory, and since the people were of the same ancestry with the Japanese, it was relatively easier to assimilate the Korean people. However, it is clear that such belief had no basis in historical facts.

Incidentally, one may wonder why the Ainu pattern in question was incorporated in the *e-zuri* for the annexation of Korea. While there are still some aspects of this that

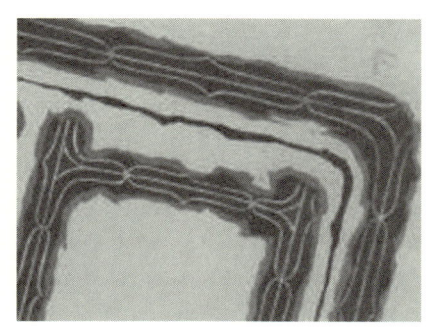

Fig. 10 Ainu pattern in Fig. 1   Fig. 11 Ainu pattern in Fig. 2

Fig. 12 Ainu pattern in Fig. 4

remain inexplicable, it is possible that the pattern was used to hint that, like the assimilation of the Ainu people as a different race, the people of the Korean Empire could also be similarly ruled by the Great Japan Empire. We can suppose that the depiction of the Ainu pattern affirmed the ruling of non-Japanese races and was used to justify the annexation of Korea.

At the time the Ainu people were clearly not given any racial group. There were four theories on the Ainu people categorizing them as descending from European race, Asian race, South Pacific race, or as a unique race—all pointing to the Ainu people as indigenous and different from the Japanese race. In addition, even intellects held "prejudice where they saw the Ainu not as people but as dogs". (Itano 2005: 200) We can deduct from these points that it was likely the prints were created in such manner to manifest Japan's pride in ruling over a 'barbaric race' under the 'Japanese version of Sinocentrism'.

Commercial postcard commemorating the annexation of Korea

The year following the annexation of Korea a New Year's greeting postcard depicting Korean girls appeared (the example shown here was purchased at a secondhand bookstore in April 2009). This commercial postcard was issued by Tokyo Zuan Insatsu Toppan-bu Naniwaya and while the year is unknown a postmark dated on January 1 can be seen. Since this was used as a New Year's greeting card, it would have been issued no later than mid-December of 1910. The design depicts young girls in traditional costumes of the Korean Empire holding Japanese New Year toys like a *hagoita* battledore and a kite, while their shadows appear to look like the number 1911. The large sun seen in the background may signify the first rising sun of the New Year, but may also have been used to show that the *hinomaru* risign sun equates to Japan being the backing support, or that the Korean Empire had just been placed under Japanese rule. In addition, the cloud covering the sun creates the map of the Korean Peninsula, showing the overlapping of Japan and Korea. The design of this postcard was created to commemorate the first New Year after the annexation of Korea and as a Yuzen print it incorporates easily discernable meanings.

Fig. 13 New Year's greeting postcard for 1911

These aspects reflect the national awareness at the time. Whether it be for a postcard or a *fukusa* cloth, it appears a great demand for designs commemorating the annexation of Korea was expected.

A century since the annexation of Korea and present day situation

Year 2010 marked 100 years since the annexation of Korea. From cultural items like Yuzen *e-zuri* and postcards of the period around the annexation, we can see that the Japanese (living in Japan proper) at the time joyfully perceived the annexation of Korea as an auspicious event. Even matters which people today feel doubtful about may have been quite the norm for the Japanese living in Japan proper at the time. It shows that the pains of the Korean and Ainu people were completely ignored.

Incidentally, it also appears that the pains of Hiroshima and Nagasaki are today little regarded in countries in East Asia today, such as South Korea. This is no doubt a complex issue, but for the people in these countries the dropping of the atomic bombs on Hiroshima and Nagasaki were the salvation that ended invasions by Japan, as well as joyful events that led to their freedom from Japan. While one feels uncomfortable with the feelings of the Japanese who celebrated the annexation of Korea, likewise it is equally unconformable when we see people today regard the Hiroshima and Nagasaki experience as something joyful.

There is a song called Iwabue by Okinawan musician Shoukichi Kina containing one verse that says: *Okinawa, Hiroshima, Nagasaki. Oh, we must never forget.* By placing Okinawa along with Hiroshima and Nagasaki, he attempts to rouse the solidarity of victims from various historical tragedies. Through equating the suffering of Okinawa to that of Hiroshima and Nagasaki, he creates a common view on the sufferings of humanity shared by all. In that sense, it is important that we do not forget such events as the March 1 independence movement of Korea and the Nanking Massacre that are no doubt great sufferings of humanity.

100 years have passed since the annexation of Korea, yet people are still unable to stand together and share the pains caused by the annexation. Social situations remain unchanged where people are unable to sympathize others who experienced similar sufferings. The *e-zuri* introduced in this paper serve to pose questions about important issues after 100 years of the event.

Conclusions

Yuzen *e-zuri* celebrating the annexation of Korea clearly show the way the society in Japan at the time. We can see from these prints that, while being sensitive to the mood of the epoch, they were also attempts to lead the trends. The designs introduced in this paper are but only a very small part of the large collection of designs and *e-zuri*. These designs were consumed, leading to further demand for new designs, resulting in great volumes of designs that ensued.

Often, traditional arts and crafts of Kyoto are given positive evaluations. However, it is important not to forget that the history of Kyoto as an ancient capital also includes histories of war. With a long and profound history of various wars, Kyoto has also been sensitive to social changes and wars. It is hard to evaluate the roles or historical experiences of Kyoto's traditional crafts through the comprehensive perception of Kyoto as a historical city.

Finally, I would like to thank the many people for their guidance and cooperation, who include Associate Professor Yuka Anzako, Professor Yoshiko Inui, Takaaki Okamoto (PD), Professor Hidemo Kanazu, Associat Professor Emiko Kida, Mr. Toshiki Toyama, Ms. Keiko Suzuki, Mr. Naoki Mizuno, Professor Keiichi Harada, Mr. Keizo Fujii, and Mr. Shinya Maezaki (PD). Gratitude is also due to the many participants of the November 2011 meeting of the Kansai section of the Society for the History of Korea for their useful advice and guidance on my presentation titled *Yūzen zuan ni egakareta kankoku heigō to urauchi bunsho* ('The Annexation of Korea Depicted in Yuzen Designs and Written Notes on the Backing').

References

Hinuma Satoru. *Kindai zuan monogatari: sono rekishi to kongo no kadai*. Kyoto: Kyoto Shoin, 1972.

Inui Yoshiko. *Zusetsu kimono-gara ni miru sensō*. Tokyo: Impact, 2007.

—, ed. *Sensō no aru kurashi*. Tokyo: Suiseisha, 2008.

Kyō Yūzen-shi Hensan Tokubetsu Iinkai, ed. *Kyō no Yūzen-shi*. Kyoto: Kyoto Yuzen Kyodo Kumiai, 1992.

Oguma Eiji. *Tanichi minzoku shinwa no kigen: nihon-jin no jigazō*. Tokyo: Shin-yo-sha, 1995.

Mizuno Naoki. 'Kyōto no naka no kindai niccho kankei-shi: Chourakukan to Kankoku heigō hōkoku saihi'. *2007 nendo enroku: kōza/jinken yukari no chi wo tazunete*. Kyoto: Kyoto Human Rights Research Institute, 2007.

Sakano Toru. *Teikoku Nihon to jinrui gakusha: 1884—1952*. Tokyo: Keiso Shobo, 2005.

Translated by Eddy Y. L. Chang

Chap.14 Sorting of the Collection of Yuzen Designs and Related Materials at Ritsumeikan University's Art Research Center

■ Masako Yamamoto

1. The collection of materials on modern dyeing and weaving at Ritsumeikan University's Art Research Center

Currently, the Art Research Center at Ritsumeikan University has a collection of materials related to modern dyeing and weaving in Japan, as well as Kyoto kimono. These include Nishiji-ori (Nishijin textile) *shō'e* (draft design with same scale and colours of the finished Nishijin textile), Yuzen dyeing designs and *e-zuri*[1], pieces of textiles, and other materials purchased from secondhand bookstores over several occasions from around 2002. In order to provide these materials to the public and conduct further research on them using a digital archive, Professor Kidachi's study group within the Kyoto Culture Group of MEXT's Global COE Program "Digital Humanities Center for Japanese Arts and Cultures" at Ritsumeikan University began full-scale sorting of the materials about three years ago. However, in the process of that, typical problems pertaining to the preservation and sorting of such great volume of materials began to surface. This paper aims to present one way of preserving, sorting and utilizing great amounts of materials from the modern period in Japan, by introducing the method of sorting—and particularly the restoration method—created as part of the center's effort to overcome the problems.

1.1. Surviving dyeing/weaving-related materials in Kyoto city and related issues

This paper will first examine the conditions of materials found in Kyoto city related to modern dyeing and weaving.

In Kyoto city, many surviving materials concerning (the industry of) modern dyeing and weaving are mainly being kept at companies, public organizations, universities and research institutions. However, the recent years have witnessed prominent cases particularly concerning materials kept at companies, where those that had been kept and passed down are removed from their original ownership through disposal as trash or being sold to secondhand bookstores as a result of factors such as the changing or termination of business operations due to recession, as people stopped wearing the kimono, or changes in the way designs are made through the use of computers. These circumstances have alerted owners of such materials, who sensed the crisis of the situation, to utilize the designs they own and begin searching for ways to do so through creating databases and publishing collections of designs. As far as the creation of databases is concerned, in the case of companies, for instance, they have begun looking for ways to use the designs they own as business content materials,[2] while public organizations such as the Kyoto Municipal Industrial Research Institute's Fiber Technology Center and the Japan Designers Association are also building their own databases[3]. However, the current state of availability of these databases makes them inefficient as research tools, due to reasons such as access to these databases not generally open to the public or requiring a fee, accessible designs only available partially, or missing fundamental information like the year of creation[4].

On the other hand, materials having been removed from their original ownership have led to increased collections at universities and research institutions. In spite of the fact that there exist some collections of actual kimonos kept as materials reflecting the history of clothing and for folklore studies, the recent years have seen a trend in the donation and purchase of collections of production process materials such as designs and pattern papers. In Kyoto city efforts being made in the past few years include our current project at Ritsumeikan University under Professor Kidachi's direction, other arts and crafts projects, and digital dyed pattern paper archives composing of *Ise katagami* (dyed pattern papers)—such as the *Ise katagami* stencils in the Sachio Yoshioka's Collection and in the collection of Kyotec Co.,Ltd. Meanwhile, Kyoto Institute of Technology has a collection of materials related to its predecessor, Kyoto College of Technology (Kyoto Kōgei Kōtō Gakkō), and Terada Tetsuro (machine-printing design artist and member of the Japan Designers Association)[5] —offering public viewing of these mainly at exhibitions held at the institute's Museum and Archives facility. The Tanaka Nao Collection at Kyoto Seika University is a collection of Ise dyed pattern papers collected by the owner of Tanaka Nao Senryoten, a dye sales company in Kyoto. The university has examined the collection using an infrared camera for checking the presence of company logo and any written notes (in black or red ink) and provides the database on the university's Library and Information Center (Joho kan) website.

The characteristic of these designs or related materials is that their existence as sets of materials can be significant. Indeed, there are many cases in the modern dyeing and weaving industry of Kyoto where well-known Japanese painters designed the sketch for Nishijin textiles or Yuzen dyeing and which could be evaluated as arts. However, a large number of the surviving materials found in Kyoto city are "tools" used for manufacturing fixed-number products. In this case, rather than a unique or finest item, these are the best kimonos or daily wear donned by the masses that reflect the interests and trends at the time. Particularly, the period between Meiji era and early Showa era was a time that saw the flourish of the kimono industry, when many variations of designs were created. Materials related to dyeing and weaving at the time, particularly when it comes to kimonos, were avidly collected privately by kimono lovers or by companies. In the case of production companies (manufacturers), the actual kimono and fabric, as well as related information such as the design artist were also kept, making many of these collections thus vital to academic research. However, the survival of more and more such materials may be in peril due to reasons described before. Consequently, materials relating to kimono designs and/or pattern papers from the modern period can, in addition to the information and significance of each and every one of the designs, provide more information as sets of materials through the fixed amount of materials being secured. In terms of future research on the dyeing and weaving (industry) and kimono design from the modern period, it will be necessary to further promote the (research-oriented) utilization of databases, particularly through sorting and preserving "large amounts" of materials and providing open access to these. In regard to the materials in the Ritsumeikan University collection, it will also be necessary to build a system where the materials can be easily accessed for research.

1.2. Materials in the Art Research Center collection

Currently, the materials we are sorting out under the guidance of Professor Kidachi are related to Nishijin textiles and Yuzen dyeing from around the late Meiji era to the early Showa period. These were purchased from secondhand bookstores over several occasions, with various shapes ranging from single sheets to albums. We are now in the process of sorting mainly the approximately 10,000-item collection of Yuzen dyeing patterns, designs and *e-zuri* in 6 sets (purchased between 2009 and 2011). Perhaps Ritsumeikan University is the only university and organization that has such a large collection of these types of research material used in actual Yuzen dyeing.

2. Making the Art Research Center collection at Ritsumeikan University available for open access

Since our 21-Century COE Program activities at Ritsumeikan University's Art Research Center we have been working on the digitizing and archiving of a diversity of materials, as well as promoting the utilization of and open access to these materials, and we are continuing that now as the Digital Humanities Center for Japanese Arts and Cultures (hereafter as "DH") under the MEXT Global COE Program[6]. In terms of the digitizing and archiving, all materials are sorted and investigated by researchers, while materials requiring repairs are adequately treated before they are digitized and archived. The restoration policies of Professor Kidachi's team also follows the general policies for restoration work at the DH Center.

At the Art Research Center of Ritsumeikan University, photographs of materials are taken on a daily basis mainly for creating a database of images of *ukiyo-e* woodblock prints and *hanpon* printed books by the DH Center's Japanese Culture Team. The materials are also being restored as part of the preparation for the photographing. Restoration work is done through repair by hand and backing of materials conducted by undergraduate and graduate students of Ritsumeikan University under the supervision of people with the expertise and experience in restoration. The entire restoration process—from the preparatory stage including *noritaki* (cooking wheat starch to make glue) to the finishing stage including book rebinding—is handled by the students. This is required to ensure the students understand each of the stages in the entire restoration process, which is conducted exactly using the same methods as those used at workshop and other places that handle restorations. While each material may require particular restoration methods, we do not change the steps and methods simply to accommodate the students.

Students who wish to partake in the restoration of materials are mainly those in the material restoration internship program offered at the Ristumeikan University. Through this program, students get a hands-on experience of nearly the entire restoration process in about a month, allowing them to acquire the skills necessary to handle any part of the process learned. Presently, items to be photographed at the Art Research Center that require restoration work are almost all restored by the students, except special cases. This is an example where restoration work conducted here at the university by students with no particular professional expertise and training can actually be done to a certain level by the students if they are given some time to familiarize themselves with the process and learn the necessary steps. It is thanks to such accumulation of experience at the Art Research Center that we were able to involve students in the sorting and restoration of the sets of *Kata-Yuzen* (Yuzen dye paper patterns) materials.

3. Sorting of Yuzen-related materials in the Ritsumeikan University collection

3.1. Overview of the sorting task of materials in the Art Research Center collection

The 6 sets of materials (purchased between 2009 and 2011) to be sorted and introduced here are believed to have been originally kept at dye shops in Kyoto city. The total number of items amount to over 10,000 pieces, comprising mainly designs of *Kata-Yuzen* where the pattern paper dyeing technique was applied and *e-zuri* that served as trial printing.

While sorting through the 6 sets of materials, it became clear that these materials were in no condition to be photographed and stored as they were. This problem was due to the fact that the materials had been folded up and placed inside boxes when they were kept by the original owners or at the secondhand bookstores, and all of the items were found creased or bent. In addition, these materials were visibly dusty or soiled, perhaps due to long years of storage. Thus, it became a pressing task to improve the condition of these materials as we sort through them for storage by cleaning and restoring each piece.

To achieve this task, undergraduate students were involved in the sorting of these items as research materials in the university's collection. The initial stage (2003 to 2009) saw several students from the Department of Japanese History and the Interdisciplinary Program volunteering to handle the task. However, as the number of items greatly increased, the sorting and restoration process now requires groups of students working as part of their lectures or tutorials. We started this new approach from academic year 2008-2009 with the Historic Archeology Seminar Practice of the Department of Humanities at Ritsumeikan University (August 4-September 23, 2008) and have until today conducted the sorting and restoration of the materials through the Museum Training course at Ritsumeikan University (August 23-27 and August 29-September 3, 2010) and winter semester sorting (February 1-11, 2011) in academic year 2010-2011, as well as the Seminar-C Practice in Kyoto Studies Program of the Department of Humanities (August 5-12, 2011) and again the Museum Training course (September 9-23, 2011) during the academic year 2011-2012.

Each session until now saw about 15 students consisting of first- to third-year students from the Department of Humanities at the university, with between 3000 and 4000 pieces photographed per session. Items requiring restoration half way through sorting are now under ongoing restoration.

The student-participated sorting first begins with the students removing the materials from their boxes. Each session was conducted in the form of a tutorial, where the students would then prepare the removed materials for photographing using a digital camera.

The next section will describe the main sorting task.

3.2. Creating inventory and numbering

Once the materials are removed from their storage boxes piece by piece, each item is then given a document number. In order to record the condition in which the materials had been kept, a numbering system was used to indicate the condition of the materials as they were stored.

For example: Box No. ▲ (of the 6 sets of boxes) + bundle ■ + item ● of that bundle → 「6-▲-■-●」

A tape measure is then used to measure the size of each item, which is then also recorded on the record sheet along with the material number. Items in special format or conditions, such as several pieces joined together, were also recorded as being so. Next, a serial number is written in pencil at the lower right-hand corner below each design.

3.3. Cleaning

This step involves using a brush to gently brush away the dust or dirt from the surface of the designs. As a precaution to prevent breathing in the dust, everyone wears a mask during this step. Utmost care was required when brushing the surface of the materials, as brushing too lightly will not successfully removed the dust and dirt, while too strongly can remove the pigment from the surface. Dust and dirt cause the deterioration of materials and can remain in the materials if the materials are restored without being completely cleaned. As a result, this cleaning step is vital before any restoration can take place.

At this point, we separate the materials into those that particularly require restoration and those that do not. In the case of the latter, we then proceed to the next step—flattening.

3.4. Flattening and sorting by size

Materials requiring no restoration work are prepared for photographing. As the pieces were found folded in their original storage boxes, they came creased and wrinkled and needed to be flattened out straight.

First, folds are flattened by finger or using other implements and the materials are then placed between two plywood boards, with Japanese paper sandwiched between every two pieces. Once there are a substantial number of items piled, a weight is then place over the top plywood board and left from half a day to over night or longer to straighten the creases.

After this the top plywood board is then removed and the flattened materials separated by size. The photographing of the materials was done with the camera fixed to a copy stand and placed directly above. Depending on the size of the material to be photographed, the distance between the camera and the material needs to be adjusted accordingly. In order to save time from readjustments, all materials are therefore first sorted by size.

3.5. Preserving and utilizing: the practice of restoration using micro-dot adhering method

A vital part of our sorting of materials is the restoration of the materials. Some of the items were found to be mildewed, possibly due to the conditions they were kept. In addition to that, the design pieces were pressed together in boxes during storage either kept by original owners or secondhand bookstores. Furthermore, as the designs were carbon-transferred onto patter papers by tracing along the designs or patterns with force, repeated use meant that outlines on the design papers had become faint, in some cases severed. As a result, many of the materials came with shredded and torn parts. Consequently, restoration work necessitated the mildew removal as well as repairing torn or creased pieces.

In regard to mildew treatment, alcohol application or fumigation was used to prevent further mildew damage. Meanwhile, there were an overwhelming number of designs with severed, shredded and torn parts that required individual handling and restoration.

In restoring such damages we were faced with the following two issues. The first is the need to restore several thousands of pieces within a limited time. The second was related to the difficulty of training or outsourcing people with specialized skills and using expensive restoration tools and materials in terms of time and cost. Such problems may not be exclusive to Ritsumeikan University and many organizations with similar collections may be facing the same issue. The aim of our current restoration project was "to allow university students conduct restoration work and achieve the purpose (photography of materials) within a given time by using inexpensive and easy-to-use tools through short-term training."

For our restoration project this time we adopted the micro-dot adhering method for repairing torn or severed materials in our collection. Micro-dot adhering method uses a dotted stamping tool to apply adhesive on materials (paper) to stick them together. This method was devised and made public by Professor Katsuhiko Masuda of Showa Women's University[7]. The actual use of this method for large-volume restoration has, however, never been reported and we believe our project is the very first to use it.

In regard to the restoration of the materials in our collection, it was conducted after the following policies were determined.

ⅰ. Degree of restoration

The purpose of our project is to eventually provide open access to our collection of materials in a digital archive. In order to achieve that, we established criteria to ensure that photographing of the materials—which is vital for creating a digital archive—is possible, and made the fulfillment of this as the requirement for the restoration.

Generally speaking, the restoration of materials is governed by certain conditions, such as ensuring the materials are not damaged, remain in their original form(at) and can be restored to the state prior to repairing. For our restoration project we also believe it is vital to ensure such conditions are met and we aim to adopt easier methods that would ensure less unsuccessful restoration. The reason for this is because a large number of students participate in the restoration by turns, which means it is important that the tasks involved require little experience, that anyone of the students can achieve the same results, and that less unsuccessful attempts are made. The micro-dot adhering method adopted for the project this time requires little glue applied to the materials, making it easily removable and having little affect on the materials. The methylcellulose used as an adhesive is water-soluble and can thus also be easily removed by applying water to it. For many reasons, it has been relatively easy to restore the damaged parts back to the original state before the restoration, and in the future, other restoration methods could also be considered and applied. This merit perfectly answers our restoration needs for the materials in our collection.

ⅱ. Skilled people for the restoration

For this project, undergraduate students (first- to third-year students) handled the restoration of materials under the tutorial guidance of Professor Eiji Suzuki of Kibi International University and Ms. Hiroe Hojioka from the Master Course at the same university (both positions held at the time of the tutorial guidance).

Participants of the restoration project first attended the demonstration and explanation session on restoration given either by Professor Suzuki or Ms. Hojioka, before beginning with simple tasks such as joining two separated designs and ironing out folds at low temperature. Ms. Hojioka supervised and provided guidance to the students as they worked on theses basic tasks, while she handled more difficult tasks.

iii. Tools for restoration

— Methylcellulose: Generally, it is common to use wheat starch paste or glue when repairing documents and other similar items. However, such adhesives require time to prepare (such as cooking in a pot) and skilled hands, while not ideal for long-term preservation, as they tend to rot fast. Consequently, these types of adhesives require skills and experience to handle. In that respect, methylcellulose can be thinned with water and thus makes it relatively easier to adjust the thickness. Being water-soluble, methylcellulose can be easily peeled off by applying water to it. In addition, it can also be kept at normal temperatures for a long time after being dissolved in water. We use Metolose made by Shin-Etsu Chemical by dissolving it with water first before application and for the restoration work this time we use Metolose SM-100 thinned to 8% concentration.

— Stamping blocks: These are rectangular blocks of wood with the hook-side of Velcro attached to one end measuring several square centimetres and used as implements for applying the adhesive onto paper.

— Petri dish: Thinned methylcellulose (8% concentration) is placed in a Petri dish, and non-woven fabric is soaked in the methylcellulose in the dish. We then dip a stamping block and ensure that the methylcellulose evenly attaches to the block.

iv. Main restoration tasks
A. Flattening

Wrinkles, twists, or severe folds or bends in the design sheets are flattened out as much as possible. Smaller creases are flattened out to a certain degree using fingers, tweezers, or a spatula. Next, the designs are turned over with the reverse side up and flattened out with water by taking care not to dissolve any of the pigments used in the drawings. Since water can both damage the design and cause mildew, excessive water is removed from the brush used to apply water on each piece of design to flatten out creases. The dampened areas are then pressed with a paper towel. The same is done to deep creases, which are then ironed out on extremely low heat over the paper towel.

B. Adhering

Ripped and severed sections of the designs are joined using strips of Japanese paper dipped in methylcellulose. To do this, thin Japanese paper strips of several square centimetres and the aforementioned stamping block prepared. Applying adhesive only to the hook-side of Velcro of the block, we then dab the attached adhesive—now applied in tiny points with the hook-side of Velcro —on the material to be restored.

This method allows us to use small amounts of high-concentration adhesive and achieve gentle adhesion under a near-dry condition. Furthermore, as the adhered area is minimized, we are able to prevent excessive water from permeating through the designs and thereby reducing undesirable effects on the design materials. When using conventional glue to adhere pieces of paper together, it is necessary to adjust the concentration and amount of glue to accommodate the type of material to be restored and the nature of the restoration. This makes it impossible for someone without any experience to determine the degree of concentration and amount of the glue to be used. In contrast, by using an adhesive requiring no special preparation using water and by using a stamping block, we can ensure less unsuccessful attempts at adhering parts while even those with no expertise on restoration can safely handle such tasks. In addition, by minimizing the facing adhering surface areas, we can reduce unnecessary strains on the materials and even remove or separate adhered parts again easily if need be.

Once strips of Japanese paper are attached to the two ends and the middle of the severed parts, we then place a weight on the adhered area to ensure that the adhesive sticks well and leave it to dry.

4. Building the *Ritsumeikan University Modern Dyeing and Weaving Designs Database* (tentative name)

We are considering providing open access to images of materials in the Art Research Center collection here at Ritsumeikan University as in the form of digital archive. In order to do that, we are sorting through the collection by numbering the materials; removing them of any folds, creases, bends, dust and dirt; and then create high-resolution images through photographing them using a digital camera.

In regard to photographing, we have chosen the method adopted by the Art Research Center, which is using a common professional camera to take photographs of the design materials by placing each piece flat on a glass panel[8].

The images taken are then given metadata to facilitate keyword search. The metadata contains such information as the numbering given to each piece in the first stage of sorting, the design(s) and pattern(s), types of document(s) attached to the reverse side of the design, and so forth.

Using digitized images created from efficient photographing to build an online digital archive will allow overviewing of large volumes of materials, while making the archive open to public access will further research use. By providing such images, we can preserve original materials through less use of the materials.

5. Conclusions

This paper described the actual practice of sorting materials from the modern period conducted at Ritsumeikan University. Often, constructing a database system with such ongoing effort would be difficult due to budget and staffing issues.

In the case of our project to sort through the large collection we have, we were able to do so through student participation. By using the micro-dot adhering method, we believe we have solved the cost and staffing issues common in specialized restoration work to a certain extent. The nature of our restoration work was of great urgency and through using this type of method it was possible to prevent the materials from further deterioration, as well as allowing the utilization of the materials as research materials. In this respect, we believe the method adopted was extremely pragmatic.

Presently, many owners or keepers of other surviving design works or modern-period documents and materials found in Kyoto city would likely be troubled by how to sort and utilize the large volumes of materials. These owners and keepers of such large volumes of modern-period materials have no other means but to constantly question the nature of their collections, the environment the materials are kept in (in various aspects) and the meaning and utilization of these materials, while searching for solutions by themselves. Although it is necessary to consider the various factors and elements involved while pushing the sorting task along, our project was fortunate in three aspects: that the collection sorted belongs to a university that provided the environment where we were able to obtain assistance from the students; that the goal of the sorting effort was clear—to prepare for open access of the sorted materials in a digital archive; and that we were able to tap into the methodology of micro-dot adhesion, which coincided with the purpose and conditions of our project. For such reasons we have now gradually overcome the issues concerning the sorting and storing of materials. While this does not necessary mean the method used in our project can be applied in other situations, we hope it can serve as an example of viable methods for sorting large volumes of modern-period materials.

＊We would like to extend our gratitude to Professor Eiji Suzuki and Ms. Hiroe Hojioka of Kibi International University for their guidance on and assistance in our material sorting. This paper is made possible thanks to their kind instructions. Our appreciation also goes to the students who volunteered and the Museum Training participants. Without their help it would not have been possible to sort through the collection of materials at Ritsumeikan University.

(1) In Yuzen traditional dyeing *kata-Yuzen* (using stencil pattern papers called katagami) is also used. The *kata-Yuzen* dyeing method requires many sheets of pattern papers. *E-zuri* is the process of evaluating how well a *katagami* would work or as a draft created for reviewing and testing the conditions of the *katagami*.

(2) Such as reported in articles in the Kyoto Shinbun newspaper: "Kyō-yuzen ishō / IT de mamore / 1000 ten gazō / Sakufū jōhō mo (Protect Kyoto's Yuzen designs — 1000 images with style information also provided), published on March 10, 2009; "Kyō-yuzen genga / Sekai e hasshin / Kyō to Ōtsu no netto-gaisha (Kyoto and Otsu Internet companies spreading original Kyoto Yuzen designs to the world)", published on December 16, 2010.

(3) Hayami Tadashi and Kitao Yoshitaka. 1998 - 1999. "Kyoto Design Utilization Project: Research on the construction of database Kata-Yuzen database", Kyoto Municipal Industrial Research Institute/Fiber Technology Center. Images courtesy of Japan Designers Association. Http://www.kyotodesign.jp/index.html (current as of September 2011).

(4) Leading databases of the history of clothing are such as the Clothing Culture Database of the National Museum of Ethnology in Osaka.

(5) Namiki Seishi, Aoki Mihoko and Yamada Yukiyo. 2005. "Shōwa shoki Kyoto ni okeru senshoku sangyo no ichisokumen: Terada shiryō no shōkai to ichizuke (An aspect of Kyoto's dyeing industry during the early-Showa period: introduction and orientation of the Terada materials)", Jinbun (Humanistic and Social Sciences)—Memoirs of the Faculty of Industrial Arts of Kyoto Technical University Vol. 54, pp. 135-145. *Koko nimo atta takumi no waza—kikai nassen—* (There's master's touch

here, too!: Machine textile printing) exhibition by the Museum and Archives of the Kyoto Institute of Technology held between August 9 and October 1, 2010. *Kyoto no modaan dezain to kindai no shima/kasuri* (Kyoto's modern designs and modern stripes/splashed patterns) exhibition by the Museum and Archives of the Kyoto Institute of Technology held between September 20 and October 28, 2011.

(6) With the following publication made: Akama Ryo and Tomida Mika (editors). 2010. *Image-database and Studies for Japanese Arts and Cultures*. MEXT Global COE Program "Digital Humanities Center for Japanese Arts and Cultures" (Ritsumeikan University). Nakanishiya Shuppan: Kyoto.

(7) Masuda Katsuhiko. 2003. "Bishoten secchakuhō ni yoru secchakuryoku to hikihagashi-ato no sonshō (Adhesive strength of the micro-dot adhesion method and the damage to paper after removal)", *The 25th Conference of the Japan Society for the Conservation of Cultural Property—Research Abstracts*. The Japan Society for the Conservation of Cultural Property, p.64-65.

—2006. "Bishoten secchakuhō no jissai—dotto sutampu to peesuto paddo (The practice of the micro-dot adhesion method: dot-stamp and paste pad)". *The 28th Conference of the Japan Society for the Conservation of Cultural Property—Research Abstracts*. The Japan Society for the Conservation of Cultural Property, pp.106-107.

(8) For detailed information on the ARC photographing method, refer to the previously mentioned *Image-database and Studies for Japanese Arts and Cultures*.

Translated by Eddy Y. L. Chang

Chap.15 The Influence of *Niwaka* Improvisational Entertainment on Movie Theatres: a Case Study on Kyoto's Shinkyōgoku District

■Atsuko Oya

Introduction

Since the modern period, entertainment districts have been newly established or restructured in urban areas of Japan. In major cities such as Tokyo, Osaka and Kyoto in particular, everything from the location to the management of theatres and permanent movie theatres of various scales were part of the city's administrative planning, with new co-existence or rivalries being created. Of these cities, Kyoto is a place with a rich history, a place where popular entertainment has been abundantly created and developed since ancient times. This is probably because much of the popular entertainment has continuously provided the place where it can be perceived by people. This rich history of entertainment went on to bring about the reception of movies as new entertainment in postmodern Kyoto. In terms of being a place where both movie production and distribution were made and distributed within entertainment districts of that same city, Kyoto was one of the very few cities in Japan at the time where Nikkatsu, the largest movie company in Japan at the time did just that since it began building a movie studio inside Kyoto during the Taisho period. How were movies distributed and how did they spread throughout entertainment districts with such close association between movie production and entertainment? The spread of movies as entertainment would not have been established without the presence and influence of already existing entertainment culture.

To put this in other words, what aspect of preexisting entertainment culture did movies draw upon or based on to establish itself through using an entertainment location? This viewpoint is an utmost prerequisite in various research areas related to the topic, and part of it is so obvious that it is commonly accepted with some sort of tacit understanding. As pointed out by Tanaka (1975) and Sato (1995) in regard to film history, even when we view movies mainly as works, we cannot sever the common elements shared with entertainment culture (namely 1. the subject, 2. the cast, 3. the production staff, and 4. the performance) from them. Meanwhile, others like Kurata (2006) and Kodama (2001) view this from the perspective of entertainment history, having focused for instance on the parallel histories of theatre and movies. Through recent case studies on Tokyo's Asakusa Kōen Rokku district, Kyoto's Shinkyōgoku and Nishijin districts by Tomita (2004), Yokota (2008) and Ueda (2009), we can now gradually see the trends and transitions of entertainment districts in detail, within which the relationship between entertainment and movies has also become more specifically defined.

By following these previous works, this paper aims to focus on 1. the characteristics of the types of entertainment provided at theatres and 2. program composition to examine the relationship of movies and pre-existing entertainment culture between the end of the Meiji period to the early years of the Taisho period, by understanding the transition of entertainment from theatres into permanent movie theatres during that period. In particular, the Shinkyōgoku entertainment district in Kyoto will be used as a case study and, while turning the spotlight on the transition of improvisational entertainment (*niwaka*) toward entertainment at permanent movie theatres as a characteristic example of the case study, this paper will clarify the influence of improvisational entertainment—that existed in the Kyoto region—on movie theatres.

1. The transitions of Shinkyōgoku

1.1. The transition of the theatres

After Japan relocated its capital to Tokyo in 1869, various policies were implemented to prevent Kyoto from falling into despair. Part of such efforts was the establishment of show tents, booths, and food shops in the vicinity of the Teramachi area to allow the area to function as an entertainment district. Teramachi is an area centering around temples and shrines as a result of the urban planning implemented by Toyotomi Hideyoshi. Its surrounding areas were visited by worshippers and many large and small show tents, booths, and food shops lined the streets there. The development of Shinkyōgoku came from the concept of Makimura Masanao, the second Governor of Kyoto at the time. The development began with a street being paved over land seized from nearby temples and shrines. Flanking the street were tents, booths and food shops. The completed Shinkyōgoku became lively through mainly its theatres, shops and food shops, with the Shinkyōgoku-dōri as its central, main street. Shinkyōgoku gradually took on the central role as Kyoto's amusement district.

By 1876 there were 3 *shibai* theatres (芝居), 3 *jōruri-seki* theatres (浄瑠璃席), 6 *gunsho-kōdan rakugo-seki* theatres (軍書講談落語席), 3 *jōruri miburi kyōgen* theatres (浄瑠璃身振狂言席), 12 *misemono* booths (見世物), 9 *daikyū* booths (大弓), 3 *hankyū* booths (半弓), and 15 *yokyū* booths (楊弓)[1]. Particularly around 1883, with permission allowing performances of great kabuki, the *Dōjō Engeki*, *Higashimukō Engeki* and *Sakaiza* theatres were each raking in a handsome amount of over 1,000 yen (value at time) per month, demonstrating thus that theatres running kabuki performances were becoming central in Shinkyōgoku. Meanwhile, besides stage entertainment, various types of entertainment performances were given at other theatres (such as *seiyō megane* (Western glasses, 西洋眼鏡), *nishiki kage-e* (錦影絵), *gidayū* (義太夫), *kyokubuki* (曲ぶき), *ikiningyō* (生人形), *jōruri* (浄瑠璃), *tejina* (magic tricks, 手品), *mukashi-banashi* (old tales, 昔噺)) (Kyoto Prefectural Library and Archives 1971), giving us a glimpse of the diversity of entertainment performances being presented at Shinkyōgoku, where kabuki performed at the three aforementioned theatres head the list of performances.

Under the *gekijō kōgyō yose torishimari kisoku* (regulations on theatres) announced in 1886, the theatres went through renovations or rebuilding, and work on developing theatres in Shinkyōgoku continued under Kyoto prefectural regulations. In addition to the various entertainment performances, we can also see that other types of entertainment (such as *teodori* (手踊り), *tamanori* (玉乗り), *niwaka* (俄), *herahera odori* (ヘラヘラ踊り) and *shinnai* (新内)) were also given at these theatres. In this way, as each theatre established its fixed type of entertainment, more and more newly created programs or entertainment types gradually changed the theatres. By 1897, the Meijiza (formerly Tokiwaza) and the Kabukiza that would go on to represent Shinkyōgoku were opened to the public one after the other, bringing the entertainment district to its first period of maturity.

1.2. The appearance of movies

During the transitions of theatres described above, it was movies that brought about the most remarkable changes. In 1897, the cinematograph brought back to Japan from France by Inahata Katsutaro, an auditor at Kyoto Mousseline Textile Company, was being used to show films at theatres and gradually extended to other venues. The films brought to Kyoto were irregularly shown at the theatres at Shinkyōgoku. The construction of a permanent movie theatre in 1907 for the purpose of showing movies brought movie viewing in Kyoto to one of its climaxes. After the opening of Minami Denkikan—the first permanent movie theatre in Kyoto—In 1908, many other theatres were built and opened one after the other, with the Kita Denkikan in 1909, the Pathé-kan, the Sanyū Club, the Yachiyokan, the Mikadokan, and the Chūō Denkikan (Chūōkan) in 1911. Furthermore, if we look at an article in the Kyoto Hinode Shimbun dated January 2, 1911, for example, we can see that most of it was about the permanent movie theatres, an indication that people at the time were starting to talk about movies. The same article, the names of Meijiza, Kabukiza and Minamiza were only given to provide performance information, with the Yokota Shōkai Katsudō Shashin-kai showing of motion pictures being held at the Minamiza. For permanent movie theatres, a list of movies showing was provided for the theatres listed, namely Chūō Denkikan, Minami Denkikan, Kita Denkikan, Nihonkan and Nishijin Denkikan. From this we can see that movies had become one of the types of entertainment at Shinkyōgoku by that time. In 1912, the second Shinkyōgoku entertainment street was opened two streets to the north of Shijō-dōri as an effort to further develop the Shinkyōgoku district as an entertainment district after the peak of permanent movie theatre constructions.

The theatres and entertainment halls at Shinkyōgoku were gradually turned into permanent movie theatres, such as the Ōtoraza that began as an improvisational theatre was relocated and reopened as the Fujikan and in its original site the Teikokukan was newly constructed in 1914, while the Nishikiza that was once a regular hall of *gidayūbushi*（義太夫節）was turned into the Asahi Club in the same year (see Fig. 1; p. 92). Shinkyōgoku maintained flexibility to constantly receive new genres of entertainment, and in being fully established as an entertainment district, it achieved its second maturity through movie entertainment.

1.3. The differentiation of theatres through changing entertainment genres and theatre renovations

The differentiation of theatres is exemplified by the Ebisuza, one of the major theatres inside Shinkyōgoku. In September 1876, the theatre was opened in front of the Shinkyōgoku Seigan-ji temple, mainly showing *jōruri miburi* (浄瑠璃身振) in the beginning, but later mostly *onna shibai* (女芝居) after around 1885. Later, from around 1902, performances were heavily focused on *shinpa* (新派) and kabuki plays, while short-term shows such as *jōruri* or *katsudō shashin* (motion pictures) were then scheduled between the major performances.

Meanwhile, the Kabukiza that was renovated from the previous Sakaiza in December 1900 was mainly providing regular kabuki performances, while allowing the Soganoya Gorō Jūrō-ichiza performing troupe to perform comedies, *sujōruri* (素浄瑠璃), *onna-jōruri* (女浄瑠璃), *ningyō-jōruri* (人形浄瑠璃), magic tricks (手品) and other performances only when the theatre was vacant due to reasons such as a kabuki performing troupe having moved to another theatre. The Kabukiza functioned similarly to the Ebisuyaza up to that stage, but around 1907 it began to include movie programs, and in 1911 the interior was renovated, while both the interior and the exterior of the building were given a Western look and all audience seating turned into chair seats in order to accommodate permanent movie showing[2]. Although newspapers reported this change as a move to expand the theatre's scope of performance genres, in actual fact, as can be seen from the programs after November that year, the Kabukiza was renovated as a permanent movie theatre, not as a stage theatre. When it was reopened to the public, it was packed with "people who were curious" or "theatre-goers who also wanted to check out the renovated interior". From this we can see that when the Kabukiza was newly turned into a permanent movie theatre, the change of its interior and exterior into Western style became one of the factors that greatly attracted people to the new theatre. From the fact that the theatre was leased to Nikkatsu by Shochiku in 1913 and the theatre opened as Nikkatsu's permanent movie theatre while the management itself also gradually changed after that, the theatre became known as a representative movie theatre in Kyoto.

However, it is hard to say that such change from being a stage theatre to become a movie theatre would have influenced the genres of entertainment or the composition of programs at the theatres. As mentioned before, just before the

Kabukiza became a permanent movie theatre, it was established as a theatre for kabuki and a venue for the Soganoya Gorō Jūrō troupe to show their performances. However, if we analyze the performacnes in 1910, the number of comedies performed by the Soganoya troupe amounted to 7 times that year, the same number of kabuki performances in the same year[3]. And while the contract condition of the Kabukiza after that is unknown, we know that movies by Fukuhōdō were shown there, with a program that had on average one actuality film, 2-3 comedy films, one action or tragedy film. For instance, the January 1912 program had 11 showings: the comedy "*Birukun to denchū*", the actuality film "*Kaitei no ikan*", the western tragedy "*Kanekashi no musuko*", three parts of the Japanese comedy "*Hato*", the comedy "*Musume no yukue*", the western history film "*Gojūnengo*", the comedy "*Damukun no shibainetsu*", and the Japanese tragedy "*Kangetsu*"[4]. This was, however, an average program at the time and did not have any influential characteristics. Meanwhile, similar programs were also provided at the Ebisuyaza that used to fit works by Yoshizawa Shōten or Yokota Shōkai between theatrical performances after 1907. In the years after that, Ebisuyaza temporarily served as a 'permanent' movie theatre during the 1920s, a fact that indicates theatres at the time were caught up in the trends of becoming permanent movie theatres, which was done according to the changing of management and the conditions of the management of the theatres. In other words, we can say that it was also likely for even major theatres that focused on kabuki performances to become permanent movie theatres.

    In regard to other small and medium-size theatres or *yose* halls, they faced more challenges. Not only did they not have the kind of theatre programs comparative to large theatres, they were also lacking facilities. As a result, these small and medium-size theatres and *yose* halls were one by one rebuilt as permanent movie theatres. For instance, the Hatsuneza *yose* hall reopened in 1909 as Kita Denkikan, the Asahiza that was used regularly by the Hyōhyōkai comedy troupe perished due to a fire in the neighborhood and was rebuilt as a permanent movie theatre in 1911, under a new name: Mikadokan. One could say that theatre managements caught on the trend of movie showing during the Meiji period and turned their theatres into permanent movie theatres at an early stage in an attempt to survive amongst competitions in the entertainment district.

    From these facts, its clear that theatres at the time were being rebuilt to enhance the entertainment genres they were presenting, with the establishment of new facilities particularly characterizing each theatre. Furthermore, despite the theatres appealing their uniqueness with specific performance genres and through the gradual establishment of kabuki and *shinpa* plays as well as comedy shows at the theatres, they still followed the same pattern of placing various performance acts between major performance genres, and there was little difference between the programs of the major performances and the minor acts that were placed in between. In particular, in the 30s of the Meiji period (the decade from 1897) the unique performance genres or programs of each theatre was already falling apart, as can be seen from the examples of Ebisuyaza and Kabukiza. It is perceivable, thus, that due to this reason the theatres were then rebuilt and given a facelift in terms of their exterior and facilities, while the management drastically changed the specialized performance genre by turning the theatres into permanent movie theatres and enhanced their specialties in order to differentiate from other theatres.

2. The locality of improvisational performances and their influence on movie showing

2.1. Improvisational performances at Shinkyōgoku

Besides the pattern of kabuki theatres becoming permanent movie theatres, as examined so far, there was also the pattern of *niwaka* or improvisational performance theatres turning into permanent movie theatres at Shinkyōgoku. The *niwaka* performance is a type of folk entertainment thought to have derived from religious ceremonies at temples or shrines, or artistic performances at pleasure quarters. In the beginning, it started as impromptu comedy act by amateurs, but gradually became what is known as *niwaka kyōgen*, performed by groups of actors as their specialized work. *Niwaka* became popular in Edo and Osaka at the same time, but in Kyoto it was particularly and frequently used as a performance for ceremonial processions at the pleasure quarters of Shimabara. In generally, this then gradually gave way to theatrical performances that would be based on ideas and plots of kabuki or *jōruri* (浄瑠璃), and by the Tenpō period (1830-1844) these were being performed at theatres and *yose* halls. During the Meiji period, *niwaka* performance in the Kansai region, particularly one troupe formed in Osaka, began expanding their popularity—such as extending performances to Tokyo—and helped create *shinpa* comedy shows. Of course, such expansion of Oasaka's *niwaka* performances also went to Kyoto and were later established as regular acts at theatres in Kyoto. By the 30s of the Meiji period (the decade from 1897), there were already several regular *niwaka* performance halls that had established their position in the entertainment districts (Enpaku, 1983).

At Shinkyōgoku, the Ōnishiza was opened in 1885 as a regular theatre for *niwaka kyōgen* performances. Apart from being regular performances, *niwaka kyōgen* would go on to be performed mainly at *yose* halls and become a popular entertainment genre at Shinkyōgoku. From the latter half of the 10s of Meiji period (the decade from 1877) *niwaka kyōgen* began to use current news topics abundantly and performances based on news and short stories became popular. The Ōtoraza[5] was newly constructed and shared popularity with Ōnishiza. Ōtoraza was so popular that apparently there was almost no space even for standing seats with the swarm of people curious to see the theatre[6]. Besides Ōtoraza such performances were also given at other *yose* halls or show tents such as Hisagoza, Kawamuraza, Panoramakan, Nakatakeza, Ichirokuza and Fukueiza. At the same time, other forms of performance, including *niwaka odori* (俄踊) dance and *shosei niwaka* (書生俄) also stemmed from *niwaka kyōgen*.

Such popularity enjoyed by *niwaka kyōgen* led to new forms of performance by *niwaka* performance troupes at theatres like Ōtoraza and Ōnishiza known as *kairyō-niwaka* (改良俄) or *shimbun-niwaka* (新聞俄). These were *niwaka kyōgen* based on short stories, incidents and love stories published in newspapers, as well as scandals reported in miscellaneous news and they were also performed at *yose* halls and theatres besides the two aforementioned regular theatres. The popularity of this kind of *niwaka kyōgen* also began to decline in the latter half of the 30s of the Meiji period (the decade from 1897), with small and medium-size theatres showing comedy acts including *niwaka kyōgen* being rebuilt and turned into permanent movie theatres one after another. After that, even Ōtoraza—as a representative *niwaka* performance theatre at Shinkyōgoku—was also rebuilt as the Minami Denkikan permanent movie theatre in July 1908. However, the Ōtoraza was immediately after reopened in Shinkyōgoku-agaru and continued to provide *niwaka kyōgen* performances. Yet in 1913 this Ōtoraza was again rebuilt and turned into the Teikokukan permanent movie theatre directly managed by Nikkatsu (See Fig. 1). After giving the performance venue twice to the showing of movies, *niwaka kyōgen* was once again performed at the Minami Denkikan permanent movie theatre, now renamed back to Ōtoraza. Nevertheless, this was eventually turned into the Fujikan permanent movie theatre and thus ending the era of *niwaka kyōgen* regular performance theatres inside

Shinkyōgoku (see Tab. 1; p. 96).

2.2. Topicality and Improvisation

Next, we will examine the content and types of *niwaka kyōgen* performed under the theatre Ōtoraza that remained until 1913 despite having to relocate several times to allow the building of permanent movie theatres. First, two characteristics can be given to the uniqueness of *niwaka kyōgen* acts being performed at Ōtoraza during the 20s (the decade from 1887) and 30s (the decade from 1897) of the Meiji period: the topicality and the improvisation of the performances.

The *niwaka kyōgen* acts performed at Ōtoraza were characteristic in that they were performed as *niwaka* acts mainly based on the serial short stories or miscellaneous news stories in newspapers such as the Kyoto Asahi Shimbun and the Osaka Asahi Shimbun. As discussed in the previous section, these were known as *shimbun-niwaka* or *kairyō-niwaka* and were a genre of *niwaka kyōgen* widely performed mainly at Ōtoraza. *Niwaka* performances of this type were created by *niwaka* artists like Tōgyoku and Bakahachi, who used Ōtoraza as the main venue of their performances (Enpaku, 1983)[7].

To give an example, there was the performance of "*Nasake no wakegushi*", a *niwaka* performance based on the murder of hairdresser Omasa in Kyoto. It was performed on the same day that the incident was reported in the Kyoto Asahi Shimbun. This performance, through its contemporary topicality represented by that of *niwaka kyōgen* performed at Ōtoraza[8] and having swiftly turnd a scandalous incident into a *niwaka kyōgen* performance, brought about a new frontier of *niwaka kyōgen* that up until then only based its ideas on kabuki or *jōruri* stories. Although the same use of current news was done also in kabuki or *shinpa* performances and presented as theatrical plays, this was something different. In the case of *niwaka kyōgen*, the characteristics of *niwaka* performance were the way stories were presented as shows and the fact that the stories were not big enough to be theatrical plays—that is, focus was given to local incidents. Particularly, there were many cases where incidents caused by the actors of Ōtoraza were directly presented as *niwaka kyōgen* acts. For instance, during a performance at Ōtoraza in 1890 Bakahachi turned an actual incident of uproar he himself had caused into a *niwaka kyōgen* performance[9]. This was based on an actual incident involving Bakahachi and the courtesans of the pleasure quarters, and many patrons of the pleasure quarters went to see the performance. In other words, this was a trial of self-production by a *niwaka kyōgen* artist that combined the important elements of topicality of current news and region-specific incidents.

Furthermore, it is also of interest that kabuki acts performed during the same period were being turned into *niwaka kyōgen*. For instance, when "*Nichirenki*" was being performed at Dōjō Shibai (Kyōkakuza), a *niwaka kyōgen* performance with the same title was also being performed at Ōtoraza[10]. Another example is the "*Shiobaratasuke no ichidaiki*" was performed in October 1889 at the Minami Engeki (Minamiza) and Sakaiza at the same time, where a *niwaka* performance based on that was also being performed[11]. These examples of drawing ideas from popular contemporary kabuki programs that were being performed everywhere and making *niwaka* performances out of them became much talked about. Even in terms of the performance programs two types of *niwaka* performances were established from around 1892, with one being *niwaka kyōgen* based on Kabuki acts and the other being *niwaka* based on miscellaneous news stories and serial stories. That is, it can be pointed out that the *niwaka* improvisational performances at Ōtoraza were characteristic in that they either following the trends of mainly kabuki theatre programs or were created by including local topics.

Next, let us examine the *sokuseki niwaka* improvisational performance at the Ōtoraza. This was a type of very popular performance where the theme of the performance was provided by the audience and based on which a *niwaka kyōgen* was improvised on the spot. This genre later copied the sumo match style and turned into *niwaka kyōgen* match performances[12]. There were a rich variety of many other types of *niwaka kyōgen* that drew ideas from other entertainment genres, such as *niwaka kyōgen* played by the group of geisha, allowing for diversified programs.

One could say that the *niwaka kyōgen* performances at Ōtoraza substantially displayed their use of topical and improvisational elements. This was particularly so if we consider the fact that many of the roles were based on those in articles and stories in newspapers and that the performances would have also been made with the readers of these newspapers in mind, thus making the creation of performance programs of various types of *kyōgen* that share common topicality and improvisations while following the trends would have been a vital element for the making of *niwaka kyōgen* at Ōtoraza.

Despite the great popularity of its *niwaka kyōgen* performances, in the 40s of the

Meiji period (the decade from 1907) Ōtoraza gradually shifted its entertainment program to other genres. One of such genres was the showing of *katsdō shashin* (motion picture). The theatre presented at least a total of four movie showings during the Meiji period[13], all of which were made by Nikkatsu. This may be partly due to the close relationship between Yokota Einosuke of Nikkatsu and Ōtoraza's manager Kobayashi Torakichi, who co-managed Teikokukan[14]. Such connection between the managers of Ōtoraza and Nikkatsu's permanent movie theatre is also considered to have led Ōtoraza under the ownership of Nikkatsu. Furthermore, when Fujikan was opened on the former location of Ōtoraza, it premiered movies featuring Onoe Matsunosuke and fellow actors, but from October 20, 1914 on it premiered *shinpa* tragedies. The reason for the change in the genre of movies premiered can be explained as follows. At the time Nikkatsu distributed movies at seven permanent movie theatres inside Shinkyōgoku[15], but its contract with three of the theatres affiliated with Shōchiku—namely the Kabukiza (*shinpa* and action movies), the Mikadokan (*shinpa* and *kyūgeki*) and the Yachiyokan (*shinpa* and *kyūgeki*)—had ended in June that year[16]. What these three theatres shared in common was that they were all showing *shinpa* movies. For Nikkatsu to lose these distribution venues, it then turned to Fujikan, one of the three major theatres for Nikkatsu including Teikokukan and Chūōkan, and made Fujikan its new venue for the premiers of its *shinpa* movies.

2.3. Regional appeal

In order to get a glance of what happened after Ōtoraza became a permanent movie theatre, his section will shed light on the features that the entertainment provided at Fujikan that was newly built over the former site of Ōtoraza, as well as the major movies shown had in common with *niwaka* performances. It is important to note that, while this permanent movie theatre solely premiered *shinpa* movies by Nikkatsu in the following years (as was necessary for Nikkatsu's movie distribution), when it was newly opened it mainly showed movies starring Onoe Matsunosuke—that is, it was a theatre for showing *kyūgeki*. First of all, Fujikan was opened in July 1914 as a permanent movie theatre managed by Nikkatsu, and its first program of movies included: 1. Actuality film "*Kōhī no Saibai*"; 2. Action comedy "*Ichimokusan*"; 3. Military epic action film "*Bakusen*"; and 4. *kyūgeki* film "*Kaibyō Taiji Akinomiyajima Ōadauchi*" (see Fig. 2; p. 99). As previously mentioned, at the time the first peak of building and rebuilding of theatres into permanent movie theatres had come to an end, the program prepared for the Fujikan—newly built at the time that movie showing had already become normalized at Shinkyōgoku—also followed the styles of other contemporary permanent movie theatres to include movies in four genres, namely actuality, comedy, action and *kyūgeki*. Here, is worth noting the *kyūgeki* movie genre. From the time Fujikan was opened to around September of that same year, the *kyūgeki* movies were being shown as main features at the end of the showing program. If we trace back to the program of the Ōtoraza years, we can see that *niwaka kyōgen* acts based on Kabuki were being performed then. Of the movies shown, there was the movie "*Tenpō Rokkasen Kōchiyama Sōshun*" premiered in September 1914 that was promoted as the movie version of "*Kōchiyama Sōshun*" performed at the Minamiza in June of the same year[17]. In other words, in the same way that theatre performances were turned into *niwaka kyōgen* acts at Ōtoraza, movies at the time also did the same to draw from theatre performances to attract audiences, indicating movie theatres were following the promotional and entertainment strategy of theatres in the past. That is to say, the devotion to kabuki plays by *niwaka kyōgen* performed in the Ōtoraza years, particularly the way they would focus on the kabuki plays performed at theatres within the same city, also worked well for the movie program of Fujikan when it was opened.

Next, let us take a look at how *shinpa* movies were shown once they became the main feature of the movie theatre program. Take for example, the first of the four "*Kachūsha*" movies shown in November 1914. The movie "*Kachūsha*" was based on Leo Tolstoy's Resurrection that was first performed as a theatrical play in March of the same year by the Geijutsuza theatrical company, with Matsui Sumako as Kachūsha and won great popularity. Nikkatsu turned this play into a movie series and premiered the movies in the same year. At the time the song "*Kachūsha-no-uta*" written by Nakayama Shinpei and sung by the actress became extremely popular, and the kineto-phonograph of her and her voice singing that song shown in Asakusa in Tokyo became a great success. Having achieved such popularity, in November of the same year this play performed by Geijutsuza, which was touring and performing at Minamiza then, was announced as a popular piece performed at Minamiza[18] and the Fujikan movie version was promoted as being based on the play at Minamiza. After the movie was premiered, many audiences from Geijutsuza[19] who would not have usually gone to Fujikan flocked to watch the movie version, showing that "*Kachūsha*" had also won great popularity in Kyoto[20]. This can be considered as one of the cases where attention was given to the entertainment program of other theatres from time to time and create new entertainment to coincide with, while successfully making such entertainment appealing even to non-usual audiences.

Conclusion

In summarizing what we have examined so far in this paper, what we can say about the case of entertainment in Kyoto is that entertainment in the form of theatrical plays and *niwaka* performances was characteristic in lending to the transition of theatres into permanent movie theatres. In regard to plays, the disappearance of the characteristic properties of each theatre that were able to survive thanks to the type of plays performed can be given as a factor in the transition. Under such circumstances, theatres began to turn toward movie showing, with many functioning as places with a maximum diversity of entertainment genres and becoming permanent movie theatres. *Niwaka* performance venues differed from play theatres; while they were places that made the characteristic properties of their entertainment genres to best use, part of the topicality and improvisational characteristics of *niwaka* performances were inherited when they turned toward movie showing and changed the entertainment genres, resulting in the promotion of movies based on theatrical performances within the same city. Permanent movie theatres became the venues for presenting theatrical programs and a rich variety of entertainment genres, while establishing themselves by basing on the potentiality of the nature of entertainment genres.

(1) *Yūbin Hōchi*, June 12, 1876.
(2) 'Engeki', *Kyoto Hinode Shinbun*, October 13, 1911.
(3) The Soganoya comedy shows were presented a total of seven times: twice in January, three times in May, and twice in September. Kabuki performances were presented a total of seven times: once in February, April and July, twice in October, and once in November. There were a total of five other performances including *engeikai* entertainment show, a magic show, *denkigeki*, *sujōruri*, and *gidayū*.
(4) 'Yengei', *Kyoto Hinode Shimbun*, January 7, 1912.
(5) Although it has been revealed that Ōtoraza became the regular venue for *niwaka* around 1882 from the Kawakita *yose* performances, the author followed newspaper

articles about the entertainment given from April 1, 1887 to determine the venue as Ōtoraza (*Kyoto Hinode Shimbun*, March 31, 1887). Meanwhile, an article in the Chūgai Denpō on March 6, 1887 also reveals that Ōtoraza was being newly built at the site of a *kanshōba* in Shikyōgoku Shijō-agaru.

(6) *Kyoto Hinode Shimbun*, September 16, 1887.

(7) See 'Gekijō Dayori', *Kyoto Hinode Shimbun*, August 30 and September 8, 1887 and 'Gekijō Tsūshin', *Kyoto Hinode Shimbun*, May 28, 1885.

(8) 'Onna kamiyui koroshi no niwaka kyōgen', *Kyoto Hinode Shimbun*, September 16, 1887. In addition, the same *niwaka* performance to match this one at Ōtoraza was also being shown on the same day at Ōnishiza.

(9) 'Bakahachi. Baka ni narazu', *Kyoto Hinode Shimbun*, May 28, 1890.

(10) Shown at Dōjō Shibai (Kyōkakuza) from February 1, 1888. In the February 17, 1888 edition of *Kyoto Hinode Shimbun*, the same *niwaka kyōgen* was reported to be performed at Ōtoraza.

(11) 'Niwaka no sensō', *Kyoto Hinode Shimbun*, October 23, 1889 and 'Shiobara Tasuke wa sōshūsha ni arazu', *Kyoto Hinode Shimbun*, October 30, 1889.

(12) 'Engei', *Kyoto Hinode Shimbun*, September 15, 1895.

(13) "*Byakkotai*" (August 11, 1910), "*Sakamoto Ryōma*" (August 1, 1911), "*Utsunomiya Tsuritenjō*" (August, 11, 1911), "*Sōma Daisaku*" (August, 20, 1911).

(14) The Teikokukan was jointed managed by the two and directly controlled by Nikkatsu.

(15) Seven theatres at Shinkyōgoku in January of the same year: Teikokukan, Daiichi Yachiyokan, Miyukikan, Kabukiza, Mikadokan, Chūōkan, and Operakan. ('Kōgyō Annai', *Kyoto Hinode Shimbun*, January 1, 1914)

(16) 'Tanoshimi', *Osaka Asahi Shimbun Kyoto Furoku*, June 20, 1914.

(17) 'Tokubetsu Kōkoku', *Osaka Asahi Shimbun Kyoto Furoku*, September 20, 1914.

(18) 'Tanoshimi', *Osaka Asahi Shimbun Kyoto Furoku*, November 20, 1914.

(19) 'Tanoshimi', O*saka Asahi Shimbun Kyoto Furoku*, November 26, 1914.

(20) Apparently the actress of the theatre play version, Matsui Sumako herself also watched the movie adaptation by hiding in the crowd. ('Tanoshimi', *Osaka Asahi Shimbun Kyoto Furoku*, November 24 and 26, 1914.)

Translated by Eddy Y. L. Chang

Chap.16 Aspects of Small-Gauge Film in Interwar Japan: Another Face of the "Cinema City" Kyoto

■ Mika Tomita

Introduction: Kyoto as Documented by Small-Gauge Film

The images below are from small-gauge films that recorded the activities of Kyoto filmmakers and scenes of the everyday[1]. They are all unique images, based on reversal development of the only original prints that are extant today, in which the fleeting moments of the times and cultures are vividly inscribed with a highly personal vision.

Figures 1 and 2 are both from images filmed by Tanaka Eiichi (1916-2007)[2], a wealthy man in Kyoto and a movie fan, when he took part in filmmaking as a camera assistant and camera operator. Figure 1 (p. 103) shows the shooting of *Kanzaki Azuma Kudari* (dir. Gotō Taizan, 1943), the first film produced at Etona Film Productions (*Etona Eigasha*), which was established by Tanaka's brother Tanaka Isuke in Omuro, Kyoto. Figure 2 (p. 103) is a commemorative film by the crew members of *Gyeongju Bulgksa and Seokguram* (*Keishū Bukkokuji to Sekkutsuan*, Dir. Nakagawa Shirō et al, 1941). Tanaka Eiichi, who was 18 years old when Etona Productions was established, passionately loved Paramount pictures and also enjoyed filming with the Cine-Kodak Special, the latest 16mm camera that all small-gauge film fans ardently yearned for[3]. Having joined Etona Productions with his beloved gadget, Eiichi, under the name of Tanaka "Seihō," (the *kanji* of which is a play on "Paramount"), became production manager and, at the same time, also flourished as an assistant cinematographer using the name of Gishi Masao. After the dissolution of Etona, Eiichi continued to engage in the field of "culture film" (*bunka eiga*) until the wartime. While *A Memory of Location* (*Rokēshon no omoide*) appears to have been filmed with his beloved Cine-Kodak Special, Eiichi, in addition to several 16mm works, also left a few works shot with 9.

5mm as well as 8mm, which had been just released at the time. With these, he filmed his own everyday life with all the varieties of small-gauge film that were available in Japan at the time. Etona Productions, through which Eiichi's interests manifested themselves strongly, attempted to produce a 16mm fiction film, *A White Mouse* (*Shiroi nezumi*) under the name of the "Small-Gauge Film Division." Although 35mm had been already become standardized for theatrical release, Etona raised its unique profile through the commercial use of "sub-standard" small-gauge films.

Figure 3 (p. 104), whose title is noted on its 9.5mm bobbin as *Atago Ski Resort* (*Atago Sukījō*), is a frame from a so-called "orphan film" whose owner or filmmaker remains unknown. Atago Ski Resort in Kyoto opened in 1929 and was active until the wartime, and the film is estimated to have been shot by the mid-1930s. In the film, a number of people who appear to be Kyoto residents are enjoying seasonal leisure at this ski resort. This work, just one and a half minutes in length, nevertheless enables us not only to witness the then-existing Atago Ski Resort, but also to be connected to people of the day – the local skiers visiting from the city of Kyoto easily by cable car, as well as a father attending to his child who has fallen over – beyond time.

Figure 4 (p. 105) was retrieved from one of the private films that belonged to Morita Sakichi (1874-1944), the president of Nikkatsu from 1937 to the end of 1941. The panoramic view of Nikkatsu Uzumasa Studio is reproduced here by overlaying panning shots (filmed at Nikkatsu Uzumasa Studio's athletic festival) one upon another. Compared to words or a still photograph, one moving image contains far more information to be processed and scholarly investigated. The scenery of wartime sports recreation, in which movie stars, studio personnel and their families all gather to commemorate the 2600th Anniversary of the Imperial Era (*Kigen 2600-nen*) at the now vanished Nikkatsu Uzumasa Studio, springs to life once again.

These small-gauge films are unique documents that portray a specific age, locality and history from personal perspectives, and their cultural, artistic, academic and historical value is indisputable.

Since the mid-1990s, the scholarly evaluation of such amateur films and home movies has grown exponentially among image archives as well as researchers. For instance, the International Federation of Film Archives (FIAF) featured amateur films in the *Journal of Film Preservation* in 1996 and in the following year held its FIAF Congress on that theme in Colombia; it has since become a driving force in the discovery and preservation of amateur films around the world. In 2002, the

Association of Moving Image Archivists (AMIA) began publication of the journal *The Moving Image*, which positions the organization as the leader in scholarly research on amateur films and home movies. In the same year, several major archivists who had propelled these issues started the "Home Movie Day" movement[4], which promotes activities to find and preserve home movies that have been buried undiscovered in more than 14 countries including Japan.

Along with such growing interests, researchers and scholars at universities as well as archives in the United States, England and France – countries where small-gauge films and home movies have been popular traditionally – have put out a number of publications that clearly articulate the substantial differences in historical traits among small-gauge films/home movies depending on their respective localities and societies[5]. Such scholarly investigations have led to the firm realization that these films are rare cultural resources capable of representing both public histories and personal memories/viewpoints (including those of minorities). Also in Japan, the Ogino Shigeji Collection, donated to the National Film Center[6], has prompted some interest in small-gauge films and amateur films[7], and the recognition of "Home Movie Day" has been growing. However, it has to be noted that the significance of the field has yet to be fully recognized especially in such institutions as universities and regional archives in Japan.

Through an overview of small-gauge film culture in Japan during the interwar period, this article attempts to examine the cultural and historical background of how aforementioned small-gauge films were produced in Kyoto from the perspective of the "local community" that the small-gauge film constructed. This article especially focuses on the process by which small-gauge films, which had cultivated vast and diverse "image cultures" (*eizō bunka*) in different places throughout Japan due to their sub-standard status, were gradually integrated into the propagandistic regime of Japanese film in wartime.

1. Introduction/Importation of Small-Gauge Film

Small-gauge films began to gain popularity in interwar Japan starting in 1922, when the Pathé Baby's 9.5mm projector and celluloid film were released by Pathé Frères in France and then immediately brought to market in Japan[8]. While the 17.5mm had already been in use, it had never become widespread in such private and public spaces as households and schools. Eastman Kodak Company introduced the 16mm to the market in the following year, and the Pathé Baby camera was released in 1924. These two formats became the prevailing currents for small-gauge films in the 1920s through the 1930s.

In both cases, the projectors and films for projection appeared on the market first to cultivate "home users" who would enjoy watching movies at home; the releases of the cameras followed in order to expand the consumer base to those who loved photography and to groups or organizations who were interested in trying filmmaking. Club activities gained momentum among small-gauge film fans by the late 1920s, and various genres of films were produced, with related contests and competitions were also held frequently. Some prominent works by active filmmakers in Japan received awards in amateur film festivals in Europe and the United States during the mid-1930s, and the introduction of Kodak's 8mm to the market completed the three main currents that comprised small-gauge film culture in interwar Japan. The fierce competition in Japan between the "French" 9.5mm (Pathé Frères) and the "American" 16mm and 8mm (Eastman Kodak) generated an unique cultural landscape distinct from that of the United States (where 16mm was dominant) or that of France (where 9.5mm was dominant).

The pivotal driving force behind the promotion of 9.5mm culture in Japan was Banno Sales Company (*Banno Shōten*) which acquired Pathé's distribution rights for the Japanese market; it also manufactured and sold its own domestic 9.5mm film, cameras and projectors. 9.5mm lovers, forming local ciné-clubs named "Baby Cinema" or "Baby Kinema," often called themselves the "Baby Party" (*Bebītō*) to demonstrate their profound attachment to 9.5mm, and they also published journals with Banno's support. The Kyoto Baby Cinema Association (*Kyoto Bebī Shinema Kyōkai*), which this article touches upon later, is one famous example of such clubs. However, along with its name, 9.5mm was occasionally ridiculed as a kids' toy, as children often appeared as users in its advertisements. Thus, 9.5mm lovers, noting the anachronism of "the acceptance of the term baby,"[9] changed its name to "Pathé cinema" (*Patē shinema*).

Meanwhile, 16mm projectors and cameras came in many varieties (including products by Bells & Howells Company), and domestically-manufactured products also gradually came to share the market. Eastman's first hubs in Japan were located at Cine-Kodak Service Japan in Osaka and Ōsawa Sales Company (*Ōsawa Shōkai*) in

Kyoto[10]. 16mm lovers in Japan established the Japanese branch of the New York-based 16mm club "Amateur Cinema League" in 1927, and in cooperation with the New York head office, the Japanese branch published a Japanese version of their the league's magazine, *Amateur Movie Makers*.

The term "small-gauge film," simply specifying the smaller size of the film gauge and the width of the film strip, was thus originally used to indicate both 9.5mm and 16mm in a neutral manner from the 1920s through the 1930s. The journal *Small-Gauge Film (Kogata Eiga)*, which began publication in 1929, was a typical vehicle for the medium, as it inclusively featured films made by non-professionals as well as professional works released for home projection or private viewing. However, "small-gauge film" began to be used as a substitute term for the hostile English-language term (*tekiseigo*, literally "the language of the enemy") "amateur movie" during the wartime. The enforcement of the Film Law (*Eigahō*) in 1939 and a general shortage of film celluloid at the time made it difficult to consume film for private/personal use, and "small-gauge film" eventually became a general term that referred to professionally produced works using sizes smaller than 35mm such as the so-called cultural film (*bunka eiga*), educational film (*kyōiku eiga*), documentary and newsreel. At the same time, this transition also means that the crucial figures who used to engage with small-gauge films in the 1920s and 30s were mobilized as primary providers of the "small-gauge films" that bore wartime propaganda in Japan.

2. The Characteristics of Small-Gauge Film

The fundamental traits of small-gauge film can be broadly classified into the six following points: 1) operability, 2) nonflammability, 3) economy, 4) film development service, 5) abundant film variations, and 6) projection image. By closely examining these six characteristics, the paper will briefly outline how small-gauge films became generally accepted in interwar Japan.

1) In regards to operability, camera, film, and projector for small-gauge film were all compact, lightweight, and could be operated as easily as pressing a button. Therefore, Kodak used women and Pathé used children in advertisements to soften the rigid and masculine image of the machine. By presenting a family-oriented new lifestyle with the image that "women and children can handle it", those advertisements, directly imported and used in Japan, circulated a Westernized modern

domestic lifestyle along with images of women. Because of those images, the small-gauge film also became a symbol that connoted the intellectual and cultural.

2) The nonflammability of the film strip was the most important element of the small-gauge film that led to its popularity. Unlike 35mm, small-gauge film eliminated the risk of fire damage, and it immediately drew attention from households and schools as a useful medium for cultural films and educational films. Around that time, the Ministry of Education promoted an educational film campaign, and in 1928, the Osaka-based Daimai Film Library and the Tokyo-based Tōnichi Film Library were both established, and began a project to lend 35mm prints to elementary schools on a national scale. In the same year, Banno Sales Company, through the intermediary of Baby Club that Banno sponsored, also started a loan service of a Pathé Baby Film Library for educational purposes[11]. Moreover, entries in *Baby Cinema*, the magazine of their nationwide organization, clearly shows Banno's interest in venturing into the field of educational film: a report that the Pathé Baby brand was chosen for school education – for its nonflammability, cost performance, and the variety of titles available for educational use – in France and England[12] appeared in 1928, and the same issue also carried an article by an elementary school teacher that emphasized the importance of small-gauge educational films[13]. In the following year, a film competition on the theme of educational film was also held[14]. As a result, 16mm film began to be used exclusively for circulation by Daimai Library in 1931 and by Tōnichi Library in 1934, and accordingly 16mm eventually became a dominant format for educational film. However, 9.5mm seemed to have been used among school educators to record their activities with students[15]. In Kyoto, unlike other prefectures, the Kyoto City Elementary School Film Education Study Group (*Kyōtoshi Shōgakkō Eiga Kyōiku Kenkyūkai*), which independently purchased and owned 16mm projectors and film prints for film projection tours, was established in 1929 within the Educational Department of Kyoto City[16]. Its activities ranged from producing films as teaching materials[17] to general promotion of the educational use of film[18].

3) The economical aspect of the small-gauge film was in striking contrast to that of 35mm. Compared to approximately 69 yen, the average monthly income of the university graduates around 1930, the cost for an imported 9.5mm camera or projector was 90yen each, and an imported 16mm camera was priced at about 450-800yen, with 540yen for a projector. However, used or domestically-manufactured products were available with far less expensive prices. Therefore, the demographic of

small-gauge film fans, which had centered initially on the upper-middle class male, both within university circles as well as educators, gradually expanded once used or domestically-manufactured equipment appeared on the market. The Prokino Movement (which will be discussed later) and the increased usage of the small-gauge film during wartime largely derived from this economic factor.

4) Kodak was especially known for starting full-fledged facilities that provided multiple services including film development. Kodak's advertizing blurb, "You Press the Lever, We Do the Rest," stressed a setup where all users had to do was to shoot, with Kodak Service Stations processing everything else. However, some small-gauge filmmakers in Japan rather preferred "self-development," which enabled them to learn ideal exposure levels and to attain more desirable results. Moreover, 9.5mm offered a favorable option that allowed reversal development, which did not require space, electricity or proper equipment. Reversal development was especially a major issue in the early 1920s, and its growth was in part deeply rooted in Tsubameya Sales Company (*Tsubameya Shōkai*) in Sanjō Karasuma in Kyoto[19].

5) Kodak's color film and panchromatic film (both released in 1928) as well as the talkie (disc type released in 1930) gave the consumers a variety of film to choose from. Due to this ample variety, works using color and talkie technologies appeared faster in small-gauge film than in theatrical Japanese films.

6) The image quality of the small-gauge film was inevitably inferior to that of 35mm, and that made it remain as a "sub-standard" format. While Kodak and other manufacturers released screens produced specifically for small-gauge film projection, "Baby Party" members in Japan claimed that using Kent paper for a screen would provide brighter images than those on the market due to its reflection ratio; sharing its method[20] in magazines, they often organized large-scale screenings with over 500 viewers in various locations. In the U.S., there are records indicating that massive screenings of around 1000 people were also held with 16mm film[21]. Some of these small-gauge filmmakers who had knowledge of projection techniques were also active as members of projection tours during the wartime.

3. Aspects of Small-Gauge Film Culture

3-1. Formation of Local Community and All Nippon

As was discussed before, small-gauge film fans established their own regional clubs to organize screenings and filming competitions, as well as publishing their journals, and their activities led to the formation of local communities. In the case of 9.5mm, most of such clubs in Japan were based in local photo studios (which sold cameras, projectors and films) or pharmacies (which handled developing chemicals), and these sites became salons for general member gatherings, screenings and publications.

The earliest and the most thriving examples can be found in the Keihanshin district, centered notably in Kyoto and Osaka. The All-Kansai Baby Kinema Club Competition was held in 1926, and many of the participants would later constitute Osaka Baby Kinema Club and Kyoto Baby Cinema Association, through which they arranged a variety of events including observation tours of Nikkatsu Kyoto Studio and Makino Studio. 1926 also saw the establishment of Tokyo Baby Cinema in Tokyo as the recovery from the Great Kanto Earthquake (1923) had progressed. Tokyo Baby Cinema built momentum to commence the National Pathé Baby Competition, which would become a nation-scale forum for small-gauge film lovers to communicate.

Kyoto Baby Cinema Association offered close exchange between professionals and amateurs: it listed up then-Nikkatsu Studio Scenario Division's Wakaba Kaoru and Mikoshiba Morio as the principal members as well as Murata Minoru and Mori Iwao as advisers, and filmmaker Suzuki Shigeyoshi and Prokino's Kimura Sotoji also frequented the group[22]. Along with Wakaba Kaoru, Tanaka Yoshitsugu and Nakano Takao, both of whom would later form Dōeisha, which produced *Perot the Chimney Sweep* (*Entotsuya Perō*, 1930), also played central roles in managing the club's activities, and they published the magazine *Baby Cinema* from the aforementioned Tsubameya in Sanjō Karasuma. In 1928, the club, under the joint sponsorship of Kyoto Ski Runner Club, hosted a filming competition on the theme of skiing[23], which laid the foundation for the aforementioned *Atago Ski Resort*. Their venues included Jūjiya Musical Instrument Store or Daimai Hall (both in Sanjō in Kyoto), and the number of participants in their regular meetings increased to over 50 by 1929, with their screenings also attracting between 500 and 600 viewers each time[24]. Yoda Yoshikata, who debuted in Nikkatsu Kyoto as a scriptwriter in 1931 on a Murata Minoru film, had already been engaged with Kyoto W.O. Cinema[25], one of the Kyoto-based 9.5mm film clubs, as an actor and scriptwriter since the 1920s, and he was also an active participant in Baby Cinema events[26]. Filled with not just film productions by seven major studios of various sizes, but also numerous small-gauge film productions and related events, including the activities of Prokino Kyoto branch, Kyoto around this time was a cinema city that weaved the professional with the amateur. Among its members was, for example, Takeuchi Yoshinosuke, whose film Sister (Ane) was awarded a prize from the London International Amateur Filmmakers Association in 1935 and selected for a 16mm world tour[27]. Etona Film Productions was also established right around this time.

The journals issued by 9.5mm or 16mm film clubs generally reported other regional club activities. Among them, it should be noted that *Baby Cinema*, the journal affiliated with Tokyo Baby Cinema Club (*Tokyo Bebī Shinema Kurabu*, later renamed as Japan Pathé Cinema Association [*Nippon Patē Shinema Kyōkai*]), which Kyoto Baby Cinema Association also belonged to, spent a number of pages to detail activities in remote locations, especially those in Korea, Manchuria, and Taiwan, rather than those in urban areas such as Tokyo, Osaka and Kyoto. Tokyo Baby Cinema Club, in parallel with aforementioned educational film libraries, initiated a system to loan prize-winning works to local screenings, and its objective was "to manifest the power of Pathé Baby by strengthening benevolent integration between Tokyo Club and other regional gatherings, as well as by expanding the field of the small-gauge film circle"[28]. While it was in part obviously a counterplot against 16mm, one club member in Hamhung in Korea reported that "I am making every effort to propagate the power of Pathé Baby throughout this Northern corner of Korea by gathering our fellow townspeople to organize a meeting"[29] and also continued that "it is true that we have now three more Pathé party members. (….) I am deeply grateful for the lending of precious films to us"; this local member in Hamhung cultivated a sense of solidarity with Tokyo Club and enthusiastically worked to build regional community through films loaned from Tokyo and journals in which her/his own contributions were printed. The editorial column also included a letter with questions from an area with no electricity. Owing to the features of 9.5mm, which cost only one sixth the cost of 16mm and which enabled users to develop the film easily with measuring cups (or to develop reversely merely with natural sunlight), 9.5mm film culture gradually spread at the grassroots level. Since Tokyo office members noted that they were "very pleased indeed to find the true significance of small-gauge film in the respectable club activities coordinated by our comrades residing in seemingly unreachable remote rural areas and islands across the border"[30], they articulated their satisfaction with this network that reached the periphery. 9.5mm and magazines transported "physically" by rail from Tokyo connected peripheral regions with central Tokyo, functioning as an apparatus that formed an awareness of constructing a notion of an "all-Japan."

3-2. Genres: From Prokino to Discipline to Touring

Small-gauge film consisted of a variety of genres including the home movie, private film (*kojin eiga*), experimental film, animation, cultural film (*bunka eiga*), educational film and documentary; however, the interwar period in Japan was marked by the films produced under Prokino or the Proletarian Film League of Japan (*Nihon Puroretaria Eiga Dōmei*).

Prokino, founded in 1929, was the first group in Japan that advocated their films as "weapons". Whereas the small-gauge films they produced – for agitation and propaganda – were screened in various locations, after oppression from the government in 1934, most leading members of Prokino ("switched" sides and) continued to develop their activities in the fields of cultural film and educational film under the propagandistic regime of Japanese government. For instance, Sasa Genjū, a representative Prokino filmmaker who practiced the agenda of "film as weapon", critically analyzed a film on the governmental policy on colonization as an "educational film merely for the publicity of the capitalist nation's colonial policy"[31] during his Prokino years. However, from the mid-1930s Sasa worked as an editor and publisher of the state-leaning magazine *Culture Film* (*Bunka Eiga*), and there he fully demonstrated the knowledge and ability he had built up in Prokino.

Prokino's branch in Kyoto marked the beginning of their activity with The *Worker-Farmer Funeral of Yamamoto Senji* (*Yamasen Rōnōsai*), which filmed with 16mm the funeral of Yamamoto Senji, who had been assassinated by a right-wing thug in 1929. Following the 10 day shooting period, this work was first screened unedited in front of those who were attending the funereal wake. As a result, the film proved the mobility, flexibility and the immediate power of small-gauge film. The Third Prokino Screening, which was held in Kyoto, was the first Prokino screening gathering outside Tokyo, and Daimai Hall, a familiar site for Baby Party members as well as small-gauge film fans in Kyoto, was selected as the venue. A total of 5 films – Prokino's *Sumida River* (*Sumidagawa*), *Children* (*Kodomo*), *May Day* (*Mēdē*), *The Eleventh Osaka May Day* (*Dai jūikkai Ōsaka Mēdē*) and Dōeisha's *Perot the Chimney Sweep* (*Entotsuya Perō*) – were screened twice a day, and all screenings were completely filled to reach a total of 1,000 viewers. "More than half [of the audiences] were students or petit bourgeois"[32], workers were about thirty percent, and the rest comprised striking union labors from Kyoto Paper Company, Sanya Copper and Brass, and Yūzen Union as well as Korean residents in Japan. Since *Perot the Chimney Sweep*, a film by Tanaka Yoshitsugu, the representative small-gauge filmmaker of the Kyoto Baby Cinema Association, was in the program, it can be thought that "students or petit bourgeois" include regular attendees of other small-gauge film screenings in Kyoto area.

Matsuzaki Keiji and Kitagawa Tetsuo, both of whose activities continued in postwar independent film productions, had been early and well-known members of the Prokino Kyoto branch and also central figures of Prokino in general. Kitagawa, who had once advocated, "All militant amateur cineastes should participate in [Prokino] as film correspondents!"[33] and who had practiced vigorous filmmaking activities in Tokyo during his Prokino years, switched sides (like Sasa Genjū) to the governmental regime and engaged in edificatory activities through nationwide projection tours. For instance, in his 1942 article "The Military Status of Small-Gauge Film" (*Kogata eiga no tōtai*)[34], Kitagawa urged all small-gauge filmmakers to submit their old works, in addition to re-edited versions based on the theme of wartime national spirit, for a projection tour throughout the Kansai area connected to political organizations such as Yokusankai, Sanpō and Sankumi. Kitagawa claimed this to be edification for small-gauge filmmakers themselves by stating that the point of those activities was to "suffer and rejoice together in living our national livelihood, and most importantly, [to] train our minds as national citizens." Moreover, in his 1943 essay titled "From Manchuria" (*Manshū kara*)[35], Kitagawa notes "how challenging and rewarding [his activities in Manchuria were] as a filmmaker"[36], while stressing the importance of film as an "enlightening entertainment" through the use of small-gauge film in vast Manchuria, which had a low literacy rate, in addition to enthusiastically discussing how Manchuria "provides [small-gauge film] with the ultimate opportunity to fulfill its primary function"[37]. Kitagawa further stated that "to screen films that give [farmers in Manchuria] energy and hope for tomorrow would be ideal and superlative cultural maneuvering"[38]. Both Sasa and Kitagawa seemingly continued practicing the "know-how" they had accumulated in their Prokino years by replacing the dichotomy between capitalist and worker/farmer with that between imperial Japan and colonies.

3-3. Amateur Films and National Agenda

In parallel with the Prokino members' turnabout, the years between the passage of the Proposal for Motion Picture and National Policy (*Eiga kokusaku kengian*) in 1933 and the prohibition on importing film and film materials in 1937 saw the strengthening of state control over the use of film as well as direction and purpose of filmmaking, and it made it difficult for small-gauge film circles to produce films, even on the individual level. Competitions also adopted subjects fitting for war propaganda, and after the enactment of Film Law in 1939, the government required small-gauge filmmakers and productions to pass a "skill qualifying examination" (*ginō shinsa shiken*) and obtain a license to screen their works legally.

The only figure from the small-gauge film world selected as a judge for the qualifying examination was Tsukamoto Kōji, then the most respected filmmaker in the groups. Tsukamoto, who had already monopolized the top prizes at various competitions since the 1920s, was a giant of the mountain genre; habitually using 9.5mm (suitable for filming on the mountains), his mastery of shooting as well as developing techniques also led to the development of new equipment, for instance for iris, fade and cranking. Tsukamoto often sat on juries at competitions in the 1930s and took a commanding role in the judging of films in line with national policy.

In his 1942 essay "The Production and Situation of Mountain Films" (*Sangaku eiga no seisaku to jikyoku*)[39], Tsukamoto, lamenting the status of small-gauge filmmaking as incapable of persuading the judges, articulated the common ground between mountain climbing and national policy as well as the purpose and necessity of making mountain films under the wartime. He argued that mountain climbing was "the most spiritual of all physical athletics and simultaneously the most directly related to national defense"[40], as well as "the home-front activity closest to the frontline"[41]. Mountains in Japan "most intensely and genuinely keep the natural beauty of our homeland concealed"[42] and therefore make one feel the "reverence for our national land that should be protected"[43]. Tsukamoto concluded by asserting that the necessity and purpose of making mountain films in times of war were to "raise the spirit of patriotism"[44]. However, beginning with the rather suggestive prefatory statement, "Escaping from the bustle of the world, mountains are a site for contemplation"[45], the essay also reaffirmed the possibility of small-gauge film as an avocation, when Tsukamoto noted that "how blissful and meaningful it is to recognize that small-gauge filmmaking as my hobby is also, even in some small degree, accorded with a national goal"[46]. This can be read as Tsukamoto, in the same way that he had expounded in these journals his views on film technologies, also announcing a technique for passing the litmus test.

This essay contains two types of ambivalences – one between policy directives of the propaganda film and methods of hobbyist small-gauge filmmaking, as well as another between the heightened awareness of evaluation from the central authority and the pride of the small-gauge film circle as a sub-standard – that epitomized characteristics of small-gauge film culture in Japan during this time.

The cultural traits of the small-gauge film in interwar Japan were formed through individual and communal activities as well as various movements in each genre and format, and Kyoto took the lead in the early formation of its basic ground. While evoking the special characteristics of each individual entity, a picture clearly emerges of the process that gradually integrated the small-gauge film into the field of propaganda media under the national regime. What becomes visible is a process through which small-gauge film spread throughout Japan as an apparatus that fostered national identity, while at the same time the dichotomized structure between the 35mm standard and the sub-standard was transformed into the other polarized consciousnesses, between 16mm and 9.5mm as well as the center and the periphery. This dynamism itself can be thought of as the idiosyncrasy of small-gauge film culture in Japan during an interwar period.

(1) Small-gauge film is the term that refers to the film width. As 35mm film was used and standardized for theatrical film, films with all other widths were considered as sub-standards. The term small-gauge film applies to films smaller in width than 35mm, including 28mm, 17.5mm, 16mm, 9.5mm, 8mm and others. Large-gauge film refers to 70mm film or films larger in width than 35mm.

(2) For the overview of Etona Film Productions and Tanaka Eiichi, please refer to my article "The Trace of Etona Film Productions: Interview Survey on Film History of Rakusei Area", *Art Research* vol.5. (http://www.arc.ritsumei.ac.jp/art_coe/work/k_05.html)

(3) Cine-Kodak Special was first advertised as multifunctional (including stop motion function) professional camera when it was released in May 1933. Direct sales retail price was $375. ((1933)"Introducing Cine-Kodak Special", *The Movie makers*, May,

198-199.)
(4) About "Home Movie Day", please refer to the main URL (http: //www. homemovieday.com/) and Japanese URL (http://www.homemovieday.jp/index/ hmd.html)
(5) Patricia R.Zimmermann. (1995) *Reel Families:A Social history of Amateur Film.* Bloomington and Indianapolis: Indiana University Press. Alan Kattelle. (2000) *Home Movies: A History of the American Industry, 1897 - 1979.* New Hampshire: Transition Publishing. Karen L. Ishizuka and Patrisia R. Zimmermann, eds. (2008) *Mining the Home movie: Excavations in Histories and Memories.* Berkeley: University of California Press. Ian Craven, eds. (2009) *Movies on Home Ground: Explorations in Amateur Cinema.* Cambridge Scholars Publishing.
(6) Using Pathé Baby and won numerous awards at film competitions from the late 1920s, Ogino Shigeji (1899-1991) was a pioneer amateur filmmaker in Japan.
(7) Nada Hisashi, "Kogata eiga no gijutsu to biteki kihan ni tsuite (1929-1932)" (On Technology of Small-Gauge Film and its Aesthetic Norm 1929-1932), *Eizōgaku* 55 (1995): 30-43/Makino Mamoru, "Senzen no Nihon kogata eigashi ni okeru shuyōna chōryu to sono tokushitsu" (Major Trends and Characterstics of the Prewar History of Small-Gauge Film in Japan), *Eizō Gakkai Kaihō* (1989): 70. Nagata Toyoomi, "Kagaku kenkyūhi hojokin [kiban kenkyū C] kenkyū seika hōkokusho: 'geinō engeki bunya no mukei bunkazai hozon no hōhō ni kansuru kisoteki kenkyū'mukei bunkazai to kiroku hozon [miyako odori no 16 miri eiga o daizai toshite" *Tokutei Hieiri Katsudō Hōjin Eiga Hozon Kyōkai Kogata Eigabu-hen* (2010)/"9.5miri firumu no chōsa kenkyū Kataoka Korekushon chōsa kenkyū" *Tokutei Hieiri Katsudou Hōjin Eiga Hozon Kyōkai Kogata Eigabu, Eiga Hozon Kyōkai Kogata Eigabu/Eiga Hozon Kyōkai Kogata Eigabu-hen* (2010)"Senzen kogata eiga shiryōsyū" *Eiga Hozon Kyōkai.*
(8) There are various views on when Pathé Baby was first released in Japan. Ōtomo Yoshisuke stated that "It [Pathé Baby] was first imported to Japan in 1922, but was interrupted by the earthquake. So it became prosperous in 1924", and Kurata Shigetarō also mentioned that "Jūjiya managing director Mr. Suzuki Ikusaburō started selling it [Pathé Baby] in 1922 saying that it is a machine like a toy we can play with" in
"Zadankai kiroku: kogata eiga no enkaku o kataru" (The Report from Round-Table: Discussing the History of Small-Geuge Film), *Kogata Eiga* 2-1 (Jan. 1930): 34. Also please refer to Mimura Kisaku, "Honpō kogata eiga hattatsu manroku: sono ichi"

(Development Chronicle of Small-Gauge Film in Japan: Part 1), *Tokyo Kogata Eiga Kyōkai Kaihō* 27 (July. 1939): 1.

(9) "Jihō kurabumei kaishō" (News: Renaming Club), *Bebī Shinema* 3-9 (Sep. 1930):12-13.

(10) In "You will find Amateur Movie Makers and Progressive Dealer at each of the following addresses. Visit them!", *The Movie Makers* (Feb. 1928): 136, only Ōsawa Shōkai was listed as Japanese branch.

(11) Fuse Makoto, "Patē Bebī kyōikuyō firumu raiburarī ni tsuite" (On Film Library for Pathé Baby Education), *Amachua Kinema* 1-3 (July. 1928): 1-2.

(12) Banno Bunzaburō, "Furansu ni okeru eiga kyōiku" (Film Education in France), *Bebī Shinema* 12 (Jun. 1928): 2/ Banno Bunzaburō, "Furansu no eiga kyōiku" (Film Education in France), *Bebī Shinema* 14 (Nov. 1928): 10.

(13) Banchō Shōgakkō, Mihoshi Masaaki, "Eiga kyōju" (Film Education), *Bebī Shinema* 12 (Jun. 1928): 3-4.

(14) The 6th Pathé Baby Filming Competition set its theme "that demonstrated the subjects of elementary school's textbooks or that incorporating their own ideas into such subjects or that could be used for school education" in "Kaikoku" (Announcement), *Bebī Shinema* 2-10 (Aug. 1929): 1. The top prize went to Tsukamoto Kōji's *The Power of Nature* (*Daishizen no chikara*), and the second prize went to Ogino Shigeji's *Until the Train Runs on Track* (*Densha ga kidō o hashiru made*) andMizumachi Noriyuki's *A Carrier Pigeon* (*denshobato*).

(15) *Bebī Shinema* received a number of opinions from licenced teachers (*kundō*). And the statictics gathered from girls' schools and junior high schools in Japan show that schools were often equipped with both 9.5mm and 16mmcameras, yet the most of schools owns only 16mm projectors. Nishimura Masami, "Gijutsuteki mondai no jūyōsei" (Importance of Technical Issues), *Bunka Eiga* 1-6 (Aug. 1938): 32-33.

(16) "Zenkoku kakuchi eiga kyōiku keiei kikan" (Throughout the Nation: Film Education Studies Manegement Institutions), *Bunka Eiga* 1-6 (Aug. 1938): 52-53.

(17) "Kurabu nyūsu Kyoto-shi kyōiku eiga kenkyūkai" (Club News: Kyoto City Educational Film Study Group), *Amachua Eiga* (*Eiga to Gijutsu*) 1-2 (Feb. 1935): 115.

(18) The lecture was given to a total of approximately 200 audiences which consisted of the graduate class of 1936 Rissei Normal School and the school teachers newly hired by Kyoto city. "Kurabu nyūsu Kyoto-shi kyōiku eiga kōshūkai" (Club News: Kyoto City Educational Film Lecture Session), *Amachua Eiga* (*Eiga to Gijutsu*) 4-6 (Dec. 1936): 417.

(19) Ōtomo Yoshisuke stated that "when we think back, after Pathé Baby was imported to Japan, reversal development was first developed in Kyoto. Especially the development by Tsubameya gained nationwide fame. Later we learned and researched hard to improve the service in Tokyo, where nowadays a number of people become our clients and appreciate our work" in "Dai kyōgikai o tsūjite mitaru rokō oyobi genzō ni tsuite" (Observation from the Film Competition: on Exposure and Development), *Bebī Shinema* 1-2 (Feb. 1928): 6-7.

(20) Wakō Ryō, "Taninzū ni miseru eisha sōchi" (A Projector to Show to the Mass Audience), *Bebī Shinema* 2-2 (Dec. 1928): 13-14.

(21) Arthur L. Gale, "Amateur Clubs: News of Group Filming." *The Movie Makers* (Oct. 1929): 652.

(22) Sakamoto Tameyuki, "Kansai amachuā eigakai no konjaku to watashi" (Overview of Amateur Film Circle in Kansai Area and Me), *Bunka Eiga* 2-7 (Oct. 1939): 44-45.

(23) "Annai: zenkoku rengō Pate Babī satsuei kyōgi taikai" (Invitation: National Federation Pathé Baby Filming Competition), *Bebī Shinema* 1-2 (Feb. 1928): 13.

(24) Ueda Kan, "Tsūshin" (Report), *Bebī Shinema* 2-11 (Sep. 1929): 2.

(25) See *D.O. Eiga Pate Bebī* (1929).

(26) Sakamoto Tameyuki, "Kansai amachuā eigakai no konjaku to watashi" 44-45.

(27) "Kurabu nyūsu I.A.C. sekai jun'ei firumu no kōkai" (Club News: the Release of I.A.C. World Tour Films), *Amachua Eiga (Eiga to Gijutsu)* 7-2 (Feb. 1938): 139.

(28) "Jihō junkai eisha" (Report Projection Tours) (1929), *Bebī Shinema* 2-6 (Apr. 1929): 2.

(29) Sagizaka Soku, "Tsūshin Keijō dayori" (Correspondence: News from Keijō), *Bebī Shinema* 2-6 (Apr.1929): 32.

(30) Yoshikawa Hayao "Baika zasshin" (Plum Blossom Notes), *Bebī Shinema* 3-3 (Mar. 1930): 14-15.

(31) Sasa Genjū, "Shokuminchi eiga ni tsuite" (On Colonial Films), *Proretaria Eiga* (Oct. 1930): 16-27.

(32) "Kōkai tōsō no kiroku Kyoto deha ikani tatakawarete kitaka" (The Document of the Struggle on View: How it has been battled in Kyoto), *Proretaria Eiga* (Aug.1930): 58.

(33) Kitagawa Tetsuo, "Purokino eiga tsūshin'in ni tsuite, sono sōan" (On Prokino Film Correspondent: a Draft), *Proretaria Eiga* (Aug.1930): 19-21.

(34) Kitagawa Tetsuo, "Kogata eiga no tōtai" (The Military Status of Small-Gauge Film), *Kogata Eiga* 2-3 (Apr.1942): 2-3.

(35) Kitagawa Tetsuo, "Manshū kara" (From Manchuria), *Kogata Eiga* 3-3 (Feb.1943): 2-3.
(36) *Ibid.*
(37) *Ibid.*
(38) *Ibid.*
(39) Tsukamoto Kōji, "Sangaku eiga no sēsaku to jikyoku" (The Production and Situation of Mountain Films), *Kogata Eiga* (Aug. 1942): 5-6.
(40) *Ibid.*
(41) *Ibid.*
(42) *Ibid.*
(43) *Ibid.*
(44) *Ibid.*
(45) *Ibid.*
(46) *Ibid.*

(Translator's note: I would like to thank Michael Chan for proofreading the earlier version of this translation.)

[Notes]
This paper is extensive re-vised version based on my presentation at the "A Symposium—The Makino Collection at Columbia: the Present and Future of an Archive"(November 2011, Columbia University).

Translated by Takuya Tsunoda

おわりに

　本書は、人文学の研究者たちが、立命館大学グローバルCOEプログラム「日本文化デジタル・ヒューマニティーズ拠点」（2007年度〜2011年度）の5年間にわたるデジタル・アーカイブ活動をとおして、それぞれの領域の膨大な史料や文化資源との対話を重ねながら、個々の特性や背景にある豊饒な文化への考察をすすめた記録でもある。執筆者の多くが、デジタル・ヒューマニティーズの前事業である21世紀COEプログラム「京都アート・エンタテインメント創成研究」（2002〜2006年度）から、アート・リサーチセンターを拠点としたデジタル・アーカイブのプロジェクトにかかわっていることを付言したうえで、本シリーズにおける本書の特殊性を述べておきたい。
　本書の内容が、他の号に比べていわゆるデジタル・ヒューマニティーズ"らしくない"、どちらかというと伝統的な知の手法にのっとった歴史、文化研究も多く含む「京都文化論」になることは、編者間でコンセプトを検討していた時点からみえていたことである。その理由として、イメージデータベースを本書のコンセプトから外したことも一因といえるかもしれないが、むしろそれ以上に、人文学の研究者にとっては、デジタル・アーカイブの活動を続け、大量のデータベースに触れ、その恩恵を日々受けながらもなお、最も関心の高いテーマは、目の前にある史料や文化資源を丹念に読み解くことであり、そしてそれらを創造した歴史や社会的、文化的コンテクストを明らかにし、記録することにあるからである。史料や文化資源それ自体と、そこに込められた情報と、背後にあるコンテクストを保存することが、デジタルも含めたアーカイブの基本であり、と同時に、デジタル・ツールや技法はそれらの共有化を飛躍的に容易にするものとして、両者はすでに不可分の存在であるといってよいだろう。その意味でも、本書の編集方針は、5年間にわたるデジタル・ヒューマニティーズの教育・

研究をとおして深めた京都文化研究の成果として、史料や文化資源、都市イメージを共通項目として設定するだけにとどめ、論考の手法を方向付けることはしなかった。各プロジェクトのデータベースやデジタル・アーカイブ、およびそれらの手法については、アート・リサーチセンターのウェブサイト（http://www.arc.ritsumei.ac.jp/index.html）を参照されたい。

　本書はまた、一つの研究成果であると同時に、途中報告でもある。なぜなら、各プロジェクトで蓄積した史料、文化資源、知的遺産の次世代への継承と、それらのデジタル・データの共有化は、アーカイブの常として永続性を前提としているからである。本書に記された史料や文化資源のデジタル・アーカイブは、共有化をとおして、さらなる国内外からの協力関係や資料の発掘へとつながり、広大かつ膨大なデジタル・ヒューマニティーズの地平を切り開くことにもなるだろう。そのためにも、この分野に秀でた若手研究者の育成と活躍の場の開拓は必須の要件であり、本著がその一助となることを期待したい。

2012年2月

編者代表　冨田美香

Afterword

The digital archiving projects of "The Digital Humanities Center for Japanese Arts and Cultures" at Ritsumeikan University Global COE program lasted for five years, academic years 2007 through 2011. During this period, many humanities researchers have examined an enormous volume of historical and cultural resources in each researcher's area of specialty and inquired into the rich culture behind the individual characteristics and background of each cultural asset. This book is a record of these long-term activities. In fact, many of the authors were engaged in digital archiving projects at the Art Research Center under the forerunner of this program during the academic years 2002 through 2006, the "Kyoto Art and Entertainment Innovation Research" program with the 21st Century COE program.

Here, I will explain the characteristic place of this book in the series. From the time when the editors began discussing the possible concepts of this book, we were already expecting this book to be less "digital-humanities-like," and more of a "theory of Kyoto culture" that includes many historical and cultural studies based on a traditional research methods. One of the reasons for this is that we excluded image databases from the scope of this book. However, another more important reason is that, for researchers of humanities, the most interesting issues arise out of close readings of the historical and cultural sources, taking into consideration the historical, social, and cultural context of such sources, and recording them. This does not change even after many years of digital archiving activities, dealing with numerous databases, and reaping their benefits. The function of archives, including digital ones, is the preservation of historical and cultural sources, their information, and contexts. At the same time, digital tools and techniques are inseparable from this function, as they make it extremely easy for us to share such archives. This is why we decided to set historical and cultural resources and urban images as common issues for the researches to address through the five years of educational and research activities, without fixing the research methods of each article. Please refer to the website of the Art Research Center (http://www.arc.ritsumei.ac.jp/index.html) for databases, digital archives, and methods that each project uses.

This book is not only reports on the achievements of each project, but also reports on works still in progress. As is common for any archive, the sharing and inheritance of digital data as well as collections of tangible historical sources, cultural resources, and intellectual heritage to future generations presumes the permanence of the archive. By sharing the digital archives of historical and cultural materials that are reported in this book, we hope to call for more cooperation from domestic and international institutions in discovering new materials; it will broaden the horizons of the digital humanities. It is necessary to raise young talented scholars in this field and widen their spheres of activity in order to achieve such a goal. We hope that this book can be step towards this goal.

February 2012
Mika Tomita, Primary Editor
(Translated by Shiho Takai)

索 引

あ 行

アイヌ文様　61,68-69
浅草公園六区　89
足利義政　7
足利義満　7,12
飛鳥井栄雅　7,123
飛鳥井雅縁　12
アンジェリコ，フラ　50
アンダーソン，ウィリアム　45-52,54-55
イーストマン・コダック（コダック）　107-110
伊勢型紙アーカイブ　75
稲畑勝太郎　90
印　35
浮世絵派　47
裏辻季福　8-10,12
映像アーキビスト協会（AMIA）　106
エトナ映画社　104,111,115
夷谷座　91,93-94
大炊御門（大路）　18,20-21,23-24
大虎座　91-101
大西座　95,101
大橋商店　67
大宮（大路）　15,17,18,20-21,23-25
大宮川　24
荻野茂二　106,116
織田信秀　5
尾上松之助　98
小野美材　3
小野流　36
お雇い外国人　45-46

か 行

改良俄　95-96
ガウランド，ウィリアム　45-47,49,51-55
括弧文　61
加藤正方　6
金森宗和　10
狩野派　45,47,51-52

歌舞伎座　90,93-94,98,101
高陽院　18,24
カラヴァッジョ　50
唐絵　2
閑院　18,20-21,24
韓国併合　58-73
灌頂　34
灌頂水　34
北川鉄夫　113-114,117-118
木立研究室　75,76
北電気館　90-91,94
喜納昌吉　72
木村荘十二　111
行基図　36
京都画壇　58
京都御所　41
京都ベビー・シネマ協会　107,110-111,113
極札　4,7,12
空海　3
芸術座　99-100
溪嵐拾葉集　36
源氏物語　2,3,5,9
工芸プロジェクト・染色型紙デジタルアーカイブ　75
光厳天皇　41
光宗　36
江談抄　3
杲宝　34
弘法大師　37
後柏原天皇　4-5
古今和歌集　2,5
国際フィルム・アーカイブ聯盟（FIAF）　105
後三条天皇　36
護持僧作法　38
呉春　45
五天竺図　30
後奈良天皇　5
近衛家　8

近衛前久	8	青蓮院流	4
近衛信尋	8	新聞俄	95-96
小林寅吉	97	朱雀（大路）	15,17-18,20-21,23,25
古筆家	2,4,12	鈴木重吉	111
古筆勘兵衛	8	成尊	36
古筆切	1-2	世尊寺流	4
古筆切所収情報データベース 1		雪舟	49-50
古筆了佐	1,6-8,10,12	山海経	29
金剛界曼荼羅	39	1910年	63
金剛頂宗綱概	34	戦争	58
金輪王	37	千宗旦	7-8
金輪聖王	39	総持抄	35

さ 行

曾我廼家五郎十郎一座　91,93

才葉抄	3	即位灌頂	34
嵯峨天皇	3	即位法	35
佐々元十	112-114,117	即席俄	97
三国観	32	尊円親王	3-5

た 行

三条西実条	5	大英博物館	47

大英博物館所蔵日本中国絵画カタログ（Descriptive and Historical Catalogue of a Collection of Japan and Chinese Paintings in the British Museum）　46

三条西実隆	4-5	大覚寺文書	6,9
三蹟	3	大極殿	35
三筆	3	胎蔵界曼荼羅	38
GIS	15,17,25	大戴礼記	33
慈円	32	大内裏	15,17,20,24
爾雅	33	大東文化大学書道研究所 11
四海	29,33-34	大日如来	36
四海印	35	大日本帝国	63
四海領掌印	35	大般涅槃経	32
慈覚大師	37	太陽暦	31
四条派	45,52	内裏	37
七条大路	15,17,20-21,25	高井蘭山	30
司馬江漢	30	高松殿	24-25
若木書法	11	武内吉之助	111
写生	45,47,49-55	武野紹鷗	2
入木抄	3	橘逸勢	3
入木道	3	伊達家	12
須弥山	29	田中英一	103,115
須弥山図解	30		
勝覚	38		
相国寺承天閣	12		
松竹	93,98		
正徹	2		

田中聖峰　104
田中喜次　111,113
池亭記　39
中央館（中央電気館）　90-91,98,101
中国派　52-53
澄豪　34
朝鮮　61-63,68-70,73
勅題　66
塚本閤治　114,117-118
土御門（大路）　17-18
土御門殿　17
鶴見大学付属図書館　1
帝国館　91,96,98,101
ディシャン　50
ディロン，フランク　45
篆刻美術館　11
天竺徳兵衛　70
天皇　28
転輪王　34
東京国立近代美術館フィルムセンター　106
東京ベビーシネマ倶楽部　111
土佐派　52
豊臣秀吉　89
ドラクロア　50

な　行

中御門（大路）　18,20-21,24
中野孝夫　111
なくさめ草　2
名古屋大学後藤文庫　1
南贍部洲　30
西洞院（大路）　15,23-25
西洞院川　24
21世紀COEプログラム　76
二条（大路）　15,17-18,20-21,23,25
日活　88,93,96,98-101,105,110-111
日葡辞書　33
日本絵画芸術（The Pictorial Arts of Japan）
　46
日本協会　45,47
日本プロレタリア映画同盟（プロキノ）　109-114,117

日本文化デジタル・ヒューマニティーズ拠点　76
日本略記　37
野路宗仲　10,13

は　行

ハート，アーネスト　45-49,51-52,54-55
パテ・ベビー（パテーベビー）　106-107,109,111-112,116-117
英一蝶　50
東三条殿　18,24
東洞院（大路）　15,20-25
微小点接着法　80-81,83,86
枇杷殿　17
福宝堂　93
藤井永観文庫　4
富士館　91,98,100
藤谷為賢　6-12
伏見天皇　4-5,36
藤原俊成　6
藤原定家　6,12
普門円通　30
粉本　45,49-50,53
平安京　28
法顕　34
法住寺殿　20-21
鳳林承章　6,7
墨跡　2
梵暦　30

ま・や・ら・わ　行

槇村正直　89
松井須磨子　99,101
松崎啓次　113
円山応挙　45,51-54
円山四条派　44-46,48-49,51,53-55
ミケランジェロ　50
南座　91,97,99
南電気館　90-91,95
明兆　50
村田実　111
明治座　90

247

森狙仙　50
森田佐吉　105
夜鶴庭訓抄　3
山科家　5
山科言継　4,5
山科言経　5
やまと絵　45,47-48,51
横田永之助　97
横田商会　91,93
吉沢商店　93
慶滋保胤　39
依田義賢　111
蘭学　31
ランドシーア．エドウィン　50

立命館大学　74,76-77,84
立命館大学アート・リサーチセンター　74, 76-77,84
両部不二　39
両部曼荼羅　37
琳派　48
ルーベンス　50
冷泉家　6
連歌　2,3,6
六波羅探題　23
若葉馨　111
和漢名数　3
早稲田大学古筆切データベース　1
和蘭天説　30,46,48-49

編者・執筆者一覧（五〇音順、＊印は編者）

彬子女王（あきこじょおう）
立命館大学衣笠総合研究機構 PD
1981年東京都生まれ。専門は在外日本美術コレクション研究、日英文化交流史。
「標本から美術へ―19世紀の日本美術蒐集、特にアンダーソン・コレクションの意義について」（『國華』1360号、2009年）、共編著『風俗絵画の文化学Ⅱ―虚実をうつす機知』（思文閣出版、2012年）、など。
担当：第4章、第12章

大矢 敦子（おおや・あつこ）
京都文化博物館学芸課映像・情報室嘱託職員、立命館大学衣笠総合研究機構客員研究員
1978年京都府生まれ。専門は日本映画史。
「『東海道中膝栗毛』関連作品に見られる歌舞伎から映画への連続性―江戸期の時空間イメージの創出―」（『イメージ・データベースと日本文化研究』、ナカニシヤ出版、2010年）、「連鎖劇における映画場面の批評をめぐって」（『アート・リサーチ』、Vol. 10、2010年）、など。
担当：第7章、第15章

川嶋 將生（かわしま・まさお）
立命館大学名誉教授・立命館大学衣笠総合研究機構特別招聘教授
1942年三重県生まれ。専門は日本文化史。
『室町文化論考―文化史のなかの公武―』（法政大学出版局、2008年）、『祇園祭―祝祭の京都―』（吉川弘文館、2010年）、など。
担当：第1章、第9章

＊木立 雅朗（きだち・まさあき）
立命館大学文学部教授
1960年石川県生まれ。専門は日本考古学、地域史。
「粘土紐接合痕の変化」（『釜山大学校考古学科創設20周年記念論文集』 釜山大学校考古学科、2010年2月）、「信楽焼陶器製地雷について―聞き取り調査と研究ノート―」（『立命館大学考古学論集Ⅴ』、立命館大学考古学論集刊行会、2010年5月）、など。
担当：第5章、第13章

＊杉橋 隆夫（すぎはし・たかお）
立命館大学文学部教授
1946年静岡県生まれ。専門は日本中世史、古文書学。
共編著『兵範記人名索引』（思文閣出版、2007年）、共編著『立命館大学京都文化講座「京都に学ぶ」⑦ 京都の公家と武家』（白川書院、2011年）、など。

田中　誠（たなか・まこと）
立命館大学大学院文学研究科博士課程後期課程
1983年栃木県生まれ。専門は日本中世史。
「初期室町幕府における恩賞方―「恩賞方奉行人」の考察を中心に―」（『古文書研究』第72号、吉川弘文館、2011年）、「康永三年における室町幕府引付方改編について」（『立命館文学』624号、2012年2月）、など。
担当：第2章、第10章

＊冨田　美香（とみた・みか）
立命館大学映像学部准教授
1966年兵庫県生まれ。専門は映画史。
共編著『イメージデータベースと日本文化研究』（ナカニシヤ出版、2010年）、共編著『山田洋次　映画を創る』（新日本出版社、2011年）、など。
担当：第8章、第16章、はじめに、おわりに

＊松本　郁代（まつもと・いくよ）
横浜市立大学学術院准教授、立命館大学衣笠総合研究機構特別招聘准教授
1974年静岡県生まれ。専門は日本宗教文化史。
『中世王権と即位灌頂―聖教のなかの歴史叙述』（森話社、2005年）、共編著『風俗絵画の文化学―都市をうつすメディア』（思文閣出版、2009年）、など。
担当：第3章、第11章

山本　真紗子（やまもと・まさこ）
立命館大学GCOE「日本文化デジタル・ヒューマニティーズ拠点」PD
1979年京都府生まれ。専門は日本文化史、芸術学。
『唐物屋から美術商へ―京都における美術市場を中心に』（晃洋書房、2010年）、「北村鈴菜と三越百貨店大阪支店美術部の初期の活動」（『Core Ethics』Vol.7、2011年）、など。
担当：第6章、第14章

シリーズ 日本文化デジタル・ヒューマニティーズ 05
京都イメージ──文化資源と京都文化──
Urban Images of Kyoto: Kyoto Culture and its Cultural Resources

2012年3月30日　初版第1刷発行

定価はカバーに表示してあります

監　修　文部科学省グローバルCOEプログラム「日本文化デジタル・ヒューマニティーズ拠点」（立命館大学）

編　者　冨田美香・木立雅朗・松本郁代・杉橋隆夫

発行者　中西健夫

発行所　株式会社 ナカニシヤ出版
〒606-8161　京都市左京区一乗寺木ノ本町15番地
Telephone 075-723-0111
Facsimile 075-723-0095
Website http://www.nakanishiya.co.jp/
Email iihon-ippai@nakanishiya.co.jp
郵便振替 01030-0-13128

Copyright © 2012 by Mika Tomita et al.
Published by Nakanishiya Publishing

装幀／白沢　正
印刷・製本／西濃印刷株式会社
Printed in Japan.
ISBN978-4-7795-0584-3 C3304